STAFFORDSHIRE AIRFIELDS IN THE SECOND WORLD WAR

2017

Martyn Chorlton

COUNTRYSIDE BOOKS
NEWBURY BERKSHIRE

The cover picture shows Wellington Mk IIIs of 30 OTU, Hixon,
and is from an original painting
by Colin Doggett

Designed by Mon Mohan

Produced through MRM Associates Ltd., Reading
Typeset by CJWT Solutions, St Helens
Printed by Cambridge University Press

*All material for the manufacture of this book
was sourced from sustainable forests.*

CONTENTS

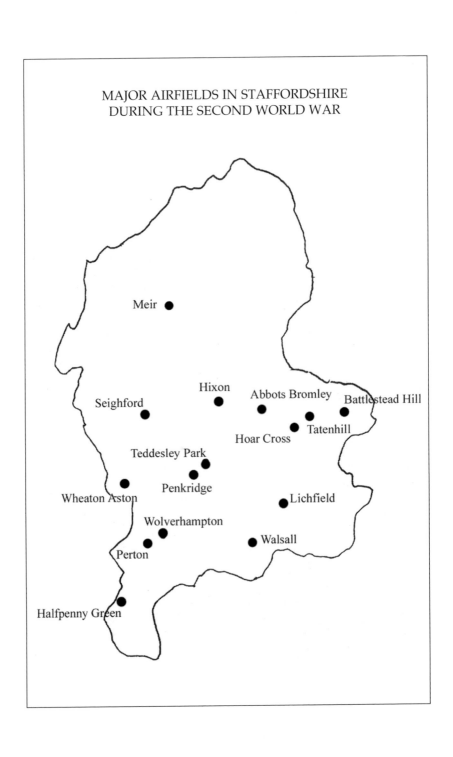

MAJOR AIRFIELDS IN STAFFORDSHIRE
DURING THE SECOND WORLD WAR

Meir

Hixon

Seighford

Abbots Bromley

Battlestead Hill

Tatenhill

Hoar Cross

Teddesley Park

Penkridge

Wheaton Aston

Lichfield

Wolverhampton

Walsall

Perton

Halfpenny Green

ACKNOWLEDGEMENTS

Special thanks to Tim Moss and the Hixon Local Historical Society for the loan of archive material. Thanks also to Ron Balding and the Staffordshire Aviation Heritage Group, and the following: J M Dews, D Marrow, DFC, Alex Finlow, S J George, Walsall Council, Staffordshire County Council, Wolverhampton Archives & Local Studies, Ken Ellis, Dave Willis, Harold (Mick) Stone, J A Douglass, Deryck (Jack) Brew and Bill Hickox, DFC and Bar.

Once again, thank you to my wife Claire for her tireless editing work which I continue to inflict upon her.

I

SETTING THE
SCENE

Before an aircraft had even been seen in the county, one particularly
significant event occurred at 115 Congleton Road, Butt Lane,
Kidsgrove, north of Stoke-on-Trent, on 20th May 1895 – Reginald
Joseph Mitchell was born. He was destined to become the designer of
24 different aircraft between 1920 and 1936, the most famous without
doubt being the Supermarine Spitfire. Sadly, Mitchell died of cancer on
11th June 1937, without seeing his wonderful design enter service or
the significant role it would play during the Second World War.

Because of the county's location, the Staffordshire airfields were
never destined to host a front-line Spitfire squadron, but operational
visitors would become commonplace as the war progressed. Flying
training would be the county's dominant role; a no less important task,
which provided the RAF with the vital aircrew it would need to defeat
the Axis powers.

However, by the time of the Second World War, Staffordshire
already had a long history of involvement in aviation. It was here in
1862 that one of the most significant events in early flying history
occurred.

Ten years earlier, Charles Green and John Welsh of Kew
Observatory had established the record balloon altitude at an
impressive 23,000 ft. Meteorologist Dr James Glaisher witnessed the
event which, in turn, inspired him to convince the British Association
for the Advancement of Science to sponsor him in 1859. Dr Glaisher's
intention was to use balloons to study the atmosphere in greater detail,
taking barometric readings, and to gain more understanding of the
solar spectrum and solar radiation at greater altitudes.

Several different balloons were looked at for the experiments,
including Charles Green's own balloon, named *Nassau*, which was the

The Mammoth *balloon at Stafford Road Gas Works in Wolverhampton, moments before its ascent on the 17th July 1862.*

same one that Dr Glaisher had observed at Kew. The launch site for the first flight was to be a central location, as far away from water and as near to a commercial coal gas producer as possible, as coal gas was more suitable than hydrogen for longer and hopefully higher flights.

The Wolverhampton Gas Company site, located on Stafford Road, Wolverhampton, was chosen for the ascent. The balloon that was eventually selected for the flights was called *The Mammoth* and was built by balloonist Henry Tracy Coxwell. With a gas capacity of 90,000 cubic ft, the balloon was made of American cloth, instead of the more traditional silk.

The first take-off of *The Mammoth* took place at 0943 hrs, 17th July 1862, from the Stafford Road site. With Henry Coxwell as pilot and Dr Glaisher also aboard equipped with a host of scientific instruments, the balloon rapidly ascended to 23,000 ft and Coxwell, fearing that they

Dr James Glaisher, who along with Henry Coxwell broke the world balloon altitude record.

might be blown out to sea, made a rapid descent. A heavy landing was made near Langham in Rutland and the intrepid pair were back in Wolverhampton that same evening. The balloonists made three more flights from Crystal Palace before returning to Wolverhampton for a second flight on 18th August. They rose to 23,700 ft and a gentler landing was carried out in Solihull. Coxwell and Dr Glaisher's third and most significant flight took place on 5th September 1862. Once again, the balloon rose at an impressive rate, but on this occasion Dr Glaisher had more time to carry out readings at the lower levels. *The Mammoth* broke cloud at 11,000 ft and after 1 hour and 40 minutes, they were at an estimated altitude of four miles. A few minutes later, the pair started to suffer the effects of lack of oxygen. At an approximate height of 29,000 ft, Dr Glaisher began to lose consciousness while Coxwell struggled with the balloon. A thermometer on board recorded the temperature at –20° F and Coxwell, also struggling for breath, could not grip anything because his hands were almost frozen. He eventually managed to bring Dr Glaisher around and the balloon began to descend at almost 2,000 ft per minute. Coxwell landed the balloon safely near Clee St Margaret, on the western side of Brown Clee Hill.

The record-breaking flight was estimated by Dr Glaisher to have reached 37,000 ft. It is more likely that the height was a little over 30,000 ft but even this height was not surpassed until 1901 and, unlike Glaisher and Coxwell, that crew carried oxygen.

Heavier-than-air flight was first recorded within the county in 1902, when the great showman Samuel Franklin Cody demonstrated one of his 'kites' in West Park, Wolverhampton. Cody developed the idea further to produce a kite capable of lifting a man and tried to sell the idea to the Army for observation work. Cody was in the town touring with his western play *Klondyke Nugget* and the kite-flying was almost

9

secondary to the show. Cody was always a headache to local police when he flew because of the size of the crowds that gathered. West Park was no exception: the police actually asked him to stop flying his kite because the crowds were trampling the flowerbeds!

It would be a further eight years before any major aviation event took place within the county; however, it was to be one of the most significant in aviation history. After months of build-up, the first all-British flying meeting was organised at Dunstall Park, Wolverhampton, between 27th June and 2nd July 1910. The event was arranged by the Midland Aero Club, whose headquarters were located at the Grand Hotel, Birmingham, and the club president was the Earl of Dartmouth.

Contemporary artist's impression of Coxwell in The Mammoth, *with an unconscious Dr. Glaisher slumped over the edge of the basket.*

The week's events included a bomb throwing competition, with a first prize of £100, and another £100 prize for the aviator flying for the longest duration. The Lord Plymouth prize was for the competitor who completed three laps of a special circuit laid out within Dunstall Park in the fastest time. The Earl of Plymouth would present the trophy to the winner. Another challenge was the Sir John Holder prize, awarded to the competitor who achieved the highest flight.

Competitors began arriving at the park from 6th June, where six wooden hangars had been erected by the Midlands Aviation Syndicate (the company running the meeting). The event attracted the great names of the day, including Charles Rolls, one partner of the fledgling Rolls-Royce, and Claude Graham-White, one of the great British aviation pioneers. Ten budding aviators were listed to take part in a variety of aircraft, including Blériot, Humber, Lane, plus locally-built Star and Hartill monoplanes. Other types included a Farman, Short–Wright and Roger Sommer biplanes, plus a Macfie Empress, Short S.27 and a Howard Wright Avis.

The week was severely disrupted by the weather which, as you can

10

The Farman biplanes were cutting-edge technology in 1910 and similar examples would have taken part in the Dunstall Park meeting.

imagine with these delicate early flying machines, was critical. All of the events listed took place, with the premier competition for the flight of the longest duration being won by Graham-White in his Farman biplane.

Also in 1910, a new model aeroplane club was formed at Burton-on-Trent in response to a rapidly growing interest in all things relating to aviation. Later in the year, the Town Council's Entertainments Committee arranged a flying week for real aeroplanes between 26th September and 1st October. The event was organised by the Burton Aviation Meeting Committee, whose president was S H Evershed. The Bass Brewery Company offered land for the event off Meadow Road within the town and also put up fences and pay-boxes. Rather than erecting pylons, as at Dunstall, for the aircraft to fly around, the course was instead marked out on the ground in whitewash. A decision to arrange other entertainments was also made in case the weather should deteriorate.

All of the aircraft taking part in the event were delivered in packing cases by rail via Doncaster and were re-assembled by mechanics in a canvas hangar on the edge of the flying field. All of the pilots taking part in the event were French and on arrival they were driven up and down the whitewashed course. The competitors were Hélène Dutrieu and L Beau, both in Farman biplanes, and Count Jacques de Lesseps and Julien Mamet, both in Blériot monoplanes. Others included Marcel Habriot in a Habriot monoplane and Emile Ladougne in a Goupy biplane.

The first day of the event was too windy to fly, much to the frustration of the large crowd which had to settle for the dulcet tones of songs by the Bijou Concert Party. The following day was better and Ladougne took to the air at 1030 hrs, circling Trent Bridge at approximately 120 ft before landing too quickly and crashing into a hangar. His aircraft was only slightly damaged and in the afternoon more flying took place, much to the delight of the local population. All work stopped in the town as planes swooped over the steeples and chimneys.

On 28th September, 15,000 people had to wait until 1600 hrs before the flying could begin. But, for the majority, it was worth the wait as a dozen further flights were made during the final two hours of the day. The event was a great success, inspiring many local people to become involved in aviation.

Spring Vale Farm, Birmingham Road, Walsall, was allocated as a refuelling stop for an air race sponsored by the *Birmingham Daily Post* on 30th September 1913. The race was between two famous aviators, Benny C Hucks and Gustav Hamel. The course of the race was 80 miles from Edgbaston via Redditch, Coventry, Nuneaton, Tamworth, Walsall, Quinton and back to Edgbaston. Thousands of locals flocked to Spring Vale Farm to witness the arrival of the two competitors who were neck and neck on their arrival at the refuelling point. The pair were on the ground for approximately 30

B C Hucks stands proudly next to his 60hp Blériot Monoplane; a popular showman, he and Gustav Hamel visited Walsall in 1913.

12

minutes before the final sprint to Edgbaston which Hamel won by a mere 4.28 seconds.

The First World War

The Royal Flying Corps (RFC) arrived in Staffordshire in 1916. Their presence was solely in response to the threat of Zeppelin attacks, the first local incident occurring on the night of 31st January. Nine Zeppelins attacked targets in the North and the Midlands and a single Zeppelin, L21, commanded by Max Dietrich, dropped 35 50 kg bombs on Tipton, Bradley and Bilston, believing it to be Liverpool, killing 33 people and injuring 20. Walsall was also hit; one notable fatality was the Mayoress, Mrs S M Slater who was in a tram in Bradford Place when a bomb fell.

Burton-on-Trent was also attacked on this night, with 15 killed and 72 injured. It was obvious that English towns and cities needed protecting against this new threat and, in response, several Home Defence squadrons were formed throughout the country with high

No 38 (HD) Squadron was first equipped with the BE.2c for Zeppelin defence. The unit operated occasionally from four landing grounds within the county, including Perton and Kingswinford.

The more capable FE.2b replaced the BE.2cs of 38 Squadron. The gunner demonstrates the clear view his position has gained with a rear-engined pusher configuration.

hopes that such units would repel or even shoot down the raiders. To defend the Midlands, 38 (Home Defence) Squadron was formed on 14th July 1916 at Castle Bromwich with BE.2cs. By September, the squadron had moved to Melton Mowbray, with three flights detached at Leadenham, Buckminster and Stamford, and an assortment of aircraft, which now included the BE.2e and BE.12. All of these were replaced in October by the more effective FE.2b, which was rear-engined giving a clearer view ahead for the gunner.

Within Staffordshire, four landing grounds were used by 38 Squadron, all of about 50 acres in size and manned by a few RFC personnel. They were located at Chasetown, Great Barr, Wall Heath near Kingswinford, and Fern Fields near Perton.

Another raid took place on 1st October 1916, mainly concentrating on the Birmingham area, but all 38 Squadron could muster was a single BE.12 from Leadenham which had to force-land with engine failure. The final of three Zeppelin raids to occur over the Midlands took place on 12th April 1918. No 38 Squadron despatched two FE.2bs from

Stamford and Buckminster but unfortunately neither aircraft saw the enemy and both crash-landed in the Coventry area.

At no stage during the First World War was an aircraft despatched from one of Staffordshire's landing grounds. Having hardly been used for flying activities, all four landing grounds were abandoned by 1919 at the latest.

Another aviation-related activity, which mainly centred on Wolverhampton during the First World War, was aircraft engine production. Clyno Cars at the Pelham Street Works produced ABC Dragonfly engines, as did Guy Motors at Fallings Park. Star Engineering of Frederick Street and H M Hobson of Cousins Street also built Renault engines and engine components.

By the end of the war, major companies with the ability to complete aircraft as well as to provide components included the following: Clyno, Guy Motors, Hobson's, Star, Sunbeam and John Martson's. The latter company produced radiators for liquid-cooled engines. Thompson Brothers of Bilston, on the edge of Wolverhampton, produced a plethora of aircraft components, including tails, various tubular frameworks and undercarriage parts.

Between the Wars

It was over ten years before any serious attempt to reintroduce civilian flying took place in the county. The landing ground at Perton had long since returned to farming but it was here in 1929 that V N Dickinson of Aero Hire Ltd was granted permission to operate a single aircraft. The machine was a de Havilland DH.60 Cirrus Moth, which he used for instructional flights.

In July 1929, Geoffrey Mander, MP, formed the Wolverhampton Light Aeroplane Club. Mander invited Dickinson, who was usually based at Castle Bromwich, to teach at the new club.

During the same year, Alan Cobham embarked on his nationwide Aerodrome Campaign, which brought him to Perton on 22nd June 1929. His visit sowed the seeds for the creation of municipal airports throughout the country and the airfields at Walsall, Pendeford and Meir became the first serious flying sites within Staffordshire.

Cobham returned to the county on 9th May 1932, with his famous 'flying circus'. His first visit was to Calderfields, near Walsall, literally

Alan Cobham in the cockpit of his de Havilland DH.50 in which he flew several record-breaking flights. He visited Staffordshire on many occasions; firstly for the positioning of future airfields and then with his Flying Circus.

in the field next to the proposed site for Walsall airport. The following year, the circus was of such a size that it split into two tours, the first visiting Walsall again on 1st June and the second going to Kitchen Lane, Wednesfield, Wolverhampton on 30th July. The Cobham shows usually consisted of aerobatics, crazy flying, flour bombing, joy riding and wing walking which, up to 1933, was performed without any kind of safety harness.

In 1933, a second flying group was formed by Charles Scott, known as the British Hospitals Air Pageant. The new pageant only lasted a single season but during its tour of 185 towns throughout the country, Stafford was one of the lucky towns visited. The aircraft flew from the Common and Miss Staffordshire (Miss Mabel Thurstone of Penkridge) was given a free flight by Charles Scott.

Cobham returned to Walsall on 8th June 1934 and the Kitchen Lane site again on 15th July 1934. The following year, his *Astra* tour visited Kitchen Lane on 6th June for the final time, followed by a visit to

Wing walking was a popular stunt which was carried out until 1933 without the aid of any kind of safety harness!

Perton on 22nd September. This put Perton on the map in aviation terms and it was officially known as 'the aerodrome' after Cobham's flying visit.

Walsall (Aldridge) Airport was opened in 1935 and scheduled services began at Meir (Stoke-on-Trent) the same year. Wolverhampton (Pendeford) Airport followed in 1936 operated by the Midland Aero Club. It was at Wolverhampton that Boulton Paul Aircraft Ltd made

17

its home in August 1936 and the first aircraft produced there, the Hawker Demon, became the county's first major association with military aircraft. The company's most famous aircraft, the Defiant, was designed, test-flown and eventually built at Pendeford.

The first military flying unit to be formed in Staffordshire before the Second World War was 28 Elementary & Reserve Flying Training School (E&RFTS) at Meir on 1st August 1938. The unit was actually civilian-run but trained reserve and new pilots for RAF service as it was becoming increasingly obvious that the clouds of war were about to descend upon Europe for the second time in living memory.

The Second World War

The Maintenance Unit

While the majority of the country was being covered by newly-built, pre-war expansion airfields, Staffordshire remained relatively untouched in the 1930s. The most significant new arrival was an airfield at Fradley, officially known as Lichfield. Initially, it was built purely for the use of 42 Maintenance Unit (MU), which after only a few months was renumbered 51 MU. MUs were the vital background machine that kept the RAF equipped with everything from teaspoons for the officers' mess to fighters and bombers for the front-line squadrons. They were incredibly flexible units, always staffed by a large cross-section of tradesmen, both RAF and civilian. No 51 MU's main task was the preparation of aircraft, which were usually delivered direct from the manufacturers, for use by operational squadrons and training units. They were joined by 82 MU in 1941, whose task was to dismantle and pack a variety of aircraft for service overseas. Civilian women, who before the war worked in the many local potteries, mainly staffed this unit; many had never even seen an aeroplane before, let alone dismantled one.

The amount and range of aircraft handled by 51 MU made Lichfield the busiest airfield within the county. This was achieved without taking into account other flying activities on the airfield. When the United States entered the war, the amount of American-built types increased the unit's inventory as more and more demands were placed on 51 MU by the Air Ministry via the Ministry of Aircraft Production

(MAP). As the war progressed, the unit carried out modification, conversion and complete rebuilds of some aircraft before they were despatched to squadrons.

When production began to outstrip the need for more aircraft, the unit started to adapt itself to the storage of vast quantities of machines, all dispersed around Lichfield and a host of Satellite Landing Grounds (SLG) allocated to it. During wartime conditions, because of the permanent threat of a potential air attack, the dispersal of aircraft put great strains on space and if it was not for the unflattering role of the SLGs then this would not have been possible. One of the landing grounds was 32 SLG at Hoar Cross, which served 51 MU from August 1941 to June 1945. Dispersed aircraft here included the Beaufighter, Boston, Hurricane, Wellington and Whirlwind.

No 51 MU continued a dual role of preparation and storage until the war's end when the latter became the priority. However, the unit would continue its work for many more years before its task was complete.

The Flying Training Unit

All of the fifteen major airfields featured within this book supported a flying training unit at some stage during the Second World War. One of the most common was the Elementary Flying Training School (EFTS) which, as the name suggests, taught the basic rudimentary flying, or *ab initio*, skills to the fledgling student pilot.

The average EFTS at the beginning of the war was equipped with the Miles Magister two-seat tandem trainer, the first monoplane trainer to enter service with the RAF. Known in RAF circles as the 'Maggie', the aircraft owed its design to the civil Cirrus-Hawk, Major, Speed Six and Hawk Trainers. A single example of the latter first entered RAF service in 1936 and the Magister followed in September 1937. Despite over 1,200 examples being produced, very few survive today and even fewer in airworthy condition. Overshadowed by the Tiger Moth, the Magister was an important trainer and an ideal stepping stone towards the new monoplane fighters of the day.

No 5 EFTS, who moved from the increasingly hectic and dangerous skies of southern England, was the first school to arrive in the county on 17th June 1940. It established itself at Meir, where 28 E&RFTS had been disbanded on the outbreak of hostilities. The unit also brought into use the county's first Relief Landing Ground (RLG) at Abbots Bromley. A typical RLG provided an alternative area for student pilots

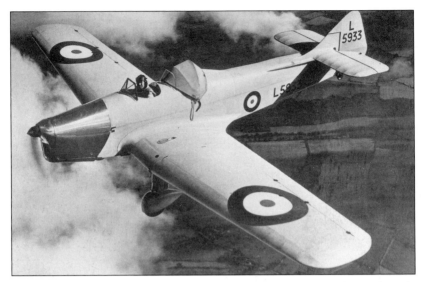

By far the most common training aircraft to be seen within the county during the early part of the Second World War was the Miles Magister.

to train away from the congestion of the home airfield. Abbots Bromley continued in this role throughout the war, serving the Tiger Moths of 16 EFTS at Burnaston, Derbyshire, after the disbandment of 5 EFTS. Battlestead Hill on the fringes of Burton-on-Trent was also brought into use specifically for 16 EFTS throughout its existence during the war.

No 28 EFTS, the second unit of its type, was formed on 15th September 1941 at Wolverhampton. Solely equipped with the ubiquitous Tiger Moth, the unit gained its own RLG at Penkridge from 19th May 1942 to 9th July 1945.

Another stage of flying training existed throughout the county – the (Pilots) Advanced Flying Units ((P)AFU), which were predominantly equipped with the twin-engined Airspeed Oxford. Along with the Tiger Moth, the Oxford would have been one of the most common aircraft to be seen during the war years. The airfields at Hixon, Perton, Seighford, Tatenhill and Wheaton Aston were all home to a (P)AFU at some stage during the war. The latter was by far the busiest, with 21 (P)AFU there from August 1943 to December 1946. On average, 140 Oxfords were on strength and spread across Wheaton Aston and at least one satellite airfield.

The de Havilland Tiger Moth had replaced the Magister as the RAF's primary trainer by 1942.

A Beam Approach Training Flight (BATF) also equipped with the Oxford supported the larger (P)AFUs. At one stage, in late 1944, Wheaton Aston had three detachments of BATFs specifically serving the training needs of 21 (P)AFU. These specially equipped Oxfords were capable of operating in very poor visibility by locating a beacon at the end of the runway in use. This groundbreaking technique of almost blind landing is taken for granted today.

The Bomber Operational Training Unit

During the 1930s and the early part of the Second World War, the training of bomber crews was a rather complicated route through a variety of training units. With the arrival of the first bomber Operational Training Unit (OTU) in April 1940, many training issues were resolved in one go. Their job was to train crews for night bomber operations on a single aircraft type and to gel that crew into an efficient team capable of navigating to and from the target.

The first unit of this type to arrive in the county was 27 OTU, which was formed at Lichfield on 23rd April 1941. Their main equipment was the Vickers Wellington IC, all of which had served with a front-line squadron before being relegated to the training role. Tatenhill was used as a satellite for a short while but was found to be unsuitable and Church Broughton in Derbyshire was used instead.

When Sir Arthur Harris took charge of Bomber Command, he was determined his aircraft would make a significant impact on the outcome of the war. He planned several ambitious '1,000-bomber' raids, which could only be carried out if aircraft were drawn from bomber OTUs as well as operational squadrons. No 27 OTU took part in three of these giant raids in 1942, losing aircraft as a result. Other raids followed making it the only unit to fly in an operational capacity from a Staffordshire airfield.

A second night-bomber training unit was formed at the newly-built airfield at Hixon on 28th June 1942. No 30 OTU also operated the Wellington I which, as with 27 OTU, was later replaced by the Wellington III and X. Both units suffered high losses typical of units of this type and many airmen, who were posted on to a bomber OTU after a tour of operations, commented that their lives were in less danger 10,000 ft over Germany!

No 27 OTU was destined to remain at Lichfield for its entire existence, being disbanded on 22nd June 1945. No 30 OTU left Hixon in February 1945 for Gamston in Nottinghamshire but was disbanded not long after the war's end.

Observers and Navigators

Bobbington, later named Halfpenny Green, was destined after completion in late 1940 to become the home of 3 Air Observer and Navigator School (AONS) on 17th February 1941. The unit was initially equipped with the highly unpopular Blackburn Botha but these, only months later, were thankfully replaced by the Avro Anson. No 3 AONS was the only unit of its type within the county and, as the name suggests, it focused on training air observers and navigators before posting them out to an OTU where they would join a crew. Reformed in October 1941 as 3 Air Observers School (AOS), the unit grew in size with, on average, 60 Ansons crammed on the airfield. At no stage during its existence did Halfpenny Green have a satellite airfield or RLG to relieve the congestion. The unit was reorganised again in April 1942 as 3 (Observers) Advanced Flying Unit ((O)AFU). Still equipped with Ansons, the role of the unit was to remain fundamentally the same throughout the war and beyond when disbandment came in December 1945.

The Airfield Factories

The Boulton Paul Aircraft Company, which had been established at Pendeford since 1935, was the most prolific aircraft producer within the county during the Second World War. After the Hawker Demon contract was completed, the next major military order was for 105 Blackburn Rocs. Destined for service with the Fleet Air Arm (FAA), the fighter was conveniently fitted with a four-gun Boulton Paul turret.

The first mass-produced Boulton Paul product was the Defiant fighter. Like the Roc, its main defence was a four-gun turret located behind the cockpit. The Air Ministry eventually ordered a total of 1,062 Defiants with production coming to an end in February 1943.

The next contract was for the Fairey Barracuda III, which was received in two batches totalling 692 aircraft. Alongside all of this aircraft production, the company was also tasked with producing and, on many occasions, fitting a variety of gun turrets.

Since their arrival at Walsall, Helliwells had been producing a steady stream of component parts for aircraft such as the Anson, Blenheim, Gladiator, Hart, Hurricane, Wellesley and Whitley. On 28th July 1940, Helliwells became part of the Civilian Repair Organisation (CRO), which successfully relieved the RAF of a huge amount of repair and maintenance work. The company was then tasked to receive the North American Harvard under the 'Lend-lease' scheme; uncrating, assembling and test flying each one on arrival at Walsall. The company also handled the Douglas Boston and Havoc in the same way and carried out Hurricane repair work as well.

Rootes Securities, which was resident at Meir from late 1941, was also heavily employed in aircraft production work. The first contract was for the Bristol Blenheim I, followed by the Blenheim IV and V. The Beaufighter VI and TFX followed and then, like Helliwells, Harvards were received in crates. Modification and conversion of newly-arrived Mustang fighters to RAF standard was also carried out before the war's end.

Post war use of the airfields

Lichfield remained the busiest airfield by far in a period of post war reorganisation and airfield closures. No 51 MU, now dedicated to storage, also prepared several types of aircraft for service with foreign air forces. The bulk of the aircraft stored at Lichfield were destined to be scrapped and this occupied most of the unit's time up until its closure on 1st July 1954. The airfield itself closed in 1962.

Other MUs made use of airfields that were now closed to flying, including 16 MU at Stafford, which took over Hixon until 1957, the airfield closing five years later. As a direct result of the enormous explosion at Fauld in 1944, 21 MU used Abbots Bromley for bomb storage until 1949 and Tatenhill until 1954.

Airfields that were abandoned or returned to the plough not long after the war included Battlestead Hill, Hoar Cross, Penkridge, Perton, Teddesley Park and Wheaton Aston, the latter probably being the most surprising of the group considering its importance during the war years.

Halfpenny Green housed 25 MU until 1956 but resurfacing of all three runways briefly reintroduced several Air Navigation School (ANS) Ansons. By 1960 the airfield was in the hands of an enthusiastic and dedicated group of civilians.

It was a military gliding school that kept the RAF in residence at Meir for many post war years. No 45 Gliding School (GS) had been at Meir since its formation in August 1942. Redesignated 632 (Volunteer)

GS in September 1955, in 1963 the gliders left Meir for Ternhill, Shropshire, where they remain today. No 632 (V)GS was replaced by the Staffordshire Gliding Club at Meir in the same year. Limited civilian aviation returned to Meir after the war, the regular users being a de Havilland Dragon Rapide and Dove. Many attempts were made to reinvigorate aviation at the airfield but by the early 1970s, the housing developers finally won when the site was earmarked for a new development. The last aircraft left Meir in August 1973.

Seighford's post war history was an interesting period, especially when it was taken over by Boulton Paul in the mid 1950s. The company needed an airfield with paved runways to test the many jet project aircraft that were being produced during this period. Boulton Paul also won contracts for English Electric Canberra overhauls and, if the TSR.2 had not been cancelled, more work would have been received. By early 1966, the sub-contract work had dried up and the airfield was abandoned.

At Wolverhampton, 28 EFTS was reformed as 25 Reserve Flying School (RFS) on 26th June 1947. Still operating the Tiger Moth, many of which had served with the old unit, the new school was also operated by Air Schools Ltd. No 25 RFS later operated the Prentice, Anson, Auster and Chipmunk before disbandment day came on 31st March 1953. No 1954 Reserve AOP (Air Observation Post) Flight became the last military unit to form and operate from the airfield on 20th July 1949. Operated by the Army, with aircraft from the RAF, the flight flew a collection of Auster AOPs and a Chipmunk. On 10th March 1957, the AOP Flight was disbanded and the association between the airfield and the RAF came to an end.

Post war civilian aviation at Wolverhampton thrived, in stark contrast to all the other airfields in the county. Light aircraft were in abundance and the formation of Wolverhampton Aviation Ltd and Derby Aviation Ltd brought commercial flights to the airfield. Wolverhampton and its Aero Club closed down in 1970 but it took several years before the airfield was cleared and developed as it is today.

Aviation in Staffordshire today

Seven of the airfields in the county can still boast a strong connection with aviation. From a non-flying point of view, the Boulton Paul factory at Pendeford still exists and is owned by a manufacturer of aircraft components. Smith's Aerospace, a direct descendant of the original company, is also the home of the Boulton Paul Aircraft Heritage Centre. The centre houses several examples of Boulton Paul aircraft, including the P.6 Biplane replica, Defiant and post war trainer the Balliol. Hixon, which was used by light aircraft up until the 1990s, is also the home of at least two aviation companies. Within the old technical site, aircraft can still be found.

Reginald Joseph Mitchell, the gifted engineer and aircraft designer who was born in Stoke-on-Trent in 1895. R J Mitchell was to become famous designing the Spitfire; sadly he died before seeing the aircraft enter RAF service.

Halfpenny Green, now known as Wolverhampton International, has a reasonably secure future and today is the busiest of all Staffordshire's remaining wartime airfields from a general aviation point of view.

Hoar Cross is now the home of the Needwood Forest Gliding Club, though whether the current gliding strip is the same area as used by the original SLG is open to debate. Despite this, the name lives on with a more peaceful form of flying now being carried on.

On the southern edge of the old RLG at Penkridge, the thriving Staffordshire Aero Club has made the airfield at Otherton their home. Like Hoar Cross, Seighford has been used for gliding since 1992 when the Staffordshire Gliding Club moved in.

Tatenhill is probably busier today than it ever was during the Second World War. The airfield now supports several different aviation companies with General Aviation aircraft, including the odd War Bird scattered all around it.

The great R J Mitchell is remembered in Stoke-on-Trent at The Potteries Museum and Art Gallery. A Supermarine Spitfire is preserved and a statue of one of the greatest 'Midlanders' of all time is also on display outside the museum. The house of his birth still exists in Congleton Road and a plaque is displayed on the outside, giving credit to a true 'local hero'.

2
ABBOTS BROMLEY

The small grass airfield at Abbots Bromley was built as a Relief
Landing Ground (RLG). Although for many airfields that would be the
first of many stages of its life, Abbots Bromley would stay a RLG
during its existence from 1941 to 1945.

The airfield was located to the west of the village, north of the
Uttoxeter road and hemmed in by Harley Lane, which followed its
northern boundary. Facilities were limited, but nine Robins provided
generous hangarage although the accommodation was small, with
provision for just 75 officers and airmen. The landing ground, which
was approximately 300 acres in size, was marked out with two 650-yd
grass runways.

The airfield came under the control of Burnaston in Derbyshire
when it first opened in early 1941. Despite this, the first aircraft to use
the airfield as a RLG was 5 Elementary Flying Training School (EFTS),
which had been established at Meir since June 1940. The Miles
Magisters of this unit used the airfield more for forced landing practice
than the traditional circuits and bumps.

Abbots Bromley officially became a RLG for 16 EFTS at Burnaston in
June 1941, purely to relieve congestion at the busy Derbyshire airfield.
Abbots Bromley, along with Battlestead Hill, replaced the unit's former
RLGs at Tatenhill and Meir. At this time 16 EFTS also operated the
Magister, but this, as in so many other elementary units, was
eventually replaced by the ubiquitous Tiger Moth.

No 5 EFTS continued to use the RLG until their disbandment in
December 1941. At least two accidents occurred during their time at
Abbots Bromley, the first on 15th October 1941 when Magister I L8131
hit a tree on approach and crashed. A second, more serious, incident
took place on 6th November. Sgt S A Holland was killed when his
Magister I L8156 struck a tree whilst flying low near the airfield.

The Tiger Moths of 16 EFTS based at Burnaston in Derbyshire used Abbots Bromley for its entire wartime existence.

Visiting aircraft were not uncommon, especially from other training schools. Other airfields were often used for 'touch and gos', simply to break up the familiarity of the pupil's own airfield. One such visitor on 5th June 1942, Magister I L8252 from 14 EFTS at Elmdon, came in too slow, stalled and spun into the ground.

No 16 EFTS made good use of Abbots Bromley during their tenure, and not many days passed without a Tiger Moth either in the circuit or heading out on a training flight. The school had a fairly low accident rate whilst operating from here.

With the war in Europe drawing to a close, the school began to shrink in size but still made use of Abbots Bromley. On 9th March 1945, Tiger Moth II DE473 was returning from a low-flying exercise when, probably unbeknownst to the pilot and instructor, Halifax VII NA317 of 1665 Heavy Conversion Unit (HCU) was carrying out a similar exercise. The Tiger Moth was on approach to land, probably at less than 1,000 ft, when the Halifax collided with the comparatively tiny trainer. Both aircraft came down north of Redmore Wood, north of Abbots Bromley village. The chances of surviving such a low altitude, high-speed impact were slim. The Halifax was operating from Tilstock

28

The old RLG's guardroom still defiantly stands by the original entrance off the Uttoxeter road. (Author)

in Shropshire, where crews were converted onto Stirling and Halifax transports for Airborne Forces squadrons.

When 16 EFTS left Abbots Bromley on 9th July 1945, it brought to an end aviation on the site. A further military use prolonged its life, however, when 21 Maintenance Unit (MU) at Fauld used Abbots Bromley as one of many sub-sites from 14th May 1945. They had another site at Tatenhill, occupied since December 1944. From July 1946, the Tatenhill sub-site took control of Abbots Bromley until the RLG's closure on 31st March 1949.

Today, the remains include a single, derelict guardroom which can be seen off the Uttoxeter road. The entrance road is in use by a local farmer and beside this, opposite the guardroom, the wooden mounting post for the entry barrier still stands. Viewed from Harley Lane, a single roofless Robin hangar also stands, along with at least one technical-looking building. The landing ground appears complete, though having long been returned to agriculture.

The only surviving Robin hangar is in a sorry state and does not give the impression that it will be around for much longer. (Author)

3
BATTLESTEAD HILL
(Burton-on-Trent)

A small landing ground located two miles west of Burton-on-Trent, Battlestead Hill spent its entire existence serving the needs of a single training unit. Many RAF and Commonwealth pilots passed through on their way to front-line postings with both fighter and bomber squadrons.

Battlestead Hill was created because of the demand for Relief Landing Grounds (RLGs) to be used by 16 EFTS (Elementary Flying Training School), based at Burnaston in Derbyshire. Formed on 10th April 1940 under the control of 51 (Training) Group, based at Moorfield House, Alma Road in Leeds, the school was growing rapidly by the beginning of 1941 and initially operated the Miles Magister. Several sites were viewed by senior officers from 16 EFTS, all of them in Staffordshire. The school briefly used Tatenhill as an RLG and then Meir in April 1941, followed by Battlestead Hill in the same month and Abbots Bromley in June.

The site at Battlestead Hill was located south of Henhurst Hill and east of Postern Road, taking its name from the hill north of the village of Tatenhill. The small landing ground would have taken up no more than 200 acres, ideal for the operation of the Miles Magister and the de Havilland Tiger Moth. The latter was the most common from 1942. Accommodation, if any, would have been tented; a few flight huts and a single hangar, probably a Robin-type, were the only buildings on the site.

Not officially taken over by 16 EFTS until May 1941, a single aircraft was recorded as being lost the previous month near Tatenhill village, which was actually closer to Battlestead Hill than to Tatenhill airfield.

A pupil pilot taxies for his first solo in his Magister – a typical scene representing the activities of 16 EFTS at Battlestead Hill during the early years of the war.

It is believed therefore that the accident occurred approaching the small RLG, when Magister I N3789 stalled and crashed on 24th April 1941.

During the early days of the RLG's existence, 30 EFTS from Wolverhampton, also flying Magisters, is said to have used Battlestead Hill. If they did, it was very briefly, as the unit was dissolved into 16 EFTS on 4th April 1941. The aircraft recorded as being at the RLG could probably have still been carrying 30 EFTS codes.

During 1942, Battlestead Hill would have been at its busiest as 16 EFTS had at least 72 Tiger Moths and 36 Magisters on strength. All were liberally spread around the supporting RLGs. By the end of the year, the Magister had been phased out and all elementary flying training was carried out using Tiger Moths.

The RLG, like much of the surrounding area, was shaken to its core by a massive explosion on 30th November 1944. Some 3,500 tonnes of explosives had blown up at RAF Fauld, located a few miles to the north. Several aircraft from Battlestead Hill were airborne at the time and some of the pilots and instructors actually witnessed the gigantic explosion. The Operations Record Book at Burnaston, which applied to the aircraft at Battlestead Hill, stated: 'Air Ministry signal received that all flying below 2,000 ft within a ten-mile radius of Fauld to cease'. No explanation was given and the witnesses of the disaster after landing back at Battlestead Hill were simply told that they did not see an explosion and never to utter a word about it.

Flying at Battlestead Hill came to an end on 9th July 1945 and it reverted, almost within weeks, to agriculture. No 16 EFTS, now with no need for RLGs, shrank in size and, still at Burnaston, was redesignated 16 Reserve Flying School (RFS) on 27th March 1947; 16 RFS, still flying the Tiger Moth, was eventually disbanded in June 1953.

Today, the majority of the old RLG site is covered in houses, but thankfully one of the roads is named Aviation Lane, giving future generations a hint of the past.

4
HALFPENNY GREEN
(Bobbington)

While generations of aircraft have come and gone, this compact, well-equipped airfield has changed little over the years. Now known as Wolverhampton Airport, the airfield is not shy of receiving regional airliners and executive jets, as well as a host of other aviation residents and visitors.

The site for a new airfield, which was initially named Bobbington, was requisitioned by the Air Ministry in the late summer of 1939. In typical style, the Ministry was all-powerful in claiming land for their purpose, as described by Mr J M Dews:

A friend of mine was living with her father and mother at Highgate Farm, where her father was farm manager. It had been an excellent season. The fields of corn and root crops were in fine condition when war was declared.

The Air Ministry had obviously had its eyes on the flat fields at Halfpenny Green and within a few days, despite the possibility of food shortages, the crops were being flattened to make the runway and bases of buildings for Bobbington Aerodrome. The family were cleared out along with the crops. Within a few days, a cottage was found for them several miles away. They never returned to the farm at Highgate.

Bobbington is a small village located to the south-west, with the hamlet of Halfpenny Green on the north side of the site. Sandwiched between three minor roads, the most southerly was closed as one of the runways passed through it, although it was still used to access the technical site from the eastern side. The three roads dictated the size of the airfield, which was effectively built with two main runways of similar length at approximately 1,200 yds each. A third runway, laid to join them in a triangular pattern, was only slightly shorter at 1,150 yds; all three were connected by a single perimeter track.

Seven Bellman hangars were constructed close together and two Enlarged Over Blisters and seven Double Enlarged Blisters were dispersed around the edge of the airfield. A bungalow-type watch office rather than a larger brick-built control tower was built in front of the hangar line. The main technical site was in a permanent pre-war Expansion style, although the bulk of the accommodation consisted of canvas tents rather than brick-built H-blocks. More comfortable Nissen huts and barrack blocks did not arrive until October 1942. The whole area was interconnected with a maze of roads and a roundabout behind the hangar line, and a parade square was also built in the centre of the airmen's billets. Bobbington was every inch a training station and this was exactly the role it was intended for when the opening was planned for February 1941.

No 3 Air Observer and Navigator School (AONS) was reformed at Bobbington on 17th February 1941 with the intention of teaching basic navigation skills using the Blackburn Botha. Originally formed in November 1939, 3 AONS had been amalgamated into 5 AONS at Weston-super-Mare, Somerset, in June 1940. No 3 AONS was one of eleven similar schools operated throughout Britain, such was the demand by Bomber Command for aircrew.

Very few newly-built airfields were ready for occupation and Bobbington's problem was poor drainage. Heavy rains had caused severe flooding and this was a problem that would take several weeks to resolve. In the meantime, 3 AONS started to receive its first Bothas. However, these were delivered to Cosford in Shropshire and the unit prepared for its first training course from that airfield. The first Botha was collected by Sqn Ldr R B Pakenham from Lyneham in Wiltshire on 4th April 1941 and two more followed later in the month.

Wg Cdr (later Gp Capt) T Q Horner took command of the airfield and 3 AONS on 18th April and, on 30th April, the unit finally moved from Cosford to Bobbington. The unit's strength quickly rose to 32 officers and 584 airmen; however, only three aircraft were available. This was reduced to two the following day when Flt Lt Fry suffered brake failure in Botha I L6342, ending up in a ditch.

Before the outbreak of the Second World War, the Air Ministry had desperately needed to re-equip the RAF's maritime squadrons. Aircraft

No 3 AONS at Bobbington was first equipped with the Blackburn Botha but after only a few months the Anson replaced it.

manufacturers were invited to tender designs and three were offered: the Blackburn Botha, the Saro Lerwick and the Bristol Beaufort. Only the Beaufort would go on to serve with distinction, the Botha and Lerwick falling woefully short of the RAF's requirements and both being withdrawn early from service.

Designed as a general reconnaissance or torpedo-bomber, the Botha only served with one front-line unit, namely 608 Squadron at Thornaby in Yorkshire. Whether it was desperation for new aircraft or over-confidence in Blackburn's products, the Air Ministry placed a large order for the Botha even before it left the drawing board. No thought was given to potential failings in the design, which mainly centred on the aircraft's serious lack of power. The Botha's two 880 hp Bristol Perseus engines were hopelessly inadequate and not particularly reliable either. The aircraft also had serious visibility problems for the pilot and crew, especially downward and laterally.

Despite these failings, 580 Bothas served with the RAF, the majority with various training schools, many of which suffered high losses and

The unit's Bothas were grounded and temporarily stored on the airfield before they were flown out for storage at a Maintenance Unit.

reliability problems. The Botha was declared obsolete in August 1943 but several continued to serve until September 1944 before the type finally disappeared from the RAF's inventory, without a tear being shed. Over 75 aircraft were destined to be lost in training accidents during its service career, several from Bobbington.

For communication duties, the unit received a single de Havilland Gipsy Moth. The ex-civilian machine, originally registered as G–AAMV, was impressed by the Air Ministry in August 1940. With the military registration of BK844, the Moth only served at Bobbington until it was struck off charge in March 1943.

On 2nd May 1941, the first few pupils arrived at the airfield, followed the next day by 47 more from Penrhos, Evanton, Manby and West Freugh – all Bombing and Gunnery Schools. These pupils were the first to undergo bombing and gunnery training before their navigation training. This was a new policy, which was designed to broaden the capability of all new navigators, air gunners and observers.

Even with only a few aircraft established at Bobbington, the airfield was still a dangerous place. Sgt G W Martin was running the engines of Botha I L6340 on 4th May when a Mr Shackleton, a civilian worker, walked into a revolving propeller. Shackleton was killed instantly.

Course No 1, with 53 pupils, began on 5th May 1941 and their instructional training followed a fortnight later. Six Bothas were now on the strength although this was still woefully short of the planned unit establishment of 35 aircraft. Nineteen aircraft had arrived by 7th June, with 15 fully trained pilots available to fly them. By the end of the day, seven Bothas were pronounced unserviceable; it was becoming increasingly obvious that the Botha was not up to the task. A typical AONS would hope to achieve up to 100 flights per day, but unserviceabilities and a shortage of pilots had reduced this to 28 flights per day. It was only a matter of time before a major flying accident would happen as a result of the pressure to get pupils through their course. Unfortunately for 3 AONS and Bobbington, two accidents would occur within 24 hours.

The first happened on 29th June 1941, when Botha I L6155 had to make a forced landing near the airfield after losing power. The pilot steered the aircraft towards Enville Golf Course. As the Botha was about to make a wheels-up landing, it struck a private car being driven by Miss E Williams of Stourbridge. In the ensuing crash, W/O AC2 J Trafford was killed and LAC Newnes de Souza, an Observer under training, was seriously injured. Sadly, Miss Williams died of her injuries later in hospital. The next evening, Botha I W5031 crashed near Enville after an engine cut following take-off. The pilot, Sgt P D K Purdon, and two Observers under training, LAC A G Chester and LAC D J Amos, were killed.

All the units operating the Botha had suffered problems with the aircraft and it was announced that from 1st July 1941 all would be grounded. The Avro Anson was to be the replacement but by now 3 AONS had received 49 Bothas, all of which were cluttered around the edge of the airfield. No flying took place until 7th July when the first six Ansons arrived at Bobbington. The following day flying training began for the first time with the Anson.

Affectionately known in RAF circles as 'Faithful Annie', the Avro Anson first entered RAF service in 1936 and continued in use until 1968. Smaller than the Botha, with a crew of three, the Anson was superior in almost all departments, bringing reliability to both air and groundcrews. Nearly 11,000 were built in Britain and Canada over an incredible 17-year production run. At its peak in 1943 and 1944, 130 aircraft were being built per month at Avro's Yeadon factory. The bulk of aircraft delivered to Bobbington were the Mk I, which had been

The Avro Anson served from 1941 until late 1945 at Halfpenny Green. The type made a surprise although brief return to the airfield during the 1950s.

converted from the general reconnaissance version to armament trainers. The Anson was fitted with a Bristol dorsal turret, armed with a single 0.303 inch Browning machine gun, making it perfect for air gunnery, combined with navigation training.

Thirteen Ansons had arrived by 14th July, but poor weather restricted their use to a few local training flights. On 22nd July, Anson I N9573 became the first of its type to be involved in an accident at Bobbington. The aircraft, which had already served with three other training units, was not seriously damaged as it went on to serve for a further three years without incident.

By the end of July 1941, flying had intensified, with some pilots achieving an amazing nine-and-a-half hours' flying time per day. Twenty-four Ansons, in addition to the forty-nine permanently grounded Bothas, were now spread around the airfield and over 1,000 personnel were accommodated at Bobbington.

The first Air Observers Navigation Course was completed on 2nd August and 49 pupils successfully passed the course. Night flying was introduced at the end of the month, which significantly increased the unit's flying hours and became a very short-term solution to overcrowding. One senior officer commented that while they were in the air they were not clogging up his airfield! At the beginning of September 1941, course numbers 5 and 6, consisting of Wireless Operators and Air Observers, were the first to be solely allocated to a single command, in this case Coastal Command.

The issue of overcrowding came to an end when the first of the troublesome Bothas were flown away to various maintenance units for storage on 14th July. This immediately created more space for Ansons, which totalled 37 by the end of September.

D Marrow, DFC, who was a navigator under training at the time, remembers the Bothas leaving:

> One of the civilian pilots who collected the Bothas was none other than Jim Mollison, the husband of the famous Amy Johnson and himself a pioneer. He asked, 'What is the matter with these Bothas?' and proceeded to perform aerobatics with one. His verdict was that there was nothing wrong with them, but we were pleased to see them go. We were quite content with the faithful old 'Annies'.

No 3 AONS suffered its first aircraft loss on 30th September 1941, luckily without loss of life. Anson I N5133 was being serviced when a

Very pistol was accidentally discharged, causing the aircraft to burst into flames. Officers and groundcrew alike were quite upset about the loss as N5133 was one of the unit's best aircraft and had recently been equipped with DF (Direction Finding) equipment, all of which had been destroyed.

Royalty descended upon the airfield for the first time on 5th October. Air Vice Marshal His Royal Highness The Duke of Kent, KG, KT, GCMG, GCVO, inspected a guard of honour, the airfield's institute, cookhouse, dining hall and sick quarters. The Duke was killed in April 1942 when the Short Sunderland he was travelling in crashed near Morven in Scotland.

October 1941 saw a reorganization of the airfield's Maintenance Wing with a transfer to civilian control. Maintenance would now be in the hands of staff from Marshall's Flying School Ltd based at Cambridge. With its generous hangarage, the work was carried out at Bobbington, with the first twelve aircraft received by Marshall's on 7th October. More changes occurred on 18th October when 3 AONS was redesignated 3 AOS (Air Observers School). Establishment of aircraft was now set at an estimated 66 Ansons, with 12 target tugs, a few Blenheims and the trusty Gipsy Moth in support.

No 3 AOS took over control of Chetton bombing range, four miles south-west of Bridgnorth in Shropshire, at the end of November. Only eleven miles from Bobbington, this was a great asset to the school, remaining under the airfield's control until the end of the war.

Increased flying hours and demands from the higher echelons for a greater throughput of courses usually resulted in a higher accident rate. Between October 1941 and the end of the year, five Ansons were involved in a variety of flying accidents and Anson I K6254 caught fire on the ground. None of these incidents caused any loss of life but two crew members were injured when an Anson crashed into a hillside near the airfield on 22nd December.

The year ended with the formation of a new Armament Flight and 1942 began with yet more reorganisation. On 31st January 1942, 3 AOS was divided up into four new flights: 'A' Flight was the already formed Armament Flight, 'B' and 'D' Flights were for Flight Day Navigation and 'C' was tasked with Night Navigation.

Part of the course training had to involve air-to-air firing, which Chetton could not support. This meant that every course was detached to 7 AGS (Air Gunnery School) at Stormy Down in South Glamorgan for this part of the training. The air-to-air firing was carried out at 7 AGS's own range at Margam, south of Port Talbot.

The unit's first fatal accident occurred on 13th March 1942. An Anson I, with two instructors and three pupils on board, crashed on the lower slope of a hill near Clee St Margaret, seven miles north-east of Ludlow in Shropshire. Two were killed outright in the accident, while the three survivors were taken to hospital. Three days later another Anson crashed near Bridgnorth, followed by another on 18th March, which crashed on the airfield, both without loss of life.

Bobbington's emergency services were tested on the evening of 25th March when two operational Wellingtons requested permission to land. The bombers were returning from a raid when they became lost. Both aircraft were brought in safely although one of the bombers clipped a tree on approach.

Despite civilian flying operations being suspended at the outbreak of the Second World War, BOAC (British Overseas Aircraft Corporation) were still operating a number of aircraft across the globe. In early 1942, they had a distinct shortage of navigators, and a solution was found after the company approached the Air Ministry. Ten navigators who graduated from Course No 10/2 were seconded for duty with BOAC on 1st April 1942. Not only was this the first time that BOAC had made such a request but it was also the first time that military-trained aircrew had been despatched for duty with a civilian company.

A third and final change was in store for 3 AOS when it was decided that all graduates of overseas training schools needed a familiarisation course on their return to Britain. The Empire Air Training Scheme was proving a success but the aircrew, trained in the vast trouble-free skies of Canada and South Africa, needed extra instruction. All ten Air Observer Schools in the country were redesignated (Observer) Advanced Flying Units, including 3 AOS which became 3 (O)AFU on 11th April 1942. The redesigned course now lasted four weeks and was still carried out on the Avro Anson. The unit had nearly 70 on strength by now. The first new AFU course arrived from PRC (Personnel Reception Centre) Bournemouth on 14th April and consisted of 30 Australians, 30 Canadians, 10 New Zealanders and 10 from the RAF Volunteer Reserve (VR).

Most units of this type had support aircraft which would be used for general communication work and, more importantly, target towing. A pair of Westland Lysanders, which were later replaced by Miles Martinets, carried out the latter. However, the Martinets were only used from spring 1943 to November of that year. A single pre-war Avro Tutor and later a Tiger Moth were also used by the unit for general flying duties.

Westland Lysander Target Tugs served at Halpenny Green before they were replaced by the locally modified Defiant.

The first 48 AFU cadets had completed their course by 11th May; all were posted to either OTUs or squadrons. Some 100 more were posted in on the same day, once again via the PRC at Bournemouth. This would be the general routine until the end of hostilities.

The increased throughput of 'under training' aircrew was reflected in a marked increase in the unit's accident rate. Many crashes occurred during low flying, which was carried out on a regular basis. During one particular low-flying reconnaissance exercise on 22nd May, Anson I N9565 struck High Tension (HT) cables. The Anson made a hasty crash landing but unfortunately hit rising ground one mile south-east of Edge Hill in Warwickshire, and burst into flames, killing all on board. Two more aircraft were lost, with all crew killed, in June; one crashing on the Isle of Man, a favourite destination for navigation exercises.

Ground accidents were common as well, with so many aircraft coming and going. A typical accident occurred on 3rd September when Anson I N5080 taxied into N9567. Neither aircraft was seriously damaged, but the pilot of N5080 was charged with gross negligence and received an endorsement in his logbook. Even visiting aircraft had mishaps; a Beaufighter overshot one of the short runways and crashed on 20th October.

Despite so many aircraft movements at Bobbington, the airfield was still only equipped with a pre-war wooden single-storey watch office. Flying control was limited and it would be several months before work began on a more permanent Type 12779 control tower which, like the original watch office, still exists today. Despite the basic facilities available at the time, a new training flight was formed under the command of Flg Off R N Teale on 8th November. The new flight was put in place purely for pilots newly 'posted in' to the unit who were not current or needed a refresher course on the Anson.

It also seems ironic that a detachment of the School of Flying Control moved into Bobbington on 22nd November. Also operating the Anson, with the odd Oxford visiting as well, the school was originally formed at Watchfield in Berkshire in December 1941, moving to Bridgnorth on 15th November 1942. Bridgnorth was not a flying station so a detachment was left behind at Watchfield to form the Airfield Controllers School while the remaining aircraft operated from Bobbington, with an average of twelve Ansons on strength.

The accident rate continued unabated throughout November 1942 and the pressure on the civilian maintenance team to keep the Ansons in the air was huge. While the majority of aircraft crashed near or on the airfield, many were a total loss when they had to ditch in the sea during a navigation exercise. One such aircraft, Anson I N9917, was traversing the Irish Sea on 13th December when the flying controls iced up and it was forced down into the cold sea off Great Ormes Head. The pilot, Sgt Wells, and a u/t (under training) navigator were lost but two others who managed to scramble into a dinghy survived.

A few days later, Sgt J P D Bartleet was flying a similar route in Anson I N4903 when the port engine failed. Bartleet performed a perfect ditching in the sea 40 miles west of Blackpool. Luckily for this crew, all made it into a dinghy and a few hours later they were rescued. Bartleet was destined to relive the experience on 26th March 1943 when he had to come down in the sea again, this time in Anson I N5382. Once again, he carried out a copybook ditching approximately 35 miles north-east of Rhyl. A British merchant vessel rescued all five crew an hour later.

The size of 3 (O)AFU in January 1943 justified the unit being divided into four training flights rather than two. 'A' and 'D' Flights were now under the command of Flt Lt Chapman and 'B' and 'C' Flights were looked after by Flt Lt Fairbank.

While better organised, the airfield was no less crowded and visitors, especially those in trouble, also increased. The local emergency services were tested again on the evening of 11th January when a Whitley made a heavy landing in poor weather, blocking one of the runways. The same night, a Wellington attempted to make a crash landing but overshot and crashed heavily about a mile outside the airfield perimeter. All of the occupants were injured, the pilot seriously. Bobbington's rescue personnel were called out again on 30th January, when another Wellington crashed on the Brown Clee Hills in Shropshire. Despite being a 20-mile drive from Bobbington, the airfield was the nearest which could offer any kind of assistance. Eight aircrew were lost in the crash and the hills are said to have claimed more lives than any other cause, with twenty-three airmen lost in six different air crashes. One of these involved a 3 (O)AFU Anson when N5379 crashed into Brown Clee on 28th April 1943, killing the pilot, Sgt W M R Lloyd, and all aboard.

Closer to home, Flg Off A L Jones was returning from a daylight flight on 9th February when, after landing, he swerved and crashed into six stationary aircraft. No one was injured but Jones was not popular with his seniors for the amount of repair work with which he had burdened the groundcrew and civilian maintenance staff. Again, on 13th February, no one was injured when Sgt L G Duncan's Anson taxied into the pilots' locker room in gusty weather. The aircraft and room were seriously damaged, but both could be repaired, and collateral damage was not as important as getting the aircrew through their training.

Flag-waving exercises were always encouraged and those involved embraced the break from the training routine. 'Wings for Victory' campaigns were being carried out all over the country in an attempt to raise money to help with the production of aircraft. On 3rd April 1943, the unit provided several Ansons to fly in formation during campaign events at Bilston and Kidderminster. Another event on 17th April at Brierley Hill saw the arrival of Lord Sherwood, Under-Secretary for Air, and Lord Wimborne at Bobbington by air en route to the event. Once again, 3 (O)AFU provided several aircraft for a formation flypast.

It was common practice for Staff Instructors throughout the Royal Air Force to be attached to front-line squadrons. This was not only for the individual to gain experience but also for the instructor to pass on current operational flying tactics to u/t airmen. A typical example was in April 1943 when WO E V Butcher spent fourteen days' operational attachment with 15 Squadron at Wyton in Huntingdonshire. The same month, Flt Lt R Quick and Sgt J L Stanley were attached to 214 Squadron at Chedburgh in Suffolk; both squadrons were flying the Short Stirling at the time.

A new Night-Flying Flight was formed at Bobbington on 26th April. This was a requirement from Group HQ and the idea was that each pilot that passed through the flight was to carry out ten successive night-training sorties. Thereafter, the individual was to continue his training during the day. This new training schedule made perfect sense as virtually all the crews would end up on front-line bomber squadrons, which carried out the bulk of their operations at night.

This also heightened the risk of accidents at the airfield and the potential for mid-air collisions. It was not long before such an event occurred when EG185 and N4925 collided on 7th May after the two aircraft formated on each other. EG185 came down near Pattingham; N4925 crashed at Patshull Park, also near Pattingham. The crews stood no chance and all were killed instantly.

The increased activity resulted in record flying-hour totals during April, May and June 1943. Some 3,628 hours were achieved in May but the unit's never-to-be-beaten record was chalked up in June with a grand total of 3,917 flying hours. All this obviously did not go without loss of life and machine, but Group HQ was more than pleased with the unit's output of trained aircrew.

From the beginning of September 1943 the airfield was renamed after the hamlet on the north side of the airfield, Halfpenny Green. Allegedly, the original name was too similar to that of a newly-built American airfield, but with so many airfields being built throughout the country the chances of landing at the wrong airfield were always high. By the war's end two other airfields also had 'Green' in their names!

One of the largest aircraft to visit the airfield was Handley Page Halifax II BB326 on transit flight to 1659 Heavy Conversion Unit (HCU) at Topcliffe in Yorkshire, on 12th November. The big four-engined bomber was a fairly good example of what the aircrew of 3 (O)AFU would end up flying over Germany. What was not expected was an example, when the aircraft attempted to depart, of how dangerous flying such an aircraft could be. Only five minutes after take-off, BB326 crashed in flames near to Bobbington village, killing seven of the eight crew members. Miraculously, the rear gunner, Plt Off T M Murdock, RCAF, was thrown clear and survived.

The School of Flying Control detachment at Halfpenny Green came to an end on 14th November 1943. The small collection of aircraft

48

returned to their original home at Watchfield, being absorbed into the Airfield Controllers School. The space the school's departure had created was quickly filled by 3 (O)AFU aircraft.

Every day, weather dependent, one night-flying and two day-flying exercises were organised as part of the training programme. By February 1944, the unit was in a position where an average of fifteen aircraft per detail were made available. This was the highest since the formation of the unit and hopes were high that this figure could be maintained. At the same time an improvised addition to the training was brought into use. A complete Anson fuselage was mounted over one of the airfield's static water tanks for dinghy drills and abandoning procedures. The fuselage was fitted with as much equipment as possible to resemble normal flying conditions and proved a great asset for training purposes.

The stark reality of Bomber Command operations once again involved the rescue services at the airfield. On the night of 15/16th March 1944, Bomber Command launched an 863-aircraft raid on Stuttgart and suffered badly at the hands of the German night-fighter crews. On their return from the raid, one aircraft, Halifax III LW413 of 425 Squadron, based at Tholthorpe in Yorkshire, was lost and running low on fuel. The pilot, Flg Off E E Kirk, RCAF, made the decision over Birmingham to abandon the aircraft to its fate. At 0340 hrs, the large crewless bomber plunged into a house in Adelaide Street, Brierley Hill, on the south-western fringes of Dudley. One person was killed and another was injured. Three houses were demolished, with a further three badly damaged. A medical team from the Station Sick Quarters (SSQ) attended the scene immediately, with further personnel from Halfpenny Green helping when daylight came. The bomber crew all survived the bale-out, although two were admitted to the airfield's SSQ.

Halfpenny Green continued to receive aircraft in trouble, including a USAAF Consolidated B–24 Liberator and a 196 Squadron Short Stirling IV from Shepherds Grove in Suffolk which overshot the runway and crashed. A USAAF Douglas C–47 also found Halfpenny Green's runways a welcome sight when an engine failed with fourteen paratroopers aboard on 12th April 1944. The crew and soldiers were accommodated overnight and the airfield's personnel were highly praised by the C–47 pilot for their assistance during the emergency.

The first signs of another unit moving into Halfpenny Green came on 23rd April 1944 when an advance party of 1545 Beam Approach Training Flight (BATF) arrived. Two days later, the main party

From April 1944, a few Airspeed Oxfords of 1545 BATF operated from the already overcrowded airfield.

followed under the command of Sqn Ldr King from Wheaton Aston, where they had been affiliated to 21 (P)AFU. Operating eight Airspeed Oxfords, as the unit's name implies, the flight specialised in landing in poor weather conditions by using a beam whose signal was picked up by special receiver equipment (beam set) inside the aircraft. One benefit of having the flight at the airfield was the information that could be passed to the resident Meteorological Officer. Virtually every day an Oxford from the BATF would fly to 10,000 ft, taking temperatures and recording cloud types and then landing and relaying the information. This kind of 'real-time' weather information was invaluable to the Met Officer.

The BATF lost its first aircraft on 5th August when Oxford I LX126 with Flt Lt E F Tween at the controls could not lower its starboard undercarriage. Tween decided to make a wheels-up landing and despite only slight damage to the propellers and belly, the aircraft was not seen as worth repairing.

The airfield's personnel were busy enough dealing with their own unit's accidents and mishaps. On 22nd August, they were called to a Wellington crash at Ellwood, near Halesowen. The aircraft belonged to

105 (Transport) Operational Training Unit based at Bramcote in Warwickshire. It is not clear whether the aircraft was flying too low or attempting a crash landing when it struck a tree and broke up, killing the three crew instantly. Only four days later, another Wellington from the same unit crash-landed on the airfield and ended up straddling a road. The pilot, Flg Off L P H Cole, survived with burns, and two others who had already baled out were uninjured.

While 3 (O)AFU's Ansons were sitting on the ground because the weather was so poor, the engines of the BATF's Oxfords would still be heard, but not necessarily seen. If the cloud base was not lower than 50 ft and the forward visibility was not less than 300 yds, then the BATF would fly. The 50 ft minimum was often pushed to the limit with at least ten approaches per day being carried out. This was increased to fifteen and such was the skill of the instructor pilots that, on 11th November, Flt Lt Tween performed an impeccable approach even without the beam set working. The same day, Sqn Ldr King carried out a single-engined approach safely with a 100 ft cloud base and visibility down to a fraction over 300 yds. These were the pioneering early days of what is commonly now known as ILS (Instrument Landing System).

Personnel from the unit were called out again on 22nd November. A pair of Mosquitos from 60 OTU at High Ercall, Salop, collided and one of the aircraft came down near West Bromwich. Sadly, the crew, Flg Off Liblikmaa and Sgt Hara, were both killed and an ambulance from Halfpenny Green brought their bodies back to the SSQ. Two aircrew from 1545 BATF were luckier when their Oxford I HN593 swung off the runway on 13th December. Plt Off D G Lee and a course pilot had attempted to take off in appalling weather with visibility down to approximately ten to fifteen yards! Because the visibility was so bad, the aircrew had no idea how close to the runway a line of 3 (O)AFU's Ansons were. Before the Oxford came to a halt it had crashed into no fewer than five Ansons, causing serious damage to them all and in turn writing off the Oxford. Despite the carnage, both aircrew aboard the Oxford escaped any serious injury.

As you can imagine, beam approaches were quite an art and to achieve them in daytime conditions was something of a feat, let alone at night. This was an important requirement at the time, giving the pilot the option to land at his home airfield rather than the traditional diversion to an airfield further away. Oxford I LB515, with flying instructor Flg Off B Smith, course pilot Flt Lt L J Morris and a single passenger, came to grief attempting such an approach on 18th December. The Oxford, which at the time was actually on 3 (O)AFU's strength, struck a tree on approach and crashed one-and-a-half miles north-east of the airfield. The aircraft was a complete wreck, but luckily Morris and the passenger, A C Mills, were only slightly injured.

The training situation for the BATF was not helped by Halfpenny Green's location, with hills all around, especially at the end of the main runway where the beam equipment was installed. The airfield was always susceptible to fog and, when the wind blew from the east, industrial haze would make the conditions even worse. To help the situation, sodium day–night lamps were installed and were lit when flights using instruments-only took place. This was commonly known at the time as QBI conditions or flying under the cloud base, which, loosely interpreted in RAF slang, was 'Quite Bloody Impossible'! The BATF were never particularly happy with the facilities at the airfield and, not long after their arrival, they were assured that they would be moved to a more suitable location. This never happened and Halfpenny Green would be their home until disbandment.

No 3 (O)AFU suffered another serious loss when two of their Ansons collided over the Isle of Man on 31st December 1944. One of the aircraft managed to crash-land on a hillside with all safe but, unfortunately, the other machine, piloted by Flt Sgt J M Penonzek, crashed with all on board killed.

From 16th January 1945, the BATF was re-affiliated to 21 (P)AFU which was still located at Wheaton Aston. While flying by the BATF at Halfpenny Green decreased, the airfield remained their home base and a few courses still passed through. The unit was another aircraft short when Oxford I NM482 came down in a snowstorm in Wassall Wood, near Kidderminster in Worcestershire, on 19th January. Both engines cut, forcing the Oxford down into the wood, injuring instructor Flt N B Worswick and course pilot Flt Sgt J R Payne and killing the passenger, Flg Off F R Miller.

A new unit was formed at Halfpenny Green in early 1945. Given the name, the Pilot-Navigation Instructors Course, very little is known about the unit. It moved to Cark, Lancashire, in October 1945 and then on to Swanton Morley in Norfolk.

When the end of the Second World War finally arrived, 3 (O)AFU reorganised itself, mainly because practice bombing exercises were no longer part of the training programme. Four new flights were formed, all with a Flight Lieutenant in charge, and a more disciplined environment began to emerge. This generally revolved around Physical Training (PT), with all Staff Pilots and Wireless Operators now having to attend a session every Saturday morning. On top of this,

An example of the diverse collection of general aviation aircraft which were evident at Halfpenny Green from the early 1960s. This is the only Kensinger KF racing aircraft built. G-ASSV was imported by Mr P G Bannister to Halfpenny but sadly it was destroyed in a crash in July 1969. (Via author)

a further hour of PT was required to be completed by all pilots during the week – usually playing squash, badminton or cricket would suffice. The new, healthy-minded regime insinuates that the unit's personnel were not at the peak of their physical fitness!

Peacetime flying activities at Halfpenny Green were no less dangerous. This was emphasised on 30th May 1945 when Oxford I NM482 of 1545 BATF collided with Anson DG799 of 3 (O)AFU, causing both aircraft to lose control and crash close to the airfield. The crew of the Oxford, instructor Flg Off J W Gooch and course pilot Flt Sgt S R Hawkins, were killed instantly.

Both of Halfpenny Green's flying units began to reduce in size as the year progressed. No 3 (O)AFU was the first to go, with flying training coming to an end on 13th November, followed by disbandment on 1st December 1945. No 1545 BATF did not last much longer, the last training flights taking place at the end of November, and it too was disbanded on 4th December 1945.

Like so many airfields throughout the country, the future for Halfpenny Green was not looking bright. Aircraft did return though, when the airfield was taken over by Maintenance Command on 1st January 1946. Halfpenny Green then became one of many sub-sites for

On 28th August 1977 an air show was organised at Halfpenny Green as a public relations exercise to improve the relations with local residents. This Dragon Rapide, owned by the Midland Metal Spinning Company, was captured on the day. (M J Willis)

25 Maintenance Unit (MU), whose main base was at Hartlebury in Worcestershire. The MU was an Aircraft Equipment Depot but several aircraft, including Dakotas and Horsa gliders, are known to have been scrapped at the airfield.

During the early 1950s, McAlpine were employed to resurface the runways in preparation for a training unit to operate from Halfpenny Green. This costly exercise was carried out in response to the lack of trained RAF aircrew, especially during the lead-up to and during the Korean War. All this refurbishment resulted in the detachment of an Air Navigation School (ANS), possibly 6 ANS from Lichfield, who operated a few Avro Ansons for just six months.

No 25 MU's association with Halfpenny Green came to an end on 15th November 1956. The airfield was immediately placed under Care and Maintenance and was officially designated as a reserve airfield.

The recently resurfaced runways would have been a major draw to an enthusiastic group led by ex-25 RFS Chief Flying Instructor, H E Gibson. During 1960, Gibson doggedly harried the Air Ministry to lease the airfield, until they buckled in March 1961. The necessary licences followed, and a group of determined volunteers laid the foundation stones for what was to become Wolverhampton Airport.

Aerial view of Halfpenny Green/Wolverhampton Airport in the early 1990s. Very little has changed over the years and this view shows all three original runways still in use.

Despite the traditional local objections and the continuing financial worries, the airfield today is well supported from all corners of general aviation.

Many original buildings survive, although only recently a few minor wartime buildings have had to be demolished because they had deteriorated so much. All three wartime runways remain in good order, mainly thanks to McAlpine, and the original control tower and three Bellman hangars are still used for their intended purpose.

5
HIXON

In 1941, the demand for fully-trained night-bomber crews was high, with Bomber Command desperately trying to make an impact on the outcome of the war. The Command required airfields dedicated to such a task and Hixon was one of many specifically built for this purpose. For many, Hixon is the perfect example of a bomber OTU (Operational Training Unit), a role that it performed for virtually all of its wartime existence.

Construction of the new airfield was begun in mid-1941 by Trollope and Cole. It was located between the villages of Stowe-by-Chartley and Hixon, hemmed in by the North Staffordshire (Euston and Manchester) and LNER Stafford and Uttoxeter railway lines. The land belonged to two farmers by the names of Marston and Jackson. Both were relocated – the Marston family was unfortunate because they were moved to a house in Blithfield destined to become the site of a reservoir only ten years later.

The railway severely restricted any expansion plans for the airfield, which was built with three runways at 1,650, 1,400 and 1,200 yards respectively. Only the latter runway, which ran in a north-west/south-east direction, had the scope to be made longer, and this was only by approximately 200 yards.

The main technical area was located on the south-eastern side of the airfield, literally on the very edge of Hixon village. Four Type T2 hangars were built on the edge of the technical site and later a Type B1 was also constructed across New Road, along with a clutch of 'pan-handle' dispersals. The latter, which totalled 30, were liberally spread around the perimeter. Two incendiary bomb stores were constructed on the western edge of the airfield; one of them was located across the North Staffordshire railway line and the other near the airfield

Hixon's Type 12779 control tower is preserved in excellent condition and still serves the airfield, now as the site's main office. (Author)

perimeter track. Additional bomb stores, including fuses, were kept on the northern side while the main fusing point was built less than 500 ft from Stowe-by-Chartley village. This meant there was not much margin for error if anything went wrong! Accommodation, while classed as temporary, catered for nearly 2,400 officers and airmen and 445 WAAFs.

The scene was now set for occupation and on 10th May 1942 a Bomber Command circular announced that Hixon would be placed within 7 Group. This was changed the following day to 92 Group and Lichfield was appointed as the parent station. The first RAF personnel to arrive on 13th May 1942 were in the form of an opening-up party. They were followed by Flt Lt J L Girling, who assumed command of the station. Wg Cdr H McC White replaced Girling a few days later on 8th June and not long after was promoted to Group Captain, becoming the first official station commander of Hixon.

It was now time for Hixon's first flying unit to be formed and this began on 28th June 1942, with 30 OTU. The unit's main equipment was to be at least 30 Vickers Wellingtons and its role was the training of night-bomber crews for Bomber Command. Before the new unit had even received any aircraft, Hixon was temporarily elevated to parent station status on 6th July. A signal from HQ Bomber Command stated

Many of the Wellingtons received by 30 OTU, if not all, had already seen operational service with a Bomber Command squadron. The Wellington IC was the first of its mark to serve at Hixon.

that Hixon would be in charge of a new airfield at Whitchurch Heath (later named Tilstock) in Shropshire where 81 OTU was being formed.

The newly posted-in ground personnel were prematurely excited when two aircraft descended upon Hixon on 15th July 1942. The first, a Wellington IC, touched down on a partly-finished runway, followed shortly afterwards by a second. The two weary bombers belonged to 12 OTU at Chipping Warden in Oxfordshire and were destined to become ground instructional training aircraft rather than being the first official 30 OTU machines. The local contractors had not yet erected any windsocks and the Wellingtons were guided in using an improvised smoke indicator and green Very lights. The same day, Hixon's controlling group changed to 93 Group, forming at Lichfield and remaining here until close to the war's end.

The Air Officer Commanding (AOC) Training for Bomber Command and AOC of 93 Group, Air Vice-Marshal Capel, visited Hixon on 17th July. Despite not a single airworthy aircraft being available, he set a target date of 4th August for flying training to begin at the airfield.

The first of three Wellingtons, which were part of the planned establishment of 30 aircraft, arrived, once again from 12 OTU, on 23rd July. More aircraft continued to fly in and the first batch of flying instructors arrived at Hixon on 28/29th July. There were eight in total; five were posted in from 25 OTU at Finningley, Yorkshire and three arrived from 16 OTU at Upper Heyford in Oxfordshire.

With only seven airworthy Wellingtons now on strength, the first course of 29 aircrew pupils arrived on 8th August 1942. The start date set by AVM Capel was, perhaps, rather ambitious and flying training did not begin until 23rd August. The same day, a second course arrived, consisting of 30 more aircrew pupils – 30 OTU were now up and running with plans to receive a new course every fortnight.

The first of many accidents which would occur at Hixon took place on 11th September 1942. Sgt Stitt in Wellington IC N2779 was carrying out circuits and landings and, on one particular approach, he came in too fast, overshot the runway, crossed the Euston to Manchester railway line and came to rest in an adjacent field. All escaped injury apart from Sgt Bakeman, an air gunner, who sustained minor cuts and slight shock. The aircraft, which originally belonged to 23 OTU at Pershore in Worcestershire, was repaired and remained at Hixon until August 1944.

After Air Chief Marshal Arthur Harris took over as Commander-in-Chief of Bomber Command in February 1942, aircraft from OTUs were regularly called upon to participate in large raids over Germany. While many other crews cut their teeth flying 'Nickel' (leaflet dropping) raids over France, the first taste of front-line operations for 30 OTU occurred over Bremen on 13/14th September 1942. Hixon dispatched four Wellingtons on the raid, which involved 446 aircraft, many from other OTUs. While the raid was deemed a success from a collateral damage point of view, 21 aircraft were lost, 13 of them from OTUs. Hixon's small contribution were lucky. Three aircraft attacked the target although a fourth failed to find it. Included in the raid was Plt Off B J Staniland in Wellington IC DV771, who bombed the target and landed at Swanton Morley in Norfolk on the way back. Plt Off R Edwards returned early with a faulty compass and landed at Tatenhill, and Flt Sgt Coles bombed the primary target from 14,000 ft and also landed at Tatenhill.

Two nights later, four more aircraft were detailed for a front-line Bomber Command operation. This time the target was Essen, with 369 aircraft taking part in the raid on a target which had proved costly and difficult to attack. Thirty-nine aircraft were lost, equating to over ten per cent of the force, of which, once again, OTU aircraft took the brunt with 18 aircraft missing in action. The 30 OTU contingent all survived, with one Wellington returning early with intercom trouble and difficulty in climbing. Flt Lt B J Duigan in DV613 returned with a full bomb load, while Plt Off Staniland and Flt Sgt E W Smith managed to bomb the target successfully.

Hixon was not yet particularly overcrowded, but a satellite airfield became available at Seighford. Originally, Wheaton Aston was proposed but this move failed to materialise and Seighford was officially taken over by 30 OTU on 16th September 1942. The use of this additional airfield would pay dividends in the near future as the unit began to increase in size.

For air-to-air firing training, 30 OTU had a pair of target tugs on strength. These were a Westland Lysander and a Boulton Paul Defiant TT Mk I, one of many converted at Pendeford. On 9th October, Plt Off R L Bartley was taxiing the Defiant around the perimeter track. Like most big tail-dragging aircraft of this design, taxiing meant steering from left to right in order to see past the aircraft's long nose. Bartley could not have noticed the horse and cart until the Defiant's wing crashed into it. The horse was badly bruised and the aircraft's wing and propeller were damaged. Ground collisions were common on busy airfields and everyone had to be wary, even the local livestock!

The first 'Nickel' raid took place from the airfield during the night of 24th October 1942. Sgt N E Burton flew the operation over north-western France, successfully dropping 700 lbs of leaflets. Burton and his crew returned to Hixon safely, despite receiving the attention of local flak defences and searchlights.

No 30 OTU's first fatal accident took place within sight of the airfield at 2050 hrs on 31st Oct 1942. W/O W L Primrose, a unit flying instructor, took off in Wellington IC Z1083, with a crew for a practice bombing exercise at night. On return to Hixon, Primrose overshot his first approach to land and, during the climb to go round again, the bomber stalled at only 500 ft. With no chance of recovery, the Wellington crashed at Grange Farm, Amerton, killing all on board.

During October 1942, Flt Lt Bill Hickox, DFC and Bar, was posted to 30 OTU as a Navigation Instructor. His job was to teach crews the necessary techniques for long-distance cross-country exercises and this would usually involve a flight of several hours. He remembers one particular day very clearly:

I recall one incident where the pilot was a trainee Warrant Officer, who was supposedly an ex-Battle of Britain fighter pilot, turning up for a briefing smelling of ale! The crew were keen to go anyway and said that he could 'take' his drink and it was the last flight they had to do before completing the course. Foolishly as it turned out, I agreed to go. Once we were out towards the Irish Sea the radio on the Wellington failed completely, which meant we had to abort the flight and turn back to base immediately. This was well before the effects of any alcohol had time to wear off and as a result the pilot needed three attempts to land, which I was not too happy about. The crew had to repeat the flight the following day and I remember giving the crew a tremendous ticking-off and telling them they must make sure they kept the pilot sober!

The first of many 'Bullseye' exercises took place from Hixon on the night of 7/8th November 1942, with three aircraft taking part. Within a few weeks, though, 30 OTU would send out an average of twelve aircraft at a time. Bullseyes were a good way of teaching aircrews to fly over long distances within a formation and over relatively safe territory. Nickels continued over France for the remainder of the year and long-distance navigation exercises, usually flown across the Irish Sea, became routine for the unit.

New Year 1943 began with an influx of aircraft and personnel from 25 OTU at Finningley in Yorkshire, which was being disbanded. Between 1st and 19th January, large parties of technical personnel and 26 Wellington IIIs with their crews were added to 30 OTU's strength. The majority of the personnel and several aircraft were immediately transferred to Seighford and by the end of the month, 30 OTU had swelled to over 2,800 personnel and 57 aircraft.

One airman was very lucky to survive when he accidentally walked into the revolving propeller of Wellington X HE428 on 2nd February 1943. These kinds of accident were considered to be inevitably fatal but the accident report simply states that 'the propeller was badly damaged'! The crew of Wellington III BK184 were equally lucky when an engine caught fire over Yorkshire the following day. The pilot, Sgt J King, managed to shut the engine down but could not maintain height, so a forced landing was the only option. The bomber, with wheels up and flaps retracted, landed successfully near Skerry Hall Farm, five miles south-east of Whitby.

It was not such a happy ending for Sgt R D Lewis, RAAF, and his crew in Wellington III BK434 on 7th February. After successfully completing a night cross-country exercise, the bomber appeared to make a good landing, but Lewis decided to open the throttles and go around again. The Wellington climbed too steeply and stalled at

At Hixon the Wellington III began to supersede the tired ICs from early 1943. This example is the prototype at Boscombe Down in Wiltshire.

1,000 ft. Before Lewis had a chance to recover, the bomber hit the ground near the Rectory, Ingestre Park, near Weston, only a mile from the southern boundary of the airfield. All five on board were killed instantly. Sadly, another crew was lost only five days later when Wellington X HE466, with Sgt E G Frezell, RCAF, at the controls crashed into Foel Grach in Snowdonia.

Up until December 1942, the unit had been solely equipped with Wellington ICs, the majority of which were becoming very tired. HQ Bomber Command made the decision that 30 OTU should be totally re-equipped with the Wellington III and X, of which several had already arrived on the unit. In February 1943, the unit held 35 Wellington IIIs, 15 Wellington Xs and only 6 Wellington ICs; the latter had already been allotted to other units. The unit was also elevated to a full OTU status.

10th April 1943 was a day to forget for 30 OTU, when two aircraft were lost at dawn within 15 minutes of each other. The first accident involved Wellington III BK179, which crashed five minutes after take-off into Ranton Woods, close to the airfield. The pilot, Flg Off R Haynes, and four crew members were killed instantly. The second Wellington III, DP611, lost power 40 minutes after take-off. The pilot, Flt Sgt R A Jones, decided to force-land on a straight piece of road near Hartington in Derbyshire. All went well, until moments before the bomber slid to a halt. The Wellington struck a solid wall, splitting open one of the bomber's fuel tanks and then quickly bursting into flames. Only two of the five crew managed to escape.

With more aircraft available and an increase in aircrew courses passing through Hixon, the unit was able to increase the number of

The Wellington X was the most prolific mark of this famous bomber ever produced. No 30 OTU received its first example in early 1943.

Wellingtons sent on Nickel operations. On average, three Nickels were being flown every month, with at least eight aircraft on each. The crews sent on the raids were generally near the end of their OTU training and recorded statistics for the unit show that very few were lost during these forays over enemy territory. The first loss did not occur until one such operation on 13/14th April 1943. While homebound and heading towards the Kent coast, Sgt H E Bull, RAAF, in Wellington III DF610, suffered a port engine failure. Bull had no choice but to ditch and this was carried out in the Strait of Dover, south of Dungeness. Despite all being injured, the crew of six survived and were quickly picked up by Air-Sea Rescue. This particular crew were posted to 460 Squadron at Breighton in Yorkshire and converted to the Lancaster III. Tragically, all but one who passed through Hixon were killed during a raid on Wuppertal on 29/30th May.

Planning the training curriculum at Hixon was becoming increasingly difficult as the unit grew in size. Divided into four flights, trainee aircrew within a flight could be at one of four stages of their training and it was obvious that the schedule needed simplifying. The solution was straightforward. On arrival at Hixon, each crew would be allocated a flight and would stay with it until the end of their training. Known as 'straight-through' training, the flight simply changed its function as each new stage of training was reached. The new system began in April 1943 and remained in place until 30 OTU disbanded.

May 1943 was one of the busiest months for Nickel operations over France. Five Nickels were flown and all but one aircraft managed to drop their cargo into the correct target area. Despite the unit being equipped with slightly newer aircraft, they were no less susceptible to technical malfunctions. On 24/25th May, outbound to France, Sgt P A J Shoreland had to turn back when he was 35 miles south of Leicester because he could not open his bomb doors and the oxygen equipment had failed.

More Nickels were carried out in June, with the main targets now being Paris, Lorent, Brest and Nantes. It was during a raid on the latter that 30 OTU lost its first aircrew on a Nickel operation. Three aircraft, including Wellington III BK559, piloted by Flt Sgt T G Dellar, RAAF, were tasked with a raid on Nantes. Dellar and his crew became lost and, at 0330 hrs, after dropping their bundles of leaflets, set course for home while very low on fuel. Still uncertain of their position and with the fuel at a critical level, Dellar gave the order for his crew to bale out. Three complied, but Flt Sgt D M Davis, RCAF, stayed with Dellar, who did not have a parachute. It is believed that the Wellington came down near Versailles. Flt Sgt Dellar is alleged to have died in the crash and Davies is thought to have been killed whilst evading capture, as his grave is several hundred miles away, near Marseilles. Of the three who baled out, two became POWs and a third, Sgt B C Reeves, managed to evade capture.

The biggest single Nickel operation from Hixon took place on 22nd/23rd June 1943. Sixteen aircraft took part: ten Wellingtons targeted Paris, two Orléans, two Le Mans and two were given Rheims. One aircraft returned early with technical problems and another landed at West Malling in Kent, after the starboard engine caught fire off Beachy Head. Wellington X HE527, piloted by Flg Sgt J Hennessy, RAAF, was reported missing and it was later discovered that the bomber had been hit by flak over Cherbourg. Three of the crew were killed, including the pilot, but three others managed to bale out, only to become POWs.

Factory-fresh aircraft for front-line operations were in no less demand by the middle of 1943. However, more war-weary aircraft were being removed from operational squadrons, providing a surplus to form additional training units. Part of the aircrew training at all bomber OTUs was in techniques in bomber defence. Fighter aircraft from a variety of different squadrons would perform mock attacks on

No 30 OTU were joined by 1686 BDTF in July 1943 operating the Curtiss Tomahawk. All six pilots belonging to the unit pose in front of the American-built fighters. (Hixon Local Historical Society)

bombers to give the air gunners an idea of what they could come up against. No 30 OTU received its own fighter affiliation unit when 1686 Bomber (Defence) Training Flight (BDTF) was formed at Hixon on 1st July 1943. It was the sixth unit to be formed and the second within 93 Group. All were equipped with the American-built Curtiss Tomahawk single-seat fighter, known in the USA as the P–40. Virtually all of the Tomahawks on the BDTFs had seen action in North Africa, with several hours on the clock. No 112 Squadron, which operated the Tomahawk as part of the Desert Air Force, were famous for applying aggressive shark-mouth markings under the nose. All of Hixon's Tomahawks either retained these markings or had them re-applied. They were ideal for fighter affiliation and proved a useful asset to the unit. No 1686 BDTF had six aircraft on strength, made up of four Tomahawk Is (AH783, 832, 850 and 852), a single IIA (AH926) and a IIB (AK128).

The loss and accident rates on Bullseye exercises were beginning to exceed all other operations from the airfield combined. A typical example occurred on the night of 6/7th July when six aircraft took off from Hixon for a Bullseye. On their return to the airfield at 0344 hrs, Wellington X HE328 crashed near Hanging Wicket, approximately two miles east of the airfield, after losing control in cloud. The pilot, Flg Off A Beare, and his crew of five were killed. One of those killed was Second Lieutenant T E Fenwick who was attached from 154 Heavy Anti-Aircraft Regiment, Royal Artillery.

The crew of a Wellington piloted by Plt Off Woodley had an unnerving experience whilst returning from a training exercise over Wales on 25th August 1943. The bomber was struck by lightning, causing one of the engines to run very roughly, with familiar signs that total failure was imminent. While the crew prepared to bale out, the engine picked up again and began to run smoothly. The flight continued until only a few miles from the airfield, over Bagots Park Bombing Range, when the guns of the front turret fired a burst without the air gunner pressing the trigger! Woodley flew back to Hixon as fast as possible and when on the ground an inspection discovered that there were big dents all along the fuselage and a large piece of a propeller blade was missing. Lightning can affect aircraft and their systems in mysterious ways.

On 30th/31st August 1943, for the first time in Hixon's short history, aircraft from the unit took part in a major bombing raid against the enemy. No 33 OTU Wellingtons, four of them from Hixon, were tasked with attacking an ammunition dump at Forêt d'Eperlecques, north of St Omer in Northern France. This was the first of a series of small raids, specifically arranged for OTU crews, where Pathfinder de Havilland Mosquitos marked the target. The experience gained by bombing a marked target would be useful once they were posted to a front-line squadron. The major distraction of a 660-aircraft raid on Münchengladbach the same night helped keep the Luftwaffe away from the OTU raid. Three 30 OTU Wellingtons dropped sixteen 500 lb bombs while the fourth aircraft, failing to see the target markers, jettisoned its bomb load into the Channel. The attack on the dump was successful with a large explosion being witnessed by many of the crews. Hixon's contingent returned home safely but two Wellingtons were lost from other OTUs.

Four more aircraft were detailed from Hixon on 31st August/ 1st September to attack another ammunition dump in Northern France. The same night, Bomber Command launched another big raid against Germany with 622 aircraft attacking Berlin. The considerably smaller force, which consisted of thirty Wellingtons, six Pathfinder

Mosquitos and five Halifaxes, set out to bomb the dump at Forêt de Hesdin. Two Wellingtons from Hixon dropped a total of sixteen 500 lb bombs on the target, but two others, failing to see the target, jettisoned their bombs into the sea. Once again, the raid was a success, without loss, in stark contrast to the Berlin raid which was deemed a failure with 47 aircraft failing to return.

A third and final trip to bomb targets in Northern France took place on 2nd/3rd September, with two Wellingtons from Hixon taking part. Thirty Wellingtons, with six Pathfinder Mosquitos and five Lancasters marking the target, bombed the ammunition dump at Forêt de Mormal. Sgt K L Perry in Wellington X HE413 dropped seven 500 lb bombs onto the target while Plt Off J Hart jettisoned the same sized load into the Channel. Another successful trip for all concerned, without loss.

On the night of 8/9th September 1943, Bomber Command gathered a mixed force of 257 aircraft to attack a German long-range gun battery at Boulogne. Several Wellingtons from OTUs contributed aircraft; in Hixon's case, three bombers took part. This particular raid also involved five USAAF Boeing B–17 Flying Fortresses. This was the first time that American aircraft had flown alongside Bomber Command aircraft during a night bombing sortie. Two of the 30 OTU Wellingtons claimed to have bombed the target, while the third, BJ986, flown by Sgt A J Sandford, returned early and dropped its bomb over Cannock range. Post-attack reconnaissance revealed that poor marking by the Pathfinder Mosquitos resulted in the gun battery being undamaged.

A routine night dual-circuit exercise by a 27 OTU Wellington from Lichfield turned into tragedy on 10th September 1943. It was common for aircraft to carry out such an exercise at another airfield and Hixon was quite used to this. Wellington III BK152, with Flg Off N G Stewart, DFM, RAAF, at the controls, came in to land at Hixon but appeared to touch down too far down the runway to stop. The throttles were opened and the bomber steadily climbed away to join the airfield circuit. After a few moments, it inexplicably plunged into a house less than a mile south-west of the airfield and killed the entire crew of six, who were all RAAF. It is possible that Stewart raised the flaps rather than the undercarriage and stalled.

Not all unit losses involved aircraft as proved by Sgt Schofield, the pilot of Wellington X HF471, on 2nd October. During a navigation exercise to the Isle of Man and back, the bomber encountered severe icing. It began to lose height and, whilst approaching the North Wales coast, Schofield gave the order to bale out over Rhyl. The wireless

A Tomahawk takes off from a snowy Hixon during the winter of 1943/44. If the runway could be cleared then aircraft would fly. (Hixon Local Historical Society)

operator, Sgt Mushet, and bomb aimer, Sgt Champion, both abandoned the aircraft, which moments later began to come back under control. Schofield continued and made a precautionary landing at Pershore in Worcestershire. It was not uncommon for aircrew to bale out in situations like this, but sadly for these two airmen, after a five-day search they were not found. It is presumed that the pair succumbed to the icy waters of the Irish Sea.

Poor weather throughout December 1943 resulted in several diversions of aircraft that were unable to land at their home airfields. A typical example occurred on 21st December 1943 when five Short Stirling IVs of 620 Squadron, Leicester East, arrived. The specially converted transport aircraft departed the next day for the short trip to their home airfield.

No 1686 BDTF suffered its first loss on 23rd December. It was not a particularly serious accident, but it could have been if the bowser that Tomahawk I AK128 taxied into had exploded! The port wing of the fighter was sufficiently damaged not to warrant repair of the aircraft.

No 30 OTU's role within Bomber Command was extended slightly from 13th January 1944. Despite being quite a few miles from the nearest coastline, Hixon's aircraft were now called upon to carry out Air-Sea Rescue (ASR) operations, specifically over the North Sea, looking for crews who had ditched returning from raids on Germany. Six aircraft took part in the first ASR sortie to search for missing Lancaster III ED826 of 15 Squadron at Mildenhall in Suffolk. The Lancaster was on a training exercise which involved flying over the sea off the Yorkshire and Lincolnshire coasts. The 30 OTU Wellingtons split into two formations for the search: (A) under the command of Flt Lt Swann and (B) under the command of Flg Off Etherton, both 30 OTU staff instructors. The ASR group spent over six hours in the air looking for the missing aircraft, but found nothing. Two Wellingtons landed at Leconfield and Pocklington, both in Yorkshire, short of fuel after flying to the very limits of their endurance. It was later discovered that the Lancaster had come down in the sea, thirteen miles south of Skegness, Lincolnshire, in the mouth of the Wash. The six crew perished and this was the first Lancaster lost by 15 Squadron after converting from the Short Stirling.

In an attempt to produce an official history of the activities of 30 OTU and specifically the training of Air Bombers, seven representatives of the press and an Air Ministry Public Relations Officer visited Hixon on 20th January 1944. Four Wellingtons were detailed for the day's activities, which would involve two aircraft dropping four 500 lb bombs on Rufford and Ragdale ranges. Six of the group, who were editorial, flew in the bombing aircraft to watch the procedure involved. The press photographers flew in the other two aircraft in an attempt to produce a pictorial record of the event. Once the bombing was completed, the four aircraft delivered the press contingent to Manby in Lincolnshire. The editorial part of the flight went very well but the weather was against the photographer and the results were not good. Despite this, a few weeks later the report appeared in the national press.

A routine practice circuit and bump exercise in the afternoon of 10th February resulted in a local workman performing an unselfish act of bravery. Sgt W E Keeler in Wellington X HF516 had his starboard engine cut whilst only at 1,000 ft. Rapidly losing height, Wheeler attempted to land on one of the shorter subsidiary runways. The Wellington did not make the runway and came down, wheels up, in a field south of New Road. The bomber swung to starboard, crashing into a concrete mixer and a pile of gravel being used for the construction of the B1 hangar near the road. After a few tense moments, the crew began scrambling clear of the bomber, which was catching fire. Sgt A J Welstead, the wireless operator, was making his escape when his parachute harness became hooked up. One of the contractors working on the hangar, Mr Cyril Fradley, ran to the burning bomber and dragged Welstead clear. Sadly, Sgt Welstead was badly burned and succumbed to his injuries in Stafford General Hospital the following day. Cyril Fradley, for his bravery, was awarded the British Empire Medal (BEM).

The Wellingtons of 30 OTU were becoming very tired by early 1944 and the unserviceability rate was increasing daily. On almost every Bullseye exercise during the year at least one aircraft returned with a technical problem or was lost as a result of one. Of the eight aircraft that took part in a Special Command Bullseye from Hixon on 11th February, half had technical faults. These ranged from engine trouble or magneto drops, to oil leaks and a sextant unserviceable.

On 16th February, only four aircraft took part in a Bullseye and all struggled back to Hixon with major technical problems. One of the Wellingtons flew the whole exercise without any trouble but on return could not get a green light to show on the port undercarriage leg, giving the pilot the impression that the leg was still retracted. Low on fuel and with visibility deteriorating, the Welllington flew over the airfield and a searchlight was illuminated on the belly of the bomber to check the position of the undercarriage. Both undercarriage legs appeared to be down and the Wellington made a normal approach and landing with the crew onboard expecting the leg to collapse at any moment. On this occasion all was well and a failed light bulb was the cause of the problem.

No 1686 BDTF, being such a small unit, could not afford to lose many of its aircraft. Now down to just five, the unit lost a second Tomahawk on 5th March 1944. AH850 suffered total oil pressure failure, causing the engine to stop abruptly. The pilot skilfully trimmed the aircraft for a glide and managed to make a successful emergency landing at Condover in Shropshire. Despite the pilot appearing to have saved the aircraft, damage to the engine was sufficient not to warrant a repair and the BDTF lost another fighter.

Less than a week later, Flg Off Chapman crashed Tomahawk I AH832 during a cross-wind take-off at Hixon on 11th March. The fighter hit the railway embankment, damaging the aircraft beyond repair; Chapman walked away unharmed. The accident card for this particular incident has a photograph of the crash donated by Flg Off Chapman, inscribed 'My second prang'. The flight was becoming desperate for aircraft, but with no more Tomahawks available, the unit

'Unlucky for Some?' Possibly one of the most famous official photographs of a Bomber Command OTU taken during the Second World War and luckily for us, from the top of Hixon's control tower. Only three serial numbers are visible out of the thirteen aircraft parked in front of the hangars in early 1944. All were lost before the war's end. How many more out of this line-up did not make it? (IWM via Hixon Local Historical Society)

had to settle for a single brand new Hurricane IIC. They were destined to lose another Tomahawk at Peplow in Shropshire on 14th April. On landing, the starboard undercarriage leg broke off, followed by the port leg as the aircraft veered off the runway.

John Cooper was an Air Gunner during the Second World War. He was part of a crew who had to retrain with a new navigator at Hixon. The crew's original navigator was removed from his position after taking their bomber into an air raid over London rather than dropping bombs over Germany! John recalls his time at Hixon:

I remember being posted only three huts away from the Coach and Horses pub which was very handy for evening socialisation! We undertook several weeks of day training in flying followed by the usual period of a month or so night flying. Following this training the complete crew with our new navigator went on a conversion course on the Lancaster at Bottesford, Leicestershire. We were then posted to 550 Squadron at North Killingholme, Lincolnshire from where we flew a successful tour of operations until the end of the war.

The social life at Hixon seems to have been pretty good, with plenty of local pubs within easy distance of the airfield. Norman Low was a Sergeant Armourer Fitter between January 1944 and March 1945:

Hixon was a very happy place to work, with regular hours and weekends that could easily be taken away on leave. I worked in the armaments section and the bombs were delivered from the bomb dump and loaded onto Wellingtons together with bullets into the turrets, which I also serviced. I remember the social side being very lively with regular visits to the Lamb and Flag, Coach and Horses, the Clifford Arms and the Woolpack – all on my normal itinerary. Another vivid memory was the dining room in the Sergeants' Mess which was painted with a mural all around by a sergeant pilot who I think came from Australia. It was mainly a landscape painting, but included a couple of planes in the sky part.

Bullseyes dominated March 1944, the general routine being only briefly disrupted by enemy action in the early hours of 24th March. For the first time since Hixon opened, the airfield came under Air Raid Warning 'Red' at 0112 hrs, but it was cleared by 0145 hrs. Considering how close to the industrial Midlands the airfield was, it is surprising that this was the only occasion a warning was sounded.

An Air Transport Auxiliary (ATA) pilot on a delivery flight with a Boulton Paul Defiant found Hixon a welcome sight on 25th March. The engine developed a major oil leak, but the pilot managed to land safely and 30 OTU ground crew quickly repaired the problem. The crew of Wellington X HF471 were not so lucky on the evening of 11th April 1944. Tasked with a night cross-country flight, Plt Off C H G Gale and his crew of five took off from Hixon at 2025 hrs. Approximately 30 minutes later, the bomber emerged from clouds and dived into fields at Sandhall Farm on the eastern bank of the River Ouse, only one mile east of Goole in Yorkshire. The crew were all killed instantly and the crash was witnessed by several locals. Despite this, Hixon had no idea as to the fate of HF471 until 1820 hours on 12th April after personnel from Holme-upon-Spalding-Moor, Yorkshire, had reported finding the wreckage at 1550 hrs that day.

On 3rd May, a secret signal was received by Hixon, prompting the airfield to prepare for the arrival of a VIP. Two days later, a 24 Squadron de Havilland Flamingo twin-engine transport from Hendon landed on the main runway. Inside was the Secretary of State for Air, Sir Archibald Sinclair, on an official visit to 16 MU at Stafford. A car was provided by the station and the Secretary's visit was brief because he was back at Hixon by 1200 hrs. His busy itinerary included Ballykelly in Northern Ireland followed by Wick in Caithness by 1700 hrs that same day!

Six Wellingtons from 'D' Flight took part in a Nickel raid in the Orléans area of Northern France on 9/10th May 1944. One aircraft, Wellington III BJ618, flown by Flt Lt R C Thorn, failed to return and hopes were not high for the crew. Whether the aircraft suffered from a mechanical failure or was hit by flak is unknown but all of the crew survived after the bomber crashed near Selles, south of Pont-Audemer. Four, including Thorn, managed to evade capture while two others became POWs. Another Wellington diverted to Tarrant Rushton in Dorset, after the navigator became ill.

The others returned to Hixon but Sgt Bowater's arrival in Wellington X LN533 was more spectacular than planned. The bomber was already having problems with its intercom, but this became secondary after what seemed to be a normal landing. Immediately after touchdown, the Wellington burst into flames. Bowater steered the bomber off the main runway, the crew vacated the burning aircraft and the emergency services were quickly on the scene extinguishing the fire. Despite the apparent ferocity of the flames, the aircraft was not seriously damaged and was quickly repaired, going on to serve with 11 AGS and remaining in service until March 1948.

High-ranking American military brass landed at Hixon on 30th June 1944. General George Patton and General William C Lee used the airfield as a staging point to visit the POW camp at Rugeley. This was one of many visits by senior American staff to POW camps throughout the country.

A group of resourceful ground engineers at Hixon came up with a design for improving the speed at which the undercarriage of a Wellington could be lowered during an emergency. If a fault occurred that affected the undercarriage, it would take a long time to crank down the gear manually and many aircraft were being belly-landed rather than landed conventionally. To avoid this situation, the Hixon engineers designed an emergency air bottle, which simply overrode the normal gear lever and blew the undercarriage down very quickly. Bomber Command approved the design and the first air bottles came into use from June 1944, saving several aircraft from unnecessary damage.

Even with an air bottle fitted, the undercarriage of Plt Off White's Wellington III BK443 would not come down when he returned from a Special Combined Bullseye exercise on 18th July. This particular exercise involved aircraft from virtually all of Bomber Command, mainly Wellington-equipped OTUs, and was of a kind becoming commonplace throughout the year. Whilst 60 miles over the North Sea, the port engine of BK443 caught fire and Plt Off White made for Coltishall in Norfolk. With the undercarriage still firmly in the raised position, White performed an impeccable crash landing at Coltishall without injury to the crew and with minimal damage to the aircraft. The bomber was repaired and remained with the unit until March 1945.

Visiting aircraft were increasing rapidly at Hixon from July 1944 onwards. Its location, near to the American 8th and 9th Air Force, Air and Service Command and the Combat Crew Replacement, all based at Stone, meant USAAF aircraft were a common sight. Douglas C–47s were regulars, Boeing B–17s and Martin B–26 Marauders were also not unusual and generally a colourful addition to the day's activities compared to the drab, camouflaged RAF Wellingtons. After the arrival of the Americans in the county, liaison and communication aircraft landed at Hixon on a daily basis. Aircraft types included the Piper L–4, Cessna UC–78, Beech UC–45A, Fairchild UC–61 and Oxfords in USAAF markings.

RAF aircraft types were also on the increase, including Albemarles and Whitleys from 42 OTU at Ashbourne in Derbyshire and Wellingtons from 28 OTU detachment at Bircotes in Nottinghamshire. Lancasters from 625 Squadron at Kelstern in Lincolnshire were diverted to Hixon on their return from a raid over Germany at the end of July. They were followed in early August by Halifaxes from 1667 HCU Sandtoft in Lincolnshire and Lindholme in Yorkshire, also diverted when the weather clamped down on their own airfields. This pattern continued until the war's end, as Hixon was always able to accommodate both visiting and resident aircraft in trouble.

After returning from a successful cross-country flight on 24th July 1944, Wellington III HF727 was parked close to Hixon's control tower. The usual mêlée of ground personnel crawled all over the aircraft preparing it for its next flight. After approximately 45 minutes, whilst the oxygen supply was being refilled, a fire broke out. Despite the fire engine getting to the scene very quickly (the fire section was located next to the control tower), the Wellington was destroyed within minutes of the blaze starting. It is presumed that spilt oxygen mixed with either engine oil or brake fluid and ignited. The Wellington had only been delivered to Hixon on 5th June, having previously served at 20 OTU, Lossiemouth in Morayshire. It had only survived this long because the fire brigade at Lossiemouth had saved it from another blaze back in January 1944. Deryck (Jack) Brew was a Corporal Armourer at Hixon and was one of many who witnessed the demise of HF727: 'I remember the tremendous heat from the fire and the propellers of the plane starting to turn simply from the hot air rising past them!'

No 1686 BDTF, with its handful of Tomahawk fighters, was disbanded on 21st August 1944. The OTU at Hixon used its own Hawker Hurricanes for fighter affiliation and the increasingly unreliable Tomahawks were withdrawn.

August 1944 was dominated by more Special Command Bullseyes. Since the Allied invasion, Nickels over Northern France had come to an end simply because the odds of being shot down had dramatically increased. While a group of aircraft was taking part in a Bullseye on 26th August, Plt Off Mettrick in Wellington X LP570 overshot the runway. The bomber came to rest on the LNER railway line with its undercarriage damaged, but the crew was uninjured. The five aircraft taking part in the Bullseye were diverted to Seighford, which was not an unusual occurrence, but was an inconvenience for the crews.

The same evening, the ground personnel were involved in moving another bomber from the railway line. Whilst on night circuits and landings, Flt Sgt R E George in Wellington X HE224 touched the runway too fast, ballooned back into the air, overshot the runway and crashed in virtually the same position as LP570 only hours before. The bomber was seriously damaged but the crew was unhurt. Because of the high probability of an aircraft crashing on the railway line, special phone lines were laid between signal boxes so that signalmen could be informed as soon as an incident took place.

Hixon played host to the 'First Annual Field Day' for the Midland Command of the Air Training Corps (ATC) on 1st October 1944. The event was recorded as a great success and competitions arranged included navigation, signals, airmanship, aircraft recognition and shooting.

Bullseye exercises continued to be the main activity with up to fourteen Wellingtons taking part at a time. Accidents occurred throughout the summer of 1944, as the Wellington IIIs and Xs were becoming tired and prone to mechanical failures. As with the earlier Mk Is, hydraulic and electrical failures became the most common reasons why an aircraft had to divert and carry out an emergency landing during a training sortie. The aircrew loss rate for 30 OTU during training sorties was reducing until October 1944, when two serious accidents claimed two more crews.

The first occurred on 12th October 1944, a particularly bad night for Bomber Command OTUs. Plt Off D J White, RAAF, in Wellington X MF698 was tasked to fly a night navigation exercise. The crew, who were all Australians apart from the rear gunner, were lost without trace somewhere in the Irish Sea. Three other Wellington Xs from other OTUs were lost that night with all their crews.

Four days later, Flt Sgt P E B Vallender, RAAF, in Wellington III X3357 was tasked with a solo navigation exercise. On its return, at 2150 hrs, the bomber collided with trees and crashed in Ingestre Park on the south-western side of the airfield. The all-Australian crew was killed instantly.

During October, the unit was reduced to three-quarters status with a smaller establishment of 40 Wellingtons and 5 Hurricanes. This was seen as an early indication that the demand for night-bomber crews was dwindling, despite Bomber Command still suffering alarming losses on raids over Germany. The reduction in status also meant that Seighford was no longer needed and on 28th October the satellite was relinquished to Flying Training Command.

The final Bullseye that 30 OTU participated in took place on 2nd

December 1944. Five aircraft of 'A' Flight took part in the operation and all returned safely to Hixon without any problems reported.

Even though the end of the war in Europe was several months away, plans were developing throughout the country for alternative uses for the hundreds of airfields which had sprung up during wartime. Hixon was no exception and on 7th December, with Air Ministry approval, the airfield was visited by the Lord Mayor of Stoke-on-Trent and two Aldermen. Their mission was to inspect the airfield and judge whether it would be suitable for use by civilian aviation after the war, but Hixon was to remain in Air Ministry hands longer than the visitors possibly imagined.

Bomber Command suffered another night of losses on 8th January 1945. No 30 OTU was hit particularly badly, losing two aircraft complete with their crews. The first incident involved Flt Sgt L J Porter, RAAF, in Wellington X LN166 who was tasked with flying a high-level bombing detail on Bagots Park range. At 1130 hrs the bomber broke up and crashed at Burton's Lane, Eccleshall, six miles north-west of Stafford. All six aircrew on board perished. The second involved Wellington X HE853, piloted by Sgt R K M Lewis on a navigation exercise. A contact was made with the aircraft at 1416 hrs but nothing more was heard and it was presumed the bomber came down in the Irish Sea with the loss of all five aircrew.

Twelve aircraft were detailed to take part in Operation Sweepstake on 14/15th January 1945, the last significant operation that 30 OTU would take part in from Hixon. It involved 126 aircraft, all from bomber OTUs, flying a diversion over the North Sea to distract the enemy from front-line Bomber Command operations. Many of the bombers involved used up more fuel than anticipated and four of Hixon's Wellingtons were diverted to Topcliffe and another to Catfoss, both in Yorkshire. Flg Off P N Hickman was ordered to divert but could not find a gap in the cloud cover. At 0020 hrs the tanks ran dry and Hickman ordered his crew to bale out. Hickman followed soon after and the bomber crashed onto tennis courts at Wilford, south of the River Trent, on the south-west side of Nottingham.

Ten minutes later another Hixon machine was being abandoned near Nottingham. Flt Sgt D Hudson in Wellington X LP830 had also run short of fuel and he and his crew successfully abandoned their aircraft. One member of this crew, complete with parachute under his arm, caught a bus from Arnold into Nottingham. A local farmer rescued another after he was caught up in the branches of a tree bordering the Henry Mellish Grammar School rugby football ground.

79

These two aircraft losses were the last to be suffered by 30 OTU while at Hixon.

Plans were already in place for a reshuffle of units throughout the country and this included Hixon. No 30 OTU's move from Hixon was carried out with great efficiency; the advance party of 16 officers, 28 NCOs and 145 other ranks began to leave on 25th January 1945. The destination was Gamston in Nottinghamshire, which had supported a bomber-training unit of its own until 86 OTU was disbanded in October 1944. The main move day occurred on 2nd February 1945 when 41 Wellingtons, 167 officers, 4 WAAF officers, 774 other ranks, 198 RAF Sgt aircrew and 314 WAAF other ranks departed Hixon for the final time. The 55th training course was continued at Gamston.

The station commander, Gp Cap F F Rainsford, honoured 30 OTU with the following comment in the unit's Operational Record Book:

Although this unit has closed for the best of reasons – the end of the European War – its dissolution will be felt by many. The cheerfulness, enthusiasm and sterling work of all ranks achieved a spirit which will be an inspiration for the tasks of peace.

While Gp Capt Rainsford's words indicate a closure of 30 OTU, the unit was not disbanded until 12th June 1945. Their most important work, however, will always be seen as occurring at Hixon.

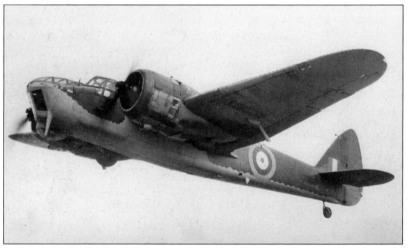

The main equipment of 12 (P)AFU was three different marks of the Bristol Blenheim, including the Mk IV depicted here.

Only a few days later, Hixon gained a new unit with the arrival of 12 (Pilots) Advanced Flying Unit ((P)AFU) from Spittlegate in Lincolnshire. No 12 (P)AFU's equipment included approximately 60 Bristol Blenheim Is, IVs and Vs. Support aircraft included Oxfords, Ansons, a Whitney Straight, a Moth and Proctors. The exact numbers of aircraft that belonged to this unit varied, but they had sufficient to warrant the need for a satellite airfield at Cranage in Cheshire. A permanent detachment was sent to Cranage as soon as the unit arrived at Hixon.

One of the last military aircraft to operate en masse from Hixon, was the Beaufort trainers of 12 (P)AFU. They were operated in the Coastal Command camouflage scheme, as displayed on this example.

One of a series of aerial photographs taken of Hixon on 11th August 1945. By now the airfield is devoid of aircraft and 16 MU is in residence. The two subsidiary runways have received a white cross, indicating that they are closed, while the main runway remains open. (Crown Copyright via Hixon Local Historical Society)

In early May 1945, 12 (P)AFU gained approximately 35 Bristol Beaufort TIIs, which had their dorsal turrets faired over and all armaments removed. These dual-controlled aircraft were finished in their original Coastal Command grey and white camouflage and they seemed out of place at Hixon with its history of drably painted machines.

The war's end at Hixon brought flying almost to a halt and on 21st June 1945, 12 (P)AFU's short time at the airfield came to an end with disbandment. All of the unit's aircraft were flown out to various MUs throughout the country; the Beauforts were flown to 44 MU at Edzell in Forfarshire, for storage and eventual scrapping.

Personnel of 16 MU pose for the camera at Hixon in 1948. (Hixon Local Historical Society)

The vast Equipment Supply Depot at 16 MU Stafford was in desperate need of sub-sites to cope with the vast influx of surplus military items. Hixon was chosen as one of such sites, 16 MU taking up residence on 31st July 1945. This latest takeover would have removed Hixon as an option for a civilian airport, which the Mayor of Stoke-on-Trent was hoping for after his visit in 1944. No 16 MU remained until 5th November 1957 when Hixon was reduced to Care and Maintenance. The Air Ministry eventually sold the airfield off in August 1962, dividing the airfield up between farming and light industrial units on the old technical site.

Today Hixon is, without doubt, Staffordshire's best-preserved wartime airfield. Three out of the original four Type T2 hangars are still in use and the Type B1 on the south side of New Road has had a dramatic facelift with a modern business façade. The entire main runway is intact and large sections of one of the subsidiary runways are also in place. The perimeter is virtually complete, much of it now a public footpath. There is a windsock pole on the north side of the airfield and the Type 12779 control tower is also preserved and occupied.

83

Aerial view of the airfield taken in the early 1990s, showing the main runway and a second shorter runway still intact. Many airfield buildings survive, the vast majority still in daily use. Hixon village is at the bottom right, having almost quadrupled in size since the Second World War.

Many of the dispersed site buildings also remain around the village, used for private dwellings or light industrial purposes. Every building still standing on the original airfield technical site is occupied by businesses, two of which are aviation related. I would highly recommend anyone, preferably just before the sun is about to set, to take a walk around this remarkable airfield.

6
HOAR CROSS
(Cross Hayes)

The workload of 51 Maintenance Unit (MU) at Lichfield was already heavy by early 1941. Safe dispersal of aircraft was becoming increasingly difficult, so alternative Satellite Landing Grounds (SLGs) were sought to relieve the pressure.

A site south of the village of Hoar Cross was one of six landing ground sites that would blossom into SLGs for the use of 51 MU. The others at Tattenhall, Blidworth, Hodnet, Grove and Hardwick Park would all fill rapidly with the aircraft that Lichfield could not cater for.

The landing ground at Hoar Cross was located just one-and-a-half miles from the Relief Landing Ground (RLG) at Tatenhill although no aerial conflict was envisaged. The first aircraft arrived at Hoar Cross on 27th July 1941, followed by an influx of personnel on 1st August, the official opening day of 32 SLG.

After only a few days, 41 airmen were accommodated under canvas and the SLG now warranted a visit by the Commanding Officer of 51 MU on 24th August. He inspected the few buildings and reviewed the cooking arrangements. Both were satisfactory but the landing ground was in a very poor state after heavy rainfall and the SLG was temporarily closed down for repairs.

During this period of inactivity, a section of the airfield was used by the South Staffordshire Regiment for a variety of courses. Under the guidance of 2nd Lieutenant Nell and Sgt Sayers, training in musketry, bayonet fighting, grenade throwing and the use of tommy guns was carried out over a period of a week in early September.

It is not recorded which aircraft first descended upon Hoar Cross but it is known that 51 MU at the time was preparing types such as the Beaufighter, Havoc, Hurricane, Wellington and Whirlwind. However,

One of the first aircraft to be dispersed at Hoar Cross was the American-built Douglas Boston.

the first incident on the SLG involved an American-built Douglas Boston twin-engined bomber which, on 27th September, suddenly burst into flames. The fire was successfully tackled by local personnel before the Burton Fire Brigade arrived, but the aircraft was considerably damaged by the incident, which was later found to have been caused by a simple short circuit. The RAF personnel were praised for their quick and correct actions and, from that day, fire fighting equipment and training were taken very seriously.

Up until 15th October 1941, the SLG's airmen were still being accommodated under canvas. With winter rapidly approaching, rather than building Nissen or Maycrete-style huts, stables were converted at the nearby Cross Hayes Farm. The stables were luxurious compared to the tents and they provided accommodation until the war's end.

Work began on the erection of aircraft hides in January 1942 at Hoar Cross. Deacons Ltd of Lichfield had been commissioned to carry out the work and the company's representative, Mr Windows, notified the SLG that work would begin on 14th January. Typically found on SLGs, the average aircraft hide incorporated natural foliage in an effort to camouflage dispersed aircraft. The combination of a drably painted aircraft, camouflage netting and surrounding woodland, virtually made them invisible from above.

Not a great success story from an operational point of view but the Westland Whirlwind certainly looked the part. Several were stored at 32 SLG, Hoar Cross during the Second World War.

The temporary closure of 35 SLG at Blidworth in Nottinghamshire resulted in an increase in the number of aircraft coming into Hoar Cross during February. The SLG catered for the new arrivals without difficulty, although camouflaging them from the air was becoming a problem. Sqn Ldr Blomfield of the Ministry of Aircraft Production (MAP) visited on 7th May 1942 to discuss camouflage and the use of Steel Camouflage Wool was recommended on the airfield.

The general condition of the SLG stood up well to torrential rains lasting for over a week during May. This was credited to the fact that Hoar Cross was covered with nearly 60,000 square yards of Square Mesh Track which not only provided a good surface for aircraft to use, but drained effectively as well.

In June 1942, a MAP Civilian Maintenance Party was employed to build a new boiler house, pump house and an extension to the ablutions block. Life was getting more comfortable at Hoar Cross for the permanent staff, whose work steadily increased during the summer months. It looked set to increase again when Flt Lt Duffy from HQ 41 Group visited on 6th August. The task was to assess the possibility of landing four-engined aircraft at Hoar Cross; this would have included such types as the Halifax, Lancaster and Stirling. However, no such aircraft ever landed here so we can safely surmise that the SLG was found to be unsuitable.

The future of Hoar Cross was in doubt by October 1942, with a debate between 51 MU and HQ 41 Group as to whether it or 37 SLG at

Hardwick Park in Derbyshire should close. Hoar Cross was chosen to stay open purely because it was closer to the parent unit. It was a good choice, as Hardwick Park would be handed over to the Airborne Forces within a year.

Despite its rural location, security began to be taken more seriously from November onwards. Eight guard dogs and their handlers arrived and, on 24th November, they were tested in a security exercise. The exercise started at 0900 hrs, continuing until 0900 hrs the following day. All RAF personnel and civilians had their identity cards and their 1250s (official RAF identity cards) checked and continuous dog patrols were carried out. At the end of the exercise, a lecture was given by a Defence NCO of 51 MU on the tommy gun and sten carbine, followed by firing both weapons on the range.

The new year began with an increased throughput of Hurricanes and the arrival of several Typhoons. Whitleys of all marks continued to be the main stock and, as 1943 progressed, the SLG steadily filled. An uneventful year was shattered on the night of 29th December, when ten Wellingtons from 30 OTU at Seighford were tasked with a Bullseye exercise. Wellington III X3883 'O', piloted by Sgt F Collett, was climbing out of Seighford when, without warning, the starboard engine caught fire. The flames raged uncontrollably and the bomber crashed at 2140 hrs just north of the SLG. Collett was the only survivor of the crash; the other five crew perished in the fire.

American-built Grumman Hellcat fighters were the only new type to pass through Hoar Cross during the year. Meanwhile, the task of preparation of Whitleys for front-line squadrons was replaced by their removal from service and eventual storage. Twenty-six Whitley Vs arrived at Hoar Cross in September 1944 – a record for the unit. Engines, propellers, instruments and wireless equipment were removed from each aircraft. The airframe that remained was collected by 34 MU at Monkmoor, near Shrewsbury, for scrapping. Sixteen more Whitleys followed in October and by the war's end, 59 in total were dispersed around the SLG.

On 28th May 1945, a civilian working party arrived to break up all of the remaining aircraft now virtually abandoned on the site. By June 1945, the airfield was clear and this very useful and busy SLG closed.

Although the airfield quickly returned to agriculture during the post war years, aviation has since come back to Hoar Cross. The Needwood Forest Gliding Club has been resident at Cross Hayes Field since 1998 and is set to stay until at least 2023 when the current lease expires.

7
LICHFIELD
(Fradley)

Easily the busiest wartime airfield in Staffordshire, Lichfield (locally known as Fradley) not only supported a variety of its own units but also provided a safe haven for many more. It was a controlling point for virtually all aviation traffic that passed through the Birmingham area during the Second World War. Lichfield saw more action and more aircraft movements than all the rest of the county's airfields put together!

Work began on the new airfield in mid-1939 before the war began and the intention was to house a large Maintenance Unit (MU) there. The location was one mile south-west of Fradley, with the Coventry Canal winding its way around the northern and eastern edges and Fradley wood bordering the western side of the site. The only option for extending Lichfield's runways was to the south and with this in mind all three were laid in that direction. The usual triangular pattern resulted in two runways at 1,100 yards and one main runway at 1,600 yards in length.

The main technical site was accessed from Ryknild Street (the A38) with many of the buildings constructed to 1930s RAF Expansion period standard. This effectively meant that the airfield had a permanent feel which many built in wartime lacked. The majority of the technical, administrative and barrack blocks were brick-built and centrally heated. Ample hangars were provided with three Type 'J's and four Type 'K's with their distinctive curved roofs; all of them measured 300 ft long and nearly 50 ft high. The only difference between these two types of hangar was usually the office and stores accommodation, which ran along each side of the buildings. Type Js were intended for operational airfields, while Type Ks were normally seen at operational stations. This mix of buildings gave a good indication of the future diversity of flying that would be possible from Lichfield. More hangars would follow, including a pair of Type T2s, a single Type B1, eight turf-covered 'L' Types and a host of Blister and Robin hangars. A large network of concrete roads was constructed which would later allow the dispersal and storage of aircraft in every corner of the airfield.

In December 1939 one of the many Aircraft Storage Units began to form. No 42 MU was to be Lichfield's first unit. However, a conflict of Maintenance Command numbers (42 Group was a maintenance group) meant that 42 MU was redesignated 51 MU on 6th March 1940. Under the control of 41 Group, based at Andover in Hampshire, 51 MU was officially opened at Lichfield on 1st August 1940 as an Aircraft Storage and Packing Unit.

With the Battle of Britain at its height, the main aircraft type to pass through Lichfield was the Hawker Hurricane I. Air Transport Auxiliary (ATA) pilots collected the fighters and delivered them direct to the front-line squadrons. Throughout August 1940, Hurricanes were collected for 32 Squadron at Biggin Hill, 310 Squadron at Duxford, 56 Squadron at North Weald and 17 Squadron at Tangmere, all in the thick of the battle.

Avro Ansons began arriving for preparation for front-line squadrons in late September. Hurricanes kept flowing through in great numbers

One of 51 MU's earliest and most important task was the preparation of Hawker Hurricanes for operational squadrons during the Battle of Britain. Hurricane I P3878 of 17 Squadron was one of many which passed through Lichfield.

The Wellington II was another aircraft prepared by 51 MU at Lichfield. The mark was the only Wellington to be fitted with Rolls-Royce Merlin engines rather than the more familiar radials.

and in early October the first of many Vickers Wellington Is arrived. A few weeks later, the personnel of 51 MU were also preparing Bristol Beaufighters.

The first loss of an aircraft attributed to the unit occurred on 25th November 1940. Flt Lt D M Barker and his crew of Cpl S G Underhill, Cpl A O Dale and LAC S Allan, all of 51 MU, took off from Honington in Suffolk to deliver Wellington IC R1173 to Lichfield. As the bomber approached the Midlands, the weather took a turn for the worse and visibility dropped rapidly. Barker turned back with the thought of landing at the small grass airfield at Desford in Leicestershire or any other safe haven he could find. It was now getting dark and fuel was running low when Barker gave the order for his crew to abandon the aircraft. Barker remained with the bomber for another twenty minutes hoping to find another airfield. Now over Lincolnshire, he set the bomber on seaward course but the Wellington came down near Alford in Lincolnshire. All survived the experience, although Barker was severely criticized for embarking on the flight in the first place.

The first Douglas Boston joined the rapidly increasing list of aircraft being prepped by 51 MU in early December 1940. Blister hangars and Robins were being readied and occupied on a daily basis throughout the month. By the year's end there were an additional twenty Robins and the larger Super Robin hangars.

Being so close to the industrial Midlands, staff at Lichfield offered a

When war broke out all civilian-owned aircraft were grounded and many, including the Miles Whitney Straight were impressed into military service. Several passed through 51 MU for modification to RAF standard.

variety of civilian training courses. One of these was the Roof Watching Aircraft Recognition Course. The first of several began on 2nd January 1941 and was attended by over 150 men representing a variety of industrial firms. Part of the course involved an aircraft being flown back and forth across the aerodrome at heights between 2,000 and 12,000 ft, with the heights indicated by different coloured Very lights fired from the aircraft. The officer in charge of flying at Lichfield gave instruction on aircraft recognition as well.

A straightforward air-test ended in tragedy on 12th January when Beaufighter Ic R2089 crashed on the airfield. Plt Off N O'Brien, a 51 MU test pilot, suffered a double engine failure after take-off. The twin-engined fighter crashed into a wooden hut occupied by 51 MU personnel. AC2 J P Rout and AC2 G Rumbold were both killed instantly in the accident, which also injured Plt Off O'Brien and eight other airmen in the hut.

Poor weather disrupted flying for several days at the end of January and the beginning of February 1941. Nine ATA pilots arrived on 24th January, with the intention of delivering nine Douglas Bostons on a short flight to Burtonwood in Lancashire. The weather was so bad that this usually easy task could not be carried out until 1st February and even then only five of the Bostons managed to leave before the weather clamped down again.

The Hurricane II and Wellington II began arriving in February and the Fairey Battle joined them in early March. The latter, by now obsolete, was only being prepared for training units. The first of several Westland Whirlwind fighters arrived in mid March although their limited use by front-line squadrons made them a relatively rare sight.

As demand for aircraft overseas increased, the work of 51 MU's packing section elevated its position into an autonomous unit. It was officially named No 53 Packing Section by the end of March 1941 and began to swell in size with the arrival of eighteen civilians of various trades from 47 MU (Packing & Storage) Sealand in Flintshire on 3rd April. The following day, the status of the unit was elevated still further when it became known as 82 MU (Aircraft Packing Depot) under the command of Flt Lt F M Milling. The new unit was given half a Type J hangar until two more large hangars had been constructed for their use. The unglamorous but important world of aircraft packing justified the existence of five other maintenance units, all under the control of 53 Wing based at Andover in Hampshire.

A reshuffle of units, a common occurrence during wartime, resulted in 51 MU coming under the control of 51 (Maintenance) Wing (Midland) area at Broughton Hall, Broughton, near Hawarden in Flintshire, on 21st April 1941. No 51 Wing controlled six other maintenance units across the Midland region and also operated several de Havilland Hornet Moths and a Miles Magister, which would often visit Lichfield.

New types continued to arrive at Lichfield, including the Douglas Havoc I and II bomber and more advanced marks of the Hurricane, such as the IIB, IIC and IID. This increase in aircraft types warranted a new shift pattern by mid-April. The airfield was split into two specific sites and on alternate nights each shift worked overtime until 2000 hours so as not to disrupt production of prepped aircraft. More civilian staff were recruited and additional RAF personnel were posted in to keep on top of the workload. To focus the main task on aircraft preparation, 51 MU passed its Storage Section to 82 MU control.

No 51 MU's place as the senior and controlling unit of Lichfield took a step back on 23rd April 1941. With little warning, the airfield was taken over by 6 Group, Bomber Command, whose headquarters were at Abingdon in Oxfordshire. The airfield's new unit was 27 Operational Training Unit (OTU), formed under the temporary command of Flt Lt R S Blackman. No 27 OTU would train night bomber crews using the Wellington IC, an aircraft that was already no stranger to Lichfield. Several of the new unit's aircraft were actually prepared at Lichfield, removing the need for an ATA pilot to deliver the Wellingtons from elsewhere.

Many months before America's entry into the Second World War, several military personnel came to view training and operational techniques. The first to arrive at Lichfield were Lt Hubert 'Hub' Zemke and three NCOs of the USAAC on 6th May 1941. Zemke would go on to command the 56th and 479th Fighter Groups before becoming a POW in October 1944. A great leader of men, the outspoken Zemke retired as a Colonel in 1966. The American group had arrived from 15 MU at Wroughton in Wiltshire, for a three-day visit. Their specialism was the Curtiss P–40 Tomahawk, of which none were on strength at Lichfield. The group, especially Zemke, accompanied 51 MU test pilots on several test flights before leaving for 29 MU at High Ercall in Shropshire.

Flt Lt Blackman's temporary command of 27 OTU came to an end on 13th May. Gp Capt O R Gayford, DFC, AFC, who arrived from Wattisham in Suffolk, took his position as officer commanding 27 OTU and Lichfield's station commander. Gp Capt Gayford was not destined to stay long at Lichfield. A posting to 152 Wing at Ouston in Northumberland beckoned and his replacement, Wg Cdr (later Gp Capt) L E Jarman, DFC, would remain at Lichfield until June 1942. No 82 MU also gained a new officer commanding when Flt Lt Milling was posted to 35 MU at Heywood in Lancashire. Flt Lt J Robertson took his place on 19th May.

Personnel from Lichfield acknowledged local fundraising efforts on 24th May. One officer and 50 airmen from 51 MU paraded in the Market Square, Lichfield, where the Mayor handed a cheque for £5,185 to Air Marshal Sir William Mitchell, KCB, CBE, DSO, MC, AFC. Sir William received the money, which had been raised by the City of

The Vickers Wellington was already a common sight at Lichfield before the formation of 27 OTU in April 1941.

Lichfield and District Spitfire Fund Appeal, on behalf of the Ministry of Aircraft Production (MAP).

The same day the first intake of pupils arrived for training with 27 OTU and by 2nd June, the unit had eleven Wellingtons on strength. Support aircraft were also beginning to arrive, including a Miles Magister and a pair of Avro Ansons. It was an example of the latter which was involved in 27 OTU's first accident, albeit a minor one, on 8th June. Sgt Earthrowl made a heavy landing in Anson I N5030 and damaged the undercarriage. Wellington IC X9600 became the first of its type to be involved in an accident on 12th June with Sgt Denby at the controls. Both aircraft in these early incidents were repaired, but both were destined to be involved in more serious accidents.

By 20th June 1941, 51 MU had over 500 personnel on strength. The vast majority were quartered in a housing estate in Lichfield with a few others living out locally. This created space for personnel from 27 OTU, who would swell the station strength to over 3,500. Aircraft being prepared by 51 MU at this time included the Anson, Hurricane IA and IIA, Wellington IA, IC and II, Whirlwind, Havoc I and II, Whitney Straight, Moth Minor, Oxford I and II, Scion and Tiger Moth, to name a few. Simultaneously, 27 OTU's strength continued to rise and, by the end of June, the unit had 25 aircraft.

With the first 27 OTU course now coming to an end at Lichfield, it would become a requirement for the final sortie to be a leaflet raid over Northern France, more commonly known as a 'Nickel'. These operations were intended to introduce the new crews to operational flying without hurling them into a major raid on Germany. The first Nickel involved three Wellington ICs, R1724, X9610 and X9611. The target was Béthune and as expected only moderate flak was experienced and all three aircraft returned to Lichfield unscathed.

As Lichfield's importance and size continued to increase, so did the number of senior visits. On 17th July, His Royal Highness the Duke of Gloucester, a military Chief Liaison Officer, visited the airfield followed by senior politicians on 24th July. With a high number of Commonwealth personnel on strength, these included the New Zealand Prime Minister, Mr Peter Fraser. All RNZAF personnel were paraded and inspected by the Prime Minister. These visits were very good for morale and similar such events would take place for the Australian and Canadian personnel who were also training at Lichfield.

By the end of August, 82 MU was increasing in size to such an extent that it had taken over one of the airfield's large Type J hangars. The unit was still packing Hurricanes for overseas shipment and

One of the first photographs taken of personnel from 27 OTU in May 1941. Lichfield's station commander and OC 27 OTU, Gp Capt O R Gayford, DFC, AFC, sits in the middle of the front row. This all-officer photograph contains all of the unit's instructors, training staff, admin officers and even the station padre.

No 82 MU was heavily involved with the dismantling and packing of the Fairey Albacore for service in the Middle and Far East.

Fairey Albacore torpedo bombers. The workforce, which was mainly female and from the local area, numbered over 300, packing an average of 30 aircraft a week.

Despite being well equipped with dispersals and hangars, it was becoming increasingly obvious that Lichfield would need several Satellite Landing Grounds (SLGs) to cope with the daily influx of new aircraft. No 51 MU brought 32 SLG at Hoar Cross and 35 SLG at Blidworth in Nottinghamshire into use on 1st August 1941. Both remained in use by the unit until late 1942, replaced by 29 SLG at Hodnet in Shropshire and 38 SLG at Grove Park in Nottinghamshire. No 13 SLG at Tatton Park in Cheshire and 37 SLG at Hardwick Park in Nottinghamshire were also used, but both had closed by September 1943. All of these SLGs proved invaluable for 51 MU, which needed dispersal areas for the large amounts of aircraft that were being processed.

No 27 OTU was in a similar position with Lichfield becoming increasingly cramped; the unit needed satellite airfields from which to operate. It had swelled dramatically with 54 Wellingtons, 18 Ansons and a pair of Lysanders on strength. Even before 27 OTU's formation Tatenhill had been earmarked as a satellite for Lichfield. From August 1941, the airfield came under Lichfield's control but it was not until November that a single flight moved in. The unit was never happy operating from Tatenhill because it lacked the facilities needed by 27 OTU. By August 1942, Tatenhill was abandoned and Church

No 27 OTU was involved in several major Bomber Command raids during the Second World War. This scene is typical of any bomber station, showing a Wellington being loaded with 250lb bombs, refuelled and prepared for the next sortie.

Broughton in Derbyshire was brought into use and remained a satellite of Lichfield until the war's end.

The first live bombing raid on enemy territory took place on 28th August 1941. Only two Wellingtons, Z8774 and Z8785, were involved in a successful bombing raid on Evreux-Fauville airfield dropping eight 250lb bombs each. Ironically, the first encounter between a 27 OTU aircraft and the Luftwaffe occurred over British territory. The crew of Wellington IC X9611 was detailed to fly a night cross-country on 1st September. Whilst on the return leg, the bomber was attacked by an enemy aircraft. A single burst of fire wounded the pilot and two other crew members. The pilot made a forced landing at North Luffenham in Rutland, where the injured crew were quickly admitted to a local hospital.

In an attempt to make life more comfortable at Lichfield, the suggestion was put forward for a large YMCA to be built. An application was made to the Council of Voluntary War Work for the building, which would provide facilities for over 1,000 personnel. It consisted of rooms for airmen and WAAFs, a spacious concert hall with a stage, a quiet room and sleeping accommodation for staff.

Sgt Nel Tarleton provided sporting entertainment on 21st October 1941. Tarleton, who was stationed at Lichfield, was the holder of the Lonsdale Belt and he boxed at the first boxing tournament of the season at RAF Hednesford.

No 27 OTU gained the use of Cannock Chase bombing range from 31st October. The unit specifically used the range for night-bombing practice and the dropping of photographic flares. From the beginning of November, 27 OTU flying operations were reorganised. The unit originally had a separate Conversion Flight (CF) which all pilots passed through on arrival before being moved on to a training flight. From 4th November, the CF was disbanded and each Wellington flight received its allotment of crews for conversion through to completion of their training. A separate Navigation Flight, operating Ansons, was also formed to give training to Air Observers and Wireless Operator/Air Gunners. This new system was intended to allocate one instructor to each crew from start to finish. The following day, the original 'A', 'B' and 'C' Flights were merged into two. 'B' Flight occupied the easterly dispersal area and 'C' Flight the south-western dispersals, while 'A' Flight was temporarily discarded. The latter was reformed a few weeks later as the unit's aircraft strength continued to rise.

By early December 1941, the workload of 82 MU showed no sign of relenting and more diverse aircraft types began to arrive. The unit received three Bell Airacobra fighters for packing on 6th December. The complicated mid-engine fighter proved to be very difficult to dismantle and the staff were not impressed when six more arrived on 13th December. Out of an original order of 675 Airacobras, only 50 were delivered, serving for a short time with only one squadron. The remainder of this order was diverted to the USAAF and the Soviet Air Force. It is quite possible that the few Airacobras which passed through 82 MU were destined for the Soviet Union. The same day, the first of many Supermarine Spitfires arrived at 82 MU; compared to the Airacobra the British-built fighter was considerably easier to pack.

The first of many operational visitors arrived on 26th January 1942. A Handley Page Hampden I of 144 Squadron, based at North Luffenham, landed after going off course from mine-laying off the French coast. The Hampden was not a type that the majority of the aircrew passing through Lichfield would serve on. Despite this, it was an opportunity for several trainees to discuss front-line operations with the crew.

Space at Lichfield became even tighter from the beginning of March

1942. More personnel were posted in from 29 MU at High Ercall for the impending arrival of the first Consolidated Liberator. This four-engined high-wing, American-built bomber first entered service with Coastal Command in June 1941. It went on to become one of the command's most effective weapons against the German U-Boats and served both Bomber and Transport Command in many theatres of war. Liberators would be a common sight at Lichfield until well after the war's end. A few weeks later, Boeing Fortresses also destined for service with Coastal Command joined the Liberators. Both of these aircraft took up a lot of space at Lichfield and dispersing and camouflaging them was becoming a big problem.

On 24th March 1942, after a weather test flight by an Oxford belonging to 51 MU, it was decided that conditions were not fit for test flying or for 27 OTU operations. Unbeknownst to a pair of ATA pilots ferrying two Wellingtons to Lichfield, thick fog was rolling in, making landing very difficult. The first aircraft, Wellington III Z1614, crashed on landing after the port engine failed on approach. The second bomber, Wellington III Z1623, overshot the main runway and force landed in an adjoining field. Both aircraft were repaired and delivered to front-line squadrons within a matter of weeks and within months both had been lost to enemy action.

The majority of Nickels flown by 27 OTU passed without incident and often without any contact with the enemy. On the night of 5/6th April 1942, four aircraft from the unit set out from Lichfield to drop leaflets in the Lille, Roubaix, Tourcoing, Lens and Béthune areas of northern France. The four bombers, the only OTU aircraft to be over France that night, dropped 126 packages of leaflets over their intended targets and set course for home. At approximately 0140 hrs, Sgt Wendon in Wellington IC X9610 was twelve miles south of Dunkirk when the rear gunner spotted an aircraft. He later described it as a twin-engined machine, which was probably a Messerschmitt Bf110 looking for an opportunity. The fighter closed to within 400 yards of the Wellington, before Sgt Wendon pushed the bomber into a steep dive. The drab camouflage on the upper surfaces of the Wellington must have done the trick because the fighter was seen no more and Sgt Wendon and his crew escaped to fight another day.

A more costly Nickel for 27 OTU occurred on 27/28th April. The night was busy for Bomber Command, with 97 aircraft raiding Cologne and 43 Halifaxes and Lancasters attacking the battleship *Tirpitz* in Trondheim Fjord, to name just two of the operations being carried out. Five aircraft from Lichfield set out for northern France

At the beginning of each course which passed through 27 OTU, a photograph of the trade group was taken. This is the NCO aircrew of No 14 Course, taken on 4th November 1941. Sgt Wendon is top-right in the group.

One of the most complicated aircraft to pass through 82 MU was the Bell Airacobra which saw limited service with the RAF. Compared to the Spitfire, the American-built fighter was very difficult to dismantle for packing.

with bombs and leaflets, all tasked with different targets. Two would not return. The first, Wellington IC X9635 flown by Flg Off L G Chick, RAAF, was lost while dropping leaflets in the Lille area. The second, Wellington IC Z8901, piloted by Sgt G A Dale, crashed at Sautour, near Philippeville in Belgium; both crews were killed.

The three remaining aircraft successfully carried out their missions, including Sgt Whittick in Wellington IC R1647. Whittick and his crew managed to drop bombs on Abbeville airfield but, despite circling the airfield, the results could not be observed. On their return to Lichfield, R1647 ran out of fuel and had to make a crash-landing near Welford Station, south of Bramcote. No injuries were caused to the crew but the aircraft suffered severe damage, including a broken back and shock loading to both engines. Incredibly, the bomber was seen as repairable and remained in service until March 1944.

Since Sir Arthur Harris had taken charge of Bomber Command, the role of the OTUs as a front-line force, rather than training, was increasing. This was highlighted on 11th May when 27 OTU was transferred along with several other similar units to the newly formed 91 (Operational Training) Group based at Abingdon in Oxfordshire. The plan by Harris to send 1,000-strong bomber raids into Germany to crush the spirit of the civilian population could only be achieved by using aircraft from the bomber OTUs.

The first of these incredible raids was organised on the night of 30th/31st May 1942 against Cologne. Of the 1,047 aircraft despatched, 365 were from OTUs, over a third of the total! Alone, 27 OTU contributed a record-breaking 21 Wellington ICs out of the 602 taking part in this historic raid. This was mainly testament to the hardworking ground crews who were suffering a 45 per cent unserviceability rate at the time.

Each aircraft departed Lichfield carrying a single 500lb bomb and an average of 360 4lb incendiaries each. No 27 OTU was lucky on this particular raid, although every man who took part had a story to tell. Flt Sgt D Stewart in X9681 witnessed a Halifax being shot down by an enemy fighter; one of three of its type brought down on the raid. Flg Off A S Caunt in N2760 at some point during the raid lost his 500lb bomb without opening the bomb bay doors! Where the bomb actually fell is unknown. Sgt H B Smith in X9608 had the opposite problem; he was unable to drop his 500lb bomb and reluctantly brought it back to Lichfield. W/O F Lupton and crew in Z8949 were lucky when both wings and the fuselage of their bomber were holed by flak. Finally, Flt Sgt N R Ross in X9883 suffered a nerve-racking ten minutes trapped in a searchlight cone. Ross dived towards the ground trying to avoid the searchlight while the two air gunners chanced their arm shooting at it.

All 21 Wellingtons returned home to Lichfield, filling the station with the sounds of a job well done. The raid was classed as a success, but the loss rate of 41 aircraft was the highest suffered by Bomber Command since the beginning of the war. Seventeen of the losses were from Bomber OTUs.

Two nights later, Harris rallied his forces for a second 1,000-bomber raid; this time against Essen. The magic number was not achieved on this occasion and Bomber Command could only muster 956 aircraft for the raid, once again relying heavily on Bomber OTU support. No 27 OTU mustered twenty Wellington ICs for the attack. Several aircrew who had flown on the Cologne raid relived the experience but on this occasion the raid was slightly less eventful.

Sgt H Richardson and his crew probably had the closest encounter with the enemy that night. Whilst over The Hague, the bomber was held in several searchlights at 8,000 ft. Richardson dived down to escape the lights and flew north out to sea while the front and rear gunners fired at the searchlights. The machine-gun fire attracted the attention of an unidentified enemy fighter, which closed in on the tail of the Wellington. The rear gunner had just enough time to fire a short burst at the fighter when the Wellington was hit by light anti-aircraft fire from a ship. Part of the geodetic structure of the bomber was damaged, an oil pipe was also ruptured and the navigator's table and chair were destroyed by the shell as it passed through the aircraft. Luckily, the navigator was up front with the pilot at the time. The offending oil pipe was repaired with chewing gum and the bomber, like all of its colleagues, returned home to Lichfield.

Compared to the first big raid, the Essen attack was not classed as successful and the bombing was very scattered. The loss rate was high, but deemed acceptable by senior authorities, with 31 bombers lost, many of them from other bomber OTUs.

A new unit relevant to 27 OTU was formed at Lichfield on 15th June. No 93 (Operational Training) Group, the last of three such groups to control several bomber OTUs within the area, made Lichfield its home. It did not stay at Lichfield long; the unit moved to Egginton Hall in Derbyshire where it remained until disbandment on 22nd June 1945.

On 17th July 1942, 93 Group Communication Flight was formed at Lichfield and, despite the main group's move to Derbyshire, the flight remained at Lichfield until 14th February 1945. It was initially formed with a pair of de Havilland Moth Minors. Other types included the

Percival Proctor, de Havilland Dominie and a very rare Foster-Wickner Warferry I. The Warferry was a single-engined high-wing cabin monoplane used for communication duties and only three served in the RAF during the war. Despite its more local positioning, 27 OTU did not join 93 Group until 1st September 1943, only to return to 91 Group control a few months before the war's end.

Sir Arthur Harris gave the bomber OTUs nearly a month to recover before he called upon them again for the final 1,000-bomber raid. The OTUs would bear the brunt of the losses on this raid, in particular 91 Group over Bremen on 25/26th June 1942. No 27 OTU readied fifteen Wellington ICs for the raid which, like the previous effort, achieved less than the 1,000, with 960 aircraft participating. On this occasion, Winston Churchill insisted that the Admiralty allow Coastal Command to participate as well, bringing the final total of aircraft involved to 1,067; greater than Cologne. The night was reasonably uneventful for 27 OTU, only marred by the loss of Plt Off T F Lamb, RAAF, in R1162. The bomber was lost without trace, along with the five crew. No 91 Group suffered the most with nearly 12 per cent of its force lost, when less than 5 per cent was deemed acceptable. The raid itself was recorded as a success with much of the city damaged or destroyed, mainly from the resulting fires.

Fifteen more Wellington ICs were prepared for a large raid on Hamburg on 28/29th July. Poor weather reduced the size of the raid and after take-off all OTU aircraft were recalled to base. Ten more of 27 OTU's Wellingtons were detailed for a 630-strong raid on Dusseldorf on 31st July/1st August. On this occasion, the raid went ahead and more than 900 tonnes of bombs were dropped on the city. Once again though, losses were high and 27 OTU lost two of its aircraft during the raid. Flt Lt E Walker in R1526 and Flg Off M G McNeil, RNZAF, in DV552, and their crews, all perished.

While the 1,000-bomber raids had been consigned to history, Bomber Command's raids were consistently large from September 1942 onwards. On 10/11th September twelve Wellington ICs took part in a Pathfinder-marked raid on Dusseldorf, which proved to be one of the most successful. For 27 OTU, no losses were recorded, probably helped by the fact that four of the group had to return early with technical problems. The latter had become an increasingly regular occurrence as the ageing Wellington ICs struggled to cope with the workload.

During the raid, Sgt A S Cook in N2735 was hit by shrapnel from exploding flak, which put holes in the wings and fuselage. Night fighters were in abundance both before and after the raid and Plt Off D M Murphy in X9707 had three follow him during the target run, but luckily managed to shake them off. Sgt R Nedoma and crew in DV883 had a close brush with the enemy at 2250 hrs and 16,000 ft, near the target. Two enemy night-fighters, believed to be Bf110s, attacked the Wellington from the rear and from the port quarter. The fighters closed in to approximately 50 yards and both fired a quick burst, which struck the hydraulics of the rear turret, putting it out of action. Luckily, it was no longer needed and the enemy encounter was over as quickly as it had begun.

The unit was in action again over Germany on 13/14th September with a return to Bremen. The force of 446 aircraft was once again made up of a large contingent from Bomber OTUs; Lichfield provided another fourteen Wellingtons. The start of the raid was marred only minutes after Sgt W J P Fletcher, RAAF, took off in L7815. The port engine failed and quickly caught fire and Fletcher attempted to return to the airfield. On the final turn to land, the bomber stalled, spun into the ground in 'C' Flight dispersal and burst into flames, killing the five-man crew instantly. A fire party from 51 MU attended the scene but not much could be done other than trying to control the flames. Nearly four hours after the crash, the four 500lb bombs detonated, killing Cpl R M S Zucker, LAC K Ward, ACI C Aveyard and ACI A Marten instantly; all members of the stand-by fire picket. The blast also damaged eight aircraft on 51 MU charge.

The raid itself was successful, with industry in the city suffering the most. The remaining aircraft of 27 OTU returned unscathed from Bremen, although the crew of N5709 were one less on return. It is not known exactly why, but between 0330 and 0345 hrs the rear gunner of N5709, Sgt N F Wallace baled out over the Papenburg. Wallace survived and became a POW, remaining at Camp 8B/344 until liberation came in 1945.

A raid on Essen on 16/17th September marked the last major operation OTUs would fly with front-line squadrons. The attrition rate was becoming too high and Harris was rapidly running out of training aircraft. The hardworking groundcrew of 27 OTU managed to ready twelve tired Wellington ICs for the attack. It was a busy night for the Lichfield crews, who contributed greatly to the successful attack that ensued on this notoriously difficult target. One bomber was lost near the target; newly promoted Plt Off F Lupton and crew in N2782.

Wellington X9876 was placed in a difficult position when a burst of flak ripped off the port aileron and put a large hole in the leading edge

From October 1942 the Wellington III began to replace the tired Wellington IC. An OTU machine taxis for take-off.

of the wing. Plt Off R A Curle and crew set course for home at an indicated airspeed of only 95 mph and at 1,500 ft. With control difficult, Curle crossed the English coast four hours later. Curle realised that the chances of getting the bomber home were nil and whilst over Andover in Hampshire he ordered his crew to bale out. The bomber plunged to the ground near Collingbourne Ducis in Wiltshire. Curle was commended for his truly remarkable flying skills and for saving his crew.

Plt Off D M Murphy was in the thick of the action again; he attracted the attentions of a searchlight off Dunkirk. Whilst at an altitude of just 50 ft, Murphy's rear gunner put the searchlight out of action. Several others from the unit had to return early because of the endless faults occurring with the early mark of Wellington; it was time for a replacement. During 1942, 117 Wellingtons from 27 OTU took part in front-line Bomber Command operations. The unit would contribute to other raids during 1943, but not on the same scale or with the same loss rate.

Many Wellington ICs continued to serve the OTU at Lichfield but from October 1942 the Wellington III replaced those that were deemed beyond repair or lost in accidents. The new mark had become the main variant in Bomber Command service with 1,519 of them seeing service. The Wellington III, with more powerful engines, was quicker, had a greater range and most importantly to the ground crew, was initially more reliable than the older Mk IC.

Several different marks of the Bristol Beaufighter were prepared by 51 MU throughout the war years.

Many of the newer Wellington IIIs were simply transferred from 51 MU or delivered direct from front-line squadrons which were in turn re-equipping with the Wellington X or changing to a four-engined bomber. No 51 MU was now handling a large number of gliders, including the General Aircraft Hotspur. The Hotspur, which was never used operationally, became the standard training glider throughout the Second World War. The North American Mustang was also present at Lichfield from late 1942 and three marks of Beaufighter were added to the colossal inventory of 51 MU. Flg Off Redwanski, a 51 MU test pilot, was lucky to escape injury when his Beaufighter V EL457 crashed on the airfield on 5th October. The twin-engine fighter was removed by 34 MU at Shrewsbury, Shropshire and repaired to fly again with 235 Squadron at Leuchars in Fife.

No 27 OTU continued to expand; having already gained 'E' Flight earlier in the year, two more flights were formed in October. A Czech Flight was created although its use was probably limited because the unit was mainly training Commonwealth aircrew, particularly Australians, by this stage of the war. A Gunnery Flight was also formed around the same time, probably making good use of the unit's Lysander and Defiant target tugs for air-to-air firing.

All previous production records were broken by 51 MU in January 1943. During the month, 142 aircraft were prepared for front-line squadrons and a further five for training units. The month also brought the unit a temporary break from the Fortress and Liberator, only to be

Aircraft being prepared at Lichfield grew in size as the war progressed, necessitating the need for Satellite Landing Grounds throughout the county and beyond. The RAF version of the B–17 Flying Fortress was handled by 51 MU.

replaced by an equally big aircraft, namely the Handley Page Halifax. The American types would return as the demand for them by Coastal Command, and eventually forces in the Far East, rose.

Nickels continued to foray into northern France with targets such as Paris and Lille being visited. With more Wellington IIIs making these trips, their success rate was on the rise again as more aircraft remained serviceable throughout the flight. Pilot error was to blame during the early hours of 14th March 1943 when Wellington III Z1681 crashed near the airfield. Plt Off G A McReath, RAAF, was returning from a night-navigation exercise when he approached too low to land and hit a tree. The force was sufficient to roll the bomber over into the ground, killing one of the crew instantly. The accident occurred only one-and-a-half miles from the airfield, but it was an incredible two hours before help arrived or Lichfield became aware that one of their aircraft had crashed. When the crash tender and ambulance arrived, it was very dark and both vehicles became bogged down trying to locate the bomber. Once the wreckage was found, it could be seen that three crew members had been thrown clear; one was already dead, a second critically injured and a third would survive. Plt Off McReath was alive but trapped in the wreckage and it took a long time before he was eventually released.

Nearly all RAF airfields were expected to use spare land for growing vegetables, especially as the 'Dig for Victory' campaign was becoming so effective with the civilian population. Lichfield was no exception and to encourage more cultivation on the airfield a station garden competition was arranged for 29th March. Personnel had been working for many months to create individual plots near their offices, hangars and living accommodation. From April to August, a £3 prize was awarded to the best garden plot within the following categories: firstly, a Section garden, then a Hut garden near an accommodation hut and finally, a WAAF garden near any WAAF site. This pastime was not only good for local fresh produce but was also a welcome distraction from wartime life.

No 27 OTU's accident rate was typical of a bomber-training unit and minor accidents happened on a weekly and, occasionally, on a daily basis. Airfields are dangerous places, especially at night and one particular accident proved this point on 14th April. At 2145 hrs, a Wellington III was about to depart on a night-navigation exercise, when the navigator Sgt K Hewitt realised that he had left some paperwork behind in the Flight Office. With the engines still running, Hewitt began his journey to retrieve his paperwork but tragically walked into one of the bomber's rotating propellers, dying of his injuries later.

Nickels to France during May 1943 included Nantes, Rouen, Lille and Paris. The unit lost another bomber over enemy territory on a Nickel to Paris on the night of 23rd/24th May. Sgt C W Astle and his crew in Wellington III BK489 were lost without trace. It was a double loss on the night of 14th June for the unit when two complete RAAF-crewed aircraft went down on navigation exercises over the North Sea. Flt Sgt W D Weir, RAAF, in Wellington III BJ672 and Flt Sgt E G Holden, RAAF, in Wellington III BJ843 were all posted as missing.

The station received a new commander on 16th June when Gp Capt C E Horrex, AFC, was posted to Uxbridge, relinquishing his post to

In early 1943, the Fortress and Liberator made way for the Handley Page Halifax. Both American types would return in greater numbers as the war progressed.

The Consolidated Liberator was another American-built type which was handled by 51 MU. Delivered in greater numbers than its stable-mate the Fortress, the Liberator served the RAF with distinction in all theatres of the Second World War.

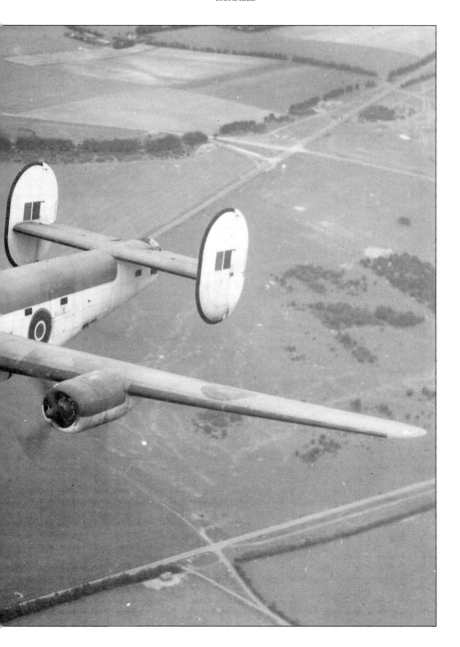

Gp Capt P G Heffernan, RAAF, AFC. With so many Australian personnel passing through 27 OTU, it seemed entirely appropriate that an Australian should command them as well. Gp Capt Heffernan was a very 'hands-on' leader and as soon as he arrived he was very keen to fly alongside the instructors and trainee crews.

Lichfield gained another unit on 17th June 1943 in the shape of 93 Group Screened Wireless Operators' School. Its role was to keep wireless operators who had already passed their training and might have already flown a tour of duty, refreshed in current techniques. How long it was at Lichfield is unknown. No 27 OTU did not become part of 93 Group itself until 1st September, a move which did not affect the unit's role and position at Lichfield.

Relentless Nickel operations from Lichfield continued throughout the summer of 1943, but by the end of August 27 OTU was once again involved in front-line Bomber Command operations. Despite the Allied invasion of Europe being many months away, it was obvious that the attack would take place along the French coast. Targets within France were gaining priority despite Sir Arthur Harris's insistence that the industrial Ruhr and targets within Germany should always be the main Bomber Command aim.

August saw the arrival of the first Wellington X, which would eventually be the standard equipment of 27 OTU. The Mk X was an improved version of the Wellington III which first entered service in December 1942. Over 3,000 were built, equipping 25 squadrons at home and overseas and, with such a prolific production rate, it was not long before they became available to the Bomber Command OTUs.

While 660 aircraft from Bomber Command attacked München-gladbach and Rheydt, the first of many small raids on ammunition dumps in the forests of Northern France by OTU aircraft was carried out on 30th/31st August 1943. The 33 OTU Wellingtons which took part, four of them from Lichfield, were led by six Pathfinder Mosquitos who marked each target. Not only was the raid good experience for the fledgling crews, but also bombing on markers was to be the main method of attacking enemy targets until the war's end. The raid was in the St Omer area, with the ammunition dump at Forêt de Eperlecques being the main target. While no aircraft were lost from Lichfield during the raid, three of them returned without dropping their bombs. A fourth 27 OTU Wellington did manage to bomb the target. The raid was described as being successful and a large explosion was witnessed during the attack.

Back at Lichfield, the sterling work being carried out by 82 MU reached a record during August. They managed to pack 201 aircraft in a single month, the first unit within the wing to achieve such figure. They then gained another type in the shape of the Hawker Hurricane IV. This rocket-equipped variant saw service in Tunisia and Italy with the Desert Air Force.

Four more 27 OTU Wellingtons took part in another attack on an ammunition dump at Forêt de Mormal in northern France on 2nd/3rd September 1943. The Lichfield contingent joined another 26 OTU Wellingtons and 5 Pathfinder Avro Lancasters on the raid, which was classed as a success, and all four from 27 OTU Wellington dropped their eight 500lb bombs on the target.

Thirty-two Wellingtons from OTUs were in action again on 3rd/4th September, this time attacking an ammunition dump at Forêt de Raismes, near Valenciennes. Six Pathfinder Halifaxes and six Mosquitos led the raid, which once again was classed as a success with no aircraft lost. All returned safely back to Lichfield, one aircraft with its bomb load still intact.

The biggest raid that 27 OTU had participated in since the '1,000-bomber' raids in 1942, took place on 8/9th September 1943. Nine Wellingtons from Lichfield joined a force totalling 257 aircraft against a long-range gun battery near Boulogne. The raid comprised 119 Wellingtons, 112 Stirlings, 16 Mosquitos and 10 Halifaxes, plus 5 USAAF Boeing B–17 Flying Fortresses flying the first night-bombing sortie of the war with Bomber Command. The Pathfinder Mosquitos were experimenting with a new marking technique, which proved to be inaccurate, and the resulting bombing left the gun battery completely unscathed. Not a single aircraft was lost during the raid and only one aircraft from Lichfield returned with its bomb load. This was to be the last major raid that 27 OTU would participate in and they were left to continue the routine of Nickel operations over France.

The last aircraft to be lost by 27 OTU on a Nickel operation over enemy territory occurred on 23rd/24th September 1943. Flt Sgt G L Dowling, RAAF, and his crew, in Wellington III X3966, was one of two aircraft tasked with a Nickel against Orléans. When in the vicinity of Rouen, the crew spotted a pair of fighters and, whilst creating distance between them, the Wellington was hit several times by flak, peppering the aircraft with shrapnel. Dowling decided to despatch his cargo of leaflets and set course for home. The fuel lines or tanks must have been punctured because fuel was being lost at an alarming rate. Once the gauges read zero, the order to bale out was given and the entire crew managed to escape the powerless bomber. They all landed in the

Beauvais area and, remarkably, the crew of five escaped capture and returned to England to resume flying duties. Flt Sgt Dowling went on to serve with 76 Squadron Halifaxes, achieving a full operational tour.

An unenviable record was achieved during the evening of 6th November 1943, when three Wellingtons from Bomber Command training units were lost through mid-air collisions on the same night. Two of the aircraft involved were from Lichfield, one of them with the station commander, Gp Capt P G Heffernan, RAAF, at the controls. The first incident took place at 2000 hrs when Plt Off M E McKiggan, RAAF, in Wellington III X3637, with an unusually large crew of six, collided with Short Stirling I R9192 from 1657 HCU (Heavy Conversion Unit) at Stradishall in Suffolk. Both aircraft were flying under cumulo-nimbus cloud, a practice that was frowned upon, when the two bombers struck each other near Saffron Waldon in Essex. The crippled Wellington went out of control and crashed at Raden Stock Farm, near Little Walden, killing all seven Australians on board. The badly damaged Stirling, with eleven personnel aboard, managed to limp back to Stradishall.

The second incident that night involved Wellington III X3924 of 26 OTU from Wing in Buckinghamshire and Wellington X LN295 from 27 OTU, with Gp Capt Heffernan, RAAF, as pilot in command. The two aircraft collided near the American-occupied airfield at Alconbury in Huntingdonshire, with the wreckage of both machines falling between the airfield's main gate and the village of Abbots Ripton. The pilot of X3924, Sgt R B Main, RCAF, was thrown clear of the wreckage and American personnel gave him first aid. Gp Capt Heffernan was the only survivor from the 27 OTU although he was seriously injured, spending many weeks in the RAF Hospital at Ely in Cambridgeshire. One of those killed in LN295 was Section Officer K L Hughes, WAAF, who had joined the all-Australian crew just for the ride. Three days later the now vacant position of station commander was filled by Gp Capt E Burton, who was posted from 5 Group headquarters at St Vincents at Grantham in Lincolnshire.

The workload of 51 MU was unrelenting by the end of 1943 and the main type being prepared by the unit was the Hawker Typhoon. The fighter-bomber was increasingly in demand for ground attack operations in northern France and it would become a key component in the success of the forthcoming invasion. Other types being handled by the unit at the time included the Fortress I and IIA, Horsa, Hotspur, Liberator IV, Magister, and Oxford I and II.

In February 1944, the unit gained another type to be prepared for

The demand for the Hawker Typhoon was at its peak during 1944. No 51 MU were tasked with fitting Rocket Projectile (RP) rails as shown here and bomb racks for 500-pounders.

frontline operations. On 29th February, a signal was received from 41 Group that the unit was to receive Grumman Hellcats and an initial batch of twenty was already allocated to 51 MU. A few days later, a further signal was received stating that 51 MU was to receive the Halifax V. These were to be prepared for 38 (Airborne Forces) Group standard, which effectively meant that the aircraft would be prepared for parachutists and glider towing. The work also included changing all four engines, plus a variety of modifications to the airframe. On top of this, the Typhoon commitment was increasing to an impressive 100 aircraft per month being prepared for operations. Many technical personnel by now were working an average of 70 hours per week but the majority cheerfully accepted this as necessary for the war effort.

Four aircraft from 27 OTU took part in a routine Nickel raid on Paris on 10/11th April 1944. While only one hour into the sortie, the port engine of Wellington X HE165 cut out. Flt Sgt V K Gratton, RAAF, was at the controls and immediately set course back to Lichfield but on approach, the undercarriage refused to lower and the bomber belly-landed on the airfield. With two fire tenders in attendance, the crew escaped injury and this was to become the last 27 OTU aircraft to be involved in an incident during a Nickel operation.

Lichfield became the home of the Rolls-Royce Development Flight from the beginning of April 1944. The flight took over one of the MAP hangars and remained in residence until the end of hostilities in Europe. The company had its own airfield at Hucknall in Nottinghamshire, which was only 40 miles north-east of Lichfield. This

Another American-built fighter to pass through Lichfield was the Grumman Hellcat carrier-borne fighter. No 51 MU prepared several for operations in the Far East with the Fleet Air Arm.

had grass runways, which were unsuitable for the operation of jet aircraft, and this is possibly why the flight moved to Lichfield. Jet flying was not actually recorded at the airfield during this period though, so the exact activities of the flight remain unknown.

In addition to Halifax modifications, 51 MU was now instructed to prepare Liberator IVs for front-line Coastal Command operations and possibly for Bomber Command in the Middle and Far East. Typhoon modifications dominated May 1944; this entailed the fitment of Rocket Projectile (RP) Rails and bomb racks for 500-pounders. The recently arrived Hellcats were creating more work for 51 MU without them actually being prepared for operations. Out of 28 Hellcats being held by the unit, 10 were found to have unserviceable engines due to corrosion and the remainder all needed new oil seals because of the internal inspections. The unit hoped to prepare no less than fifteen of the fighters for the Fleet Air Arm (FAA) per month, but the hold-up with spares meant that only eight actually left Lichfield over the same period.

Another American type passed through 51 MU in June when the Douglas Dauntless arrived. Only seven examples of the dive-bomber ever served with the FAA so it is quite possible that all of them passed through Lichfield.

Unscheduled visits by aircraft returning from front-line operations over Germany and France were becoming increasingly commonplace. During July, a Lancaster from 460 Squadron at Binbrook in Lincolnshire and another Lancaster from 300 Squadron at Faldingworth, also in Lincolnshire, were diverted to Lichfield. August saw the arrival of a Halifax, this time from 51 Squadron at Snaith in Yorkshire. On 5th August, a single Halifax arrived from Skipton-on-Swale, followed by eight Lancasters from 12 Squadron at Wickenby in Lincolnshire. More Halifaxes and Lancasters were diverted throughout the month, making it the busiest for such arrivals during the whole war. Later in the year, Lichfield provided a safe haven for nine USAAF B–17 Flying Fortresses returning from a raid on Germany on 16th November 1944.

The advance through France by the Allies following the invasion on 6th June was painfully slow, but progress was being made. It was becoming increasingly difficult and dangerous for Nickel operations to continue in the crowded French skies. Morale-boosting leaflets were becoming unnecessary, as it was now obvious that every effort was being made to liberate France and her people. With this in mind, the last Nickel operation to be flown by 27 OTU took place on 17th August 1944 when two aircraft dropped leaflets on Tours and Blois. Lichfield's Wellingtons had flown an impressive 274 Nickel operations since the unit's formation.

The demand, as expected, was high for 51 MU's RP-equipped Typhoons, the main recipient being the 2nd Tactical Air Force operating in Northern France. During August, 198 Typhoons were dispatched to front-line squadrons.

No 82 MU continued its packing work which, by September 1944, was still diversifying. Albacores were being packed for the Royal Navy, as well as Spitfires for the Mediterranean Air Command (MAC), India and Australia. Hurricanes were dismantled and packed for India

Stinson Reliant communication aircraft were dismantled and packed for use in the Middle and Far East by 82 MU during late 1944.

121

and Typhoons for MAC, and Stinson Reliants plus a variety of component parts for 40 Group. The unit also took on extra work from 25 MU at Hartlebury in Worcestershire that included packing ten Wellingtons. Additional work from 16 MU at Stafford was taken on and involved packing no less than 50 Airspeed Oxfords. All this was taken on by 82 MU without difficulty or complaint.

No 86 OTU, based at Gamston in Nottinghamshire, was beginning to wind down and several intakes of part-trained pupils were received by 27 OTU. The first, a group of Canadians, arrived at Lichfield on 12th October 1944. Others followed, although with the outcome of the war all but decided, the need for bomber OTUs steadily declined. No 83 OTU at Peplow in Shropshire was also being closed down and an intake of pupils was received at Lichfield on 26th October. The first sign of 27 OTU's own demise came at the end of October when the bomb dump at Lichfield was systematically relieved of its bombs and pyrotechnics, all of which were returned to various MUs. Only a few practice bombs and small-arms ammunition were retained for training purposes. By the end of November, the bomb dump was made available to RAF Fauld for ammunition storage.

Meanwhile, 51 MU seemed to be getting busier, with even more demand for the Liberator VI and the Typhoon, which continued fighting its way across Europe. The very last Mustang prepared by the unit left during October, the first indication that 51 MU's hard labours might be coming to a conclusion. Fifty more Hellcats arrived in December and a sign of the future role for 51 MU came when 41 Group decided that 75 Auster V airframes should be stored at Lichfield. Almost all MUs of this type, that had spent the entire war preparing aircraft, continued their post war existence storing and sadly breaking many of the aircraft that they had originally prepared. No 51 MU received its first Republic Thunderbolt fighter in early December, followed by the first of many Hawker Tempest Vs on 12th December 1944.

An unlucky run for the station commanders of Lichfield continued on 17th December 1944 when Gp Capt E Burton was injured in a car accident. He was admitted to the RAF Hospital at Cosford in Shropshire where he remained for many weeks. He was replaced by Gp Capt H I Dabinett, who was posted in from Ossington, which was rapidly running down and no longer required a Group Captain in charge.

No 51 MU was quite used to receiving signals demanding more Typhoons for the front-line squadrons fighting in Europe. However,

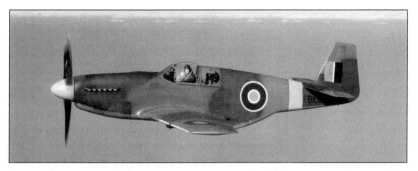

The North American Mustang was a common site at Lichfield throughout the war. The last was prepared by 51 MU in October 1944.

on this occasion, the request was from a training unit, namely 56 OTU, which had been reformed at Milfield, Northumberland to train pilots on the ground-attack Typhoon. Instructions were received from headquarters 41 Group that a total of 40 Typhoons were urgently required for the Milfield unit. Half of the requirement was needed by 1st January 1945, but 51 MU went slightly better and had 23 ready by 31st December.

Before the year was out, 27 OTU experienced reductions of its own personnel when large numbers of the Servicing Wing were posted out to various units. Plans were already in place for the unit's disbandment although at this stage they were a little premature. No 27 OTU was returned to 91 Group control again on 22nd January but, as with the previous moves, very little changed at Lichfield. However, on this occasion, 27 OTU ceased to be RAAF and all future pupils were destined just for RAF service.

It was during January 1945 that the unit experienced the last of far too many fatal air accidents. On many occasions during the war, training aircraft were called upon to form large formations, flying a predetermined course to give the enemy the impression that they were part of or the actual main part of a bombing raid. Several Bullseye operations were used for this purpose but by this stage of the war a separate entity known as Operation Sweepstake was employed. On the 14/15th January, 126 aircraft, all from training units, were tasked to fly over the North Sea as a diversionary tactic while a major raid took place on Leuna and two minor raids on Grevenbroich and Dülmen. One of several aircraft from 27 OTU that was involved was Wellington III X3465, piloted by Flg Off K E Cranley, RAAF. On return from the exercise, Cranley encountered very poor weather and diverted to Wymeswold in Leicestershire. Whilst attempting to land, the bomber crashed, injuring all aboard and killing the rear gunner, Flg Off E R Peace, RAAF.

No 51 MU reached the very maximum it could handle of multi-engined aircraft during February 1945. With 59 on strength, mainly Liberators and Halifaxes, all of which needed to be parked on hard standings, Lichfield was literally full. From April, with the end of the war clearly in sight, 51 MU commenced a 'Preparation for Long-Term Storage' programme in accordance with a policy laid down by 41 Group several months previously. Not only was this a major turning point in the kind of work being carried out at Lichfield, but it also meant that dispersal of stored aircraft was far less difficult than before. More aircraft could be positioned closer together without fear of them being destroyed by air attack.

In May 1945, with the war now over, 27 OTU's workload tailed off dramatically with only a fraction of the wartime training sorties being flown. The airfield was no less dangerous and it is sad to record that the last casualty from 27 OTU was once again by walking into a revolving propeller. On 22nd May 1945, Sgt R G Withrington, an air gunner on Wellington X HE331, was killed instantly when the propeller struck him.

The satellite used by 27 OTU at Church Broughton was closed down on VE Day and the main party who had been working there since 1942 returned to Lichfield on 18th June, followed by the rear party a few days later. The flying sortie by the unit took place from Lichfield on 22nd June 1945 and the unit was officially disbanded the same day. Between 1st and 9th July, all remaining 27 OTU aircraft and equipment were ferried away to various MUs, facing an uncertain future. Several of the Wellington Xs were given a second flying career after conversion to T Mk 10 standard, many serving into the early 1950s.

Ending as it had begun back in 1939, Lichfield was returned to the control of Maintenance Command on 9th July 1945. Now under the control of 41 Group, Lichfield still housed 51 MU and 82 MU, both units continuing the same line of work. No 51 MU's immediate post war work included converting Liberators to transport standard and the long-term storage programme continued. Plans were received in August to store 150 Oxfords followed by 230 Mosquitos of all marks. Many Typhoons, which were originally prepared by 51 MU, ended their days in open storage at Lichfield. To cope with the amount of aircraft being received by the unit, 51 MU gained Church Broughton as a sub-site from August 1945, followed by Stoke Heath in Shropshire on 15th November 1948.

The end of the demand for packed aircraft to be sent overseas also brought about the end of 82 MU in October 1945. The final aircraft handled by the unit were the Spitfire XIV and Tempest II, the last of which had been cleared by September. The service personnel employed by the unit were transferred to 76 MU at Wroughton in Wiltshire but sadly the loyal civilian workforce were all laid off. Instructions were received to close down on 31st October and the resulting redundancies were reported to the District Manpower Board and the Local Office of the Ministry of Labour and National Service. This bureaucratic-sounding department was tasked with finding the civilian workers of 82 MU alternative employment.

To cope with the influx of aircraft being delivered to 51 MU, an additional ferry unit was formed on 30th November 1945. Known as No 3 Ferry Pool (FP), a typical busy day was recorded as an example of their workload in January 1946. The small unit ferried nine Lincolns, three Lancasters, one Wellington, two Martinets, two Warwicks, three Mosquitos, one Firefly and a single Hornet Moth. Despite their workload, 3 FP moved to Polebrook in Northamptonshire on 15th March 1946, once again leaving Lichfield with just 51 MU in residence.

Throughout 1946, the unit was involved in preparing the Miles Magister for civilian use and various marks of Mosquito for service with foreign air forces. These included Belgium, Czechoslovakia, Denmark, France, Israel and Sweden.

By 1947, the unit had broken up 150 Flying Fortresses, 500 Liberators and an incredible 900 Typhoons. This systematic scrapping of such quantities of aircraft at Lichfield inevitably began to create space on and around the airfield and 51 MU slowly shrank in size.

A flying unit returned to Lichfield in May 1947 in the shape of reformed 43 Gliding School (GS). Originally formed at Walsall in October 1943, it had been closed down in December 1946. The school flew Cadet and Sedbergh gliders and remained operating at Lichfield until 1st September 1955, becoming the last flying unit to do so.

From June 1948, the many Oxfords that were already in storage plus a host of new arrivals were being prepared for use with a variety of foreign air forces, mainly in the Middle East. The Oxford preparation work took until March 1950, followed by the arrival of several Avro Lincolns. These were kept in storage for potential use during the Malayan Conflict until 1953, when this became the main task for the unit.

Some of the last RAF aircraft to be operated from Lichfield were the Vickers Valetta T3s of 6 ANS. WJ467 served the unit during the mid 1950s.

Up until the mid-1990s, as seen here looking east, the airfield was virtually complete. Today it has been developed almost into obscurity, but all the hangars that can be seen in the photograph still stand and are all in use.

No 104 Flying Refresher School was formed at Lichfield on 23rd July 1951 to train reserve pilots for the bomber role. The unit operated the Wellington T10 and Oxford I and personnel totalled over 2,000 at the unit's peak. The school was redesignated as 6 Air Navigation School (ANS) on 15th February 1952. The new school retained its Wellingtons for a while but these were replaced by the Vickers Valetta T3 and, just before its disbandment, the Vickers Varsity T1. By 1st December 1953, the unit was disbanded.

No 51 MU's association with Lichfield came to a sad end on 1st July 1954 when the unit was officially disbanded. In its final years, 99 MU, 5003 Airfield Construction Squadron and the Maintenance Command Ground Defence School used Lichfield. The airfield was closed in April 1958 and in May 1962 the Air Ministry disposed of the site for £240,000.

Up until the late 1990s, the airfield was virtually complete with runways, perimeter track and dispersals intact. Over the last decade, remarkable changes have occurred and a visit in 2007 found the airfield rapidly disappearing under large, modern warehouses and offices. What remained of the runways has been allocated for housing but virtually all of the hangars still exist and the majority have been refurbished and are being used for industrial purposes.

8
MEIR
(Stoke-on-Trent)

Along with every other significant town in the country, in the late 1920s Stoke-on-Trent felt the need for a municipal airport. Areas of suitably level land were few and far between around Stoke but sites at Wetley Common, Weston Coyney and Meir were inspected by the City Council Aerodrome Committee.

The Air Ministry gave them its advice and 182 acres of land were purchased at Lower Normacot Farm, Meir which was by far the most suitable choice and the original recommendation of the committee: 'Meir at the time was a village located on the southeastern side of Stoke and was rapidly growing into a suburb of Longton. The airfield was located south of the Uttoxeter Road between Longton and Blythe Bridge on to the main rd. It is capable of housing six Tutors. This belongs to the Stoke-on-Trent Civil Flying Club and there is a ground engineer there. The Club at present has only one aircraft (Miles Hawk).' It was hoped that the airfield would be suitable to house a detachment from 5 FTS (Flying Training School) at Sealand in Cheshire. While the unit did adopt the airfield as a landing ground, being so distant, very little if any military activity was recorded at this time.

Several small airlines had been keeping a close eye on Meir's development and the first scheduled service began on 12th August 1935. The aircraft was DH.86 G–ACVY *Mercury* of Railway Air Services (RAS) based at Croydon in Greater London, and the service, which operated between London, Belfast and Glasgow, landed at Meir on request at a set time. Passengers alighting at Meir could also fly to Manchester, Liverpool, Blackpool, the Isle of Man and Belfast as part of the same route offered by RAS. Floodlights, landing lights, a radio

De Havilland DH.86 G–ACVY 'Mercury' of Railway Air Services carried out the first scheduled commercial flight from Meir on 12th August 1935.

room and waiting rooms were among many facilities which were added as a direct result of the RAS operation.

In April 1936, the subject of military flying cropped up again when Mr A McLaren, MP for Stoke-on-Trent, wished to know if a service or auxiliary flying unit could be based at Meir. In his next breath, he said how much of a burden the aerodrome was on the ratepayers and that there was much opposition to it from members of the Council. Lack of housing was a major problem at the time and the use of the land for this purpose would have been preferred by many officials. The latter point would be raised continually through the airfield's history and would eventually be a major factor in its demise.

A few months later, it was confirmed that Meir would become home to one of twenty new Elementary and Reserve Flying Training Schools (E&RFTS) being formed throughout the country. An E&RFTS operated military aircraft with RAF instructors, but civilian contractors generally serviced the aircraft. Basic flying skills were taught to new pilots during the week and RAFVR (Volunteer Reserve) pilots flew at the weekends to keep their flying hours up. The new training school would require more buildings including a pair of T2 hangars with a variety of ancillary buildings attached, such as lecture and briefing rooms.

The new school, designated 28 E&RFTS, was formed on 1st August 1938 within 26 (Training) Group, whose headquarters were at Buntingsdale Hall at Market Drayton in Shropshire. It was one of four

The Hawker Hart was obsolete when 28 E&RFTS was formed at Meir in August 1938. Along with the Hind, the Hart continued to serve as a training and support aircraft into the early years of the Second World War.

schools operated by Reid & Sigrist Ltd. Aircraft on strength included the Hawker Hart, Hawker Hind, Miles Magister, and later the Avro Anson.

The airfield continued to expand throughout the remainder of 1938 with an additional 150 acres purchased on the southern side. The RAF also suggested that they would need more hangar space and a Bellman type hangar was planned for construction. Instead, the corporation built a hangar of 40,000 square ft in front of the Flying Club hangar at a cost of nearly £34,000. The RAF unintentionally gained a far superior building because it was not completed until after the beginning of the Second World War and went straight into military service. When the war did arrive on 3rd September 1939, flying was prohibited at all civilian flying clubs throughout the country. This also included the civilian-run 28 E&RFTS and literally overnight Meir fell quiet.

It was several months before moves within Air Ministry circles intimated that a new unit would make use of Meir. On 10th February

1940, Wg Cdr J A C Wright, AFC, TD, DL, MP, arrived at Ternhill in Shropshire, as officer commanding 1 Practice Flying Unit (PFU). Although over twenty miles away, Ternhill was the nearest permanent RAF station and an ideal assembly point for an 'opening-up party' to organise itself before moving to Meir.

No 1 PFU was formed to accommodate 120 acting pilot officers and 120 sergeant pilots who had already completed an advanced course at a Flying Training School (FTS). The PFU was the first unit of its kind and its main objective was to keep these pilots current in both aerial and ground training techniques. On arrival at Meir on 12th February 1940, the opening party's first problem was a distinct lack of accommodation. This was solved by requisitioning three large houses for the officers; one doubled as a mess and sleeping accommodation, the remaining two were used solely for accommodation. The non-commissioned officers were billeted at Longton Town Hall while all permanent staff, officers and airmen were accommodated at various houses around the airfield. Locally hired civilian buses transported the staff and pupils to and from the airfield and various mess halls.

Reid & Sigrist, which originally looked after the aircraft of 28 E&RFTS, won the contract to service the machines of the PFU. The company also carried out maintenance of the unit's mechanical transport (MT) and parachutes. The intended establishment of the PFU was 27 Hawker Hectors and 27 de Havilland Dominies, although this figure was never quite reached.

The Hector was a large, reasonably powerful biplane which started life in 1933. Designed for Army Co-Operation duties, the Hector served with front-line squadrons until June 1940. It went on to serve with several gliding schools, finding a new lease of life as a tug.

No 1 PFU was officially formed on 4th March 1940 within 23 Group, established at South Cerney in Gloucestershire. It was not until 20th March that the first aircraft, six Hectors, arrived from 5 Maintenance Unit (MU) at Kemble in Gloucestershire. Hawker Hind Trainers were added to a small fleet of aircraft in early April and it was one of these which became the PFU's first casualty. While taking off from Aston Down in Gloucestershire, Flg Off M D H Wilson's Hind (T) K6837 ended up on its nose, causing enough damage to write the aircraft off.

The PFU also became involved in local military exercises by simulating air and parachute assaults. On 13th May, Col McAlaster of the Staffordshire Regiment visited Meir to make arrangements for an exercise involving aircraft carrying troops and dropping parachutists against the airfield itself. The simulated attack took place at 1600 hrs

An early photograph of a Hawker Hector. By the beginning of the war they were relegated to second line units such as 1 PFU at Meir.

and within fifteen minutes of the siren sounding all aircraft were dispersed and all defensive positions were manned and ready. It was recorded that the PFU by this stage had 40 Hectors and Hinds on strength.

The following day it was the turn of the PFU aircraft to be the enemy with a mock attack on a military post at Alton Towers. Nine aircraft took part in the exercise, which once again involved troops from the Staffordshire Regiment. On 16th May, the Staffordshire Regiment returned to Meir to practise more anti-parachutist defence techniques including selecting posts and positions for machine guns.

The first indication that a new unit might move into Meir occurred on 5th June 1940. Flt Lt Ellis and Flt Lt Bailey from 5 Elementary Flying Training School (EFTS), based at Hanworth in Middlesex, visited Meir under instructions from Flying Training Command. With the Battle of Britain about to begin, the south-east of England was no place for a Miles Magister-equipped training unit. A move to relatively safer skies further north was logical and 1 PFU's demise came swiftly when instructions were received on 15th June to close the unit down the following day. The original intention had been to form several similar units, this being why the one and only PFU was numbered, but this never came to fruition.

Known as 15 E&RFTS during its pre-war existence, the unit was reformed as 5 EFTS at the outbreak of the Second World War. Originally, the school operated a host of different aircraft but by now only flew the single-engined, low-wing Magisters, of which over 40 were on strength. On arrival at Meir on 16th June accommodation was a problem, especially on the airfield. The remnants of 1 PFU were still *in situ* and Reid & Sigrist still occupied a considerable proportion of offices, hangars and storerooms. A single new hangar was made available to the school and the attached offices were immediately turned into lecture rooms with the remainder occupied by the commanding officer, an Orderly Room, an office for the Chief Flying Instructor (CFI) and a Civil Officer Section.

To accommodate pilots under training, two more civilian houses were requisitioned, named 'Goddesburg' and 'The Grove'. Initially, though, these houses were used to accommodate a temporary mess and house all instructors, commissioned and non-commissioned, and the senior civilian personnel. Pupils were accommodated at Longton Town Hall under very poor conditions. The hall was permanently blacked-out, ventilation was poor and the location was two miles from the airfield. Flying Training Command rules at the time stated that special transport would not be provided for service personnel living more than two miles away. To overcome this, Meir's MT section provided lorries to transport the pupils to and from the airfield. This was not an ideal solution but one that worked until conditions improved.

Despite the difficulties in getting established at Meir, 5 EFTS began normal flying instruction at 0845 hrs and normal ground instruction at 0900 hrs on 17th June. The disruption of the move did very little to slow up the flying rate as 3,171 hours and 25 minutes of flying time were still achieved during the month.

By the end of June, Reid & Sigrist had cleared almost all of their stores and aircraft, releasing a great deal more space to 5 EFTS. Rooms were now being used for their intended role, including purpose-built lecture rooms which had been used as stores for spare parts. Another positive move was the sudden availability of Meir Drill Hall, which had been handed over from the Army to the RAF. The hall was less than half a mile from the airfield and arrangements were made to move the pupils there from Longton Town Hall. Work also began on constructing kitchens and a dining hall next to the Drill Hall, making life considerably more pleasant for the pupils passing through the school. The move, however, still would take take place until October 1940.

No 5 EFTS were used to operating from Hanworth under more 'war-like' conditions, but on arrival at Meir found the airfield in a comparatively unprepared state. No defences of any kind had been built and there was no control or 'pass system' in operation. Both were implemented by the end of June, with barbed wire and defence posts now scattered around the perimeter of the airfield.

Sadly, the first recorded incident involving a 5 EFTS Magister was a fatal one. On 3rd July 1940, Plt Off R C Sankey and Sgt D A Green were carrying out low-flying practice in N3852 near Trentham Park. The small trainer struck some high tension (HT) cables, burst into flames and crashed, killing both occupants instantly. The resulting enquiry stated that the area where the accident took place was 'most unsuitable for low flying'.

On a lighter note, there was an act of human kindness in Longton on 6th July when Flg Off Broomhall was out on his lunch break. He was approached by a lady who handed him an envelope and requested that he should give it to his Officer Commanding (OC) for the benefit of the 'boys at Meir'. On opening the envelope, the OC found it contained £100 in notes. This impressive gift was used to provide additional facilities for the airmen and also the necessary capital to open a canteen. The mystery donor was eventually traced as Mrs Wyatt of 12 Cemetery View in Longton.

Several air raids occurred around the airfield during July 1940, most focusing on the many potteries located around Stoke. One particular incident involved a single enemy aircraft dropping 74 incendiary bombs within half a mile of Meir; the damage could have been worse, as 30 of the bombs did not go off. Another raid on 13th October, also probably unwittingly, came close to hitting the airfield. At midnight, several enemy aircraft were circling the district when a stick of three bombs was dropped. The first bomb landed in the garden of a house on the edge of the airfield. Luckily, no-one was injured and no damage was inflicted on RAF property.

With no sign of a concrete runway being laid at Meir by November 1940, the grass surface was starting to become muddy. The situation was aggravated by defensive barbed wire and trenches, which had encroached on the tarmac apron near the hangars. The barbed wire was eventually removed to make more room for aircraft to manoeuvre. Another problem which was noted during the month was the poor visibility encountered when flying directly over the airfield. This was attributed to industrial smog and haze from the local pottery towns and the ground formation around the airfield. From an aircraft, Meir was actually more visible from a few miles away and this was to prove a great handicap to inexperienced trainee pilots. A Relief Landing Ground (RLG) was needed. Abbots Bromley was chosen and on many occasions diversions helped airmen in trouble. A Forced Landing Ground (FLG) was also available at Stone and, like Abbots Bromley, helped many pilots to get down safely.

With an aircraft such as the Magister, forced landings were generally a straightforward procedure which usually did not result in damage to the aircraft or injury to the pilot. Anything up to six forced landings in a single day could be carried out by pilots from Meir, the majority without problems. 3rd November 1940 was a typical day with four aircraft involved in various incidents. LAC Dickson became lost and force-landed near Burton-on-Trent, and LAC Moorfoot got himself in a similar situation near Leek. LAC Watson took being 'lost' even further when he force-landed and wrecked his Magister I L8514 near Gisburn in Lancashire, over 70 miles north of the airfield. More serious was another victim of HT cables during a low-flying exercise, when Instructor Sgt M C Pope and LAC C R Boraston crashed in Magister I T9700 near Shelton-under-Harley. Both pilots were taken to Staffordshire Royal Infirmary.

On the orders of Flt Lt Bailey, a very disillusioned essay written by members of the senior course at the time was published for all on the unit to read. The individuals who penned the work remained anonymous but their comments reflected the thoughts of many who passed through basic flying training. The first gripe was bad

This Magister is daubed in pre-war, all-yellow training colours which were replaced with drab camouflage when war broke out.

136

accommodation, followed by a lack of sufficient leave to see families. Another more alarming complaint stated that there were faults in certain individual instructional methods. No action was recorded as being taken against the authors of the work, indicating that their complaints were taken seriously and that action to remedy the situation was taken.

From 12th November, aircraft were no longer picketed out in the open because the damp caused deterioration of the Magister's wooden structure. This meant more work for the ground crew who had to bring the aircraft into the hangars at night, but less work for engineers repairing the machines.

A typical course to pass through 5 EFTS came to a conclusion on 13th November 1940. Out of 60 pupils who attended No 11 War Course, 40 completed their training. Three pupils were transferred to the following-on course, all of whom were expected to pass. This gave a wastage figure of 28 per cent, which was average for the time. The same day, a further 61 pupils arrived from 3 Initial Training Wing (ITW) at Torquay in Devon in preparation for No 12 War Course.

5th December was another eventful day at Meir, which involved two forced landings and LAC Best crashing on his first solo landing. The same day, Blenheim I L1218 from 13 OTU at Bicester in Oxfordshire landed downwind and crashed. The aircraft was not seriously damaged.

The quick thinking of one of the unit's flying instructors probably saved the lives of two pupils and two aircraft at the same time. On 15th December, LAC Williams of 'B' Flight crashed on landing in Magister I T8262 and collided with another Magister which had instructor Sgt Parker and pupil LAC Clark aboard. Sgt Parker leapt out of his machine and switched off Williams' engine and then assisted LAC Clark, who had been badly cut in the face by a piece of his own aircraft's propeller. A fire broke out underneath the entwined aircraft, which Sgt Parker tackled with a fire extinguisher.

The dearth of accommodation at Meir was a continuous problem, highlighted on 17th December when No 14 War Course arrived. The 60-strong course could not believe their luck when they were all sent away on six days' leave due to the lack of available accommodation. The break must have done them all the power of good because when the course ended in January 1941, all 60 pupils passed!

Morale was given a boost at Meir when a concert party was arranged on 10th December. Several personnel from the airfield helped to produce the play, helped by local artists, and 775 people attended.

The Lord Mayor of Stoke-on-Trent presented RAF brooches to female helpers in the canteen at the end of the performance.

Friendly fire has been a common occurrence since warfare began and, during the confusion of war, mistakes can happen. One such incident was witnessed by Flg Off Howard and LAC Bateman whilst carrying out forced landing practice west of Stone in Magister I N3776 on 23rd December. The airmen watched as the anti-aircraft defences of the Royal Ordnance Factory at Swynnerton opened up on a Handley Page Harrow transport. Luckily, the Harrow did survive but was forced down into a field in an attempt to escape the deadly shelling. Several shells also burst close enough to Flg Off Howard's Magister for him to hear the explosions above the noise of the engine.

From Christmas 1940 through to March 1941, the weather was very poor and the unit struggled to achieve even a fraction of its planned flying hours. Industrial haze was becoming a permanent problem, aggravated in January by up to four feet of snow.

February began badly with a fatal accident on the 2nd of the month. Plt Off G C Blunt and LAC J A Ashley of 'A' Flight in Magister I N3776 spun onto the airfield out of control, killing both airmen instantly. Another tragic accident occurred on the edge of the airfield a week later. Air Transport Auxiliary (ATA) pilot L A Phillips crashed his Spitfire near to Meir; sadly he died of his injuries before reaching hospital.

Equally horrific-looking accidents occasionally resulted in the pilot and passenger surviving practically unharmed. On 5th March, Flg Off McCarthy-Jones and his pupil LAC Griffiths of 'A' Flight crashed their Magister into houses near the airfield. The chances of surviving such an accident were always slim but McCarthy-Jones got away with a broken leg while Griffiths suffered a slight burn to his face. A fire broke out in the wrecked aircraft but the quick actions of the civilian householders brought it under control. The same day, LAC Grindod of 'D' Flight experienced a similar crash when his Magister I T9703 struck a farm building on the edge of the airfield. Grindod was attempting to go around after a bad landing. The aircraft was a total wreck but Grindod was not seriously hurt.

The weather by March was on the turn and a more respectable 2,185 hours were achieved by 5 EFTS compared to 380 hours during February. April was even better with an increase to 3,473 flying hours, but at the cost of another pupil's life on 9th April. LAC L H Smith of 'D' Flight was killed when his Magister I L8085 crashed at Wood Farm near Leigh in Shropshire.

No 16 EFTS at Burnaston in Derbyshire was in need of another RLG in April 1941. Meir is recorded as having been used by the Magisters in this unit until June but considering how busy Meir was at the time, it would be very doubtful if 16 EFTS made much use of the airfield.

Another fatal accident occurred on 1st May when LAC Tuffin of 'D' Flight crashed in Magister I L8158. Tuffin lost control and came down on Groundslaw Farm, Tittensor four miles south-west of the airfield; sadly he died of his injuries later in the day.

Not all pupil pilots were cut out for flying and one individual proved the point on 20th May. LAC Pears of 'C' Flight overshot, stalled and crashed onto the Uttoxeter Road, adjacent to the airfield. Uninjured, Pears flew again the following day but, rather embarrassingly, crashed on the airfield once more. He was suspended from further flying training and it can only be presumed that he was remustered to a ground trade. This was not an unusual occurrence; it was exceptional for all of the No 14 Course mentioned earlier to pass with flying colours.

July 1941 proved to be the most successful that 5 EFTS had achieved since arriving at Meir – 4,402 flying hours were achieved by the unit's busy Magisters, a figure that was never surpassed. But while July was one of the most successful flying months, it also proved to be the most costly. Five airmen from the unit lost their lives and another four were injured in a variety of flying accidents. The first fatal accident of the month took place on 7th July when Sgt Jones and LAC Golder of 'A' Flight were killed in a flying accident. Four days later, Plt Off A W Amos and LAC Healy collided in mid-air with LAC Whiting, resulting in three more deaths.

August proved to be much better but several aircraft were wrecked in the five forced landings that took place. Six others crashed on the airfield and LAC Smith of 'A' Flight was lucky when he damaged his wing in a mid-air collision on 11th August. Surprisingly, this was one of the quieter months for accidents; the worst by far for the unit was to be October 1941.

During October, 29 pupil pilots had to force-land at various locations; a few had mechanical problems but the majority were simply lost. Twelve others crashed on the airfield and another four were involved in taxiing accidents, including LAC T Blake who trundled into a petrol bowser on 8th October. The most serious accident occurred on 17th October when LAC J R Meadows crashed Magister I L8157 near Rough Close. Remarkably, no pilot was seriously injured during this abundance of incidents.

With upper surfaces camouflaged this would be a typical scene at an EFTS during the war, complete with a smartly dressed civilian prop swinger.

The status of 5 EFTS was changed in October from a Class A unit with an establishment of 72 aircraft and 120 pupil pilots, to a Class B unit. This downgrade was an attempt to reduce congestion and the establishment was reduced to 54 Magisters and 90 pupil pilots.

This reduction was reflected in the amount of pilots who force landed during November; numbers were now down to a mere 22 forced landings, and a more acceptable 7 crashes. The smaller 5 EFTS did not warrant four flights any more and only 'A' and 'B' Flight now functioned.

December 1941 proved to be the quietest on record for the unit, mainly because news had been received back in October that 5 EFTS would be disbanded before Christmas, and also because the weather was poor for the majority of the month. On 15th December, the bad weather brought about the unexpected arrival of the biggest aircraft to land at Meir so far, when a Vickers Wellington I of 109 Squadron, on detachment at Boscombe Down in Wiltshire, was forced to put down.

On 20th December, all flying ceased and 5 EFTS was officially disbanded on 23rd December. On 31st December, all instructors were posted out and Meir was placed under Care and Maintenance, already unsure of its future so early in the war.

Almost the whole of 1942 proved to be very quiet for Meir, which firmly remained under Care and Maintenance. A reasonably-sized RAF contingent was always in residence and, on 24th January, Flt Lt S F Baden-Lea was appointed as the commanding officer. It was not until August that another RAF unit was formed at Meir with 45 Gliding School (GS). The school was to become the longest serving unit to exist at Meir and during its history, it flew the Cadet I, II and TX3, Prefect TXI, Falcon III and Sedbergh TXI, all accommodated in a Robin hangar on the north-western side of the airfield. The school also operated a permanent detachment at Long Mynd in Shropshire where gliding still takes place today. During wartime, it was only possible for the unit to operate at the weekends, but this was carried out almost without fail, only the worst of the weather ever stopping them flying. Still at Meir, the unit was reformed as 632 (Volunteer) GS on 1st September 1955 and remained at the airfield until it was moved to Ternhill in Shropshire in 1963.

In late 1941, construction of a factory complex began on the southern side of Grindley Lane, near to Blythe Bridge. It was thought that the large building would be taken over by an RAF Maintenance Unit but instead, the site was developed as a shadow factory for Avro. The plan was for the Manchester-based company to produce the Tornado for Hawker's, but this aircraft came to nothing mainly because of problems with its Rolls-Royce Vulture engine. When redeveloped, the Tornado evolved into the more successful Typhoon, the majority of which were eventually built by the Gloster Aircraft Company. The new Grindley Lane factory was also considered for Armstrong Whitworth Albemarle production, also built by Avro, but this did not come to fruition either.

The first occupants were Rootes Securities Ltd, a group made up of Singer, Humber, Hillman and Sunbeam–Talbot. The companies were brought together in the early 1930s by Reginald and William Rootes and, not long after, expressed an interest in aircraft production. William Rootes had already approached the Bristol Aeroplane Company with a view to producing the Blenheim. A new factory at White Waltham in Berkshire was planned but this fell through and an alternative factory at Speke in Liverpool was used for Blenheim production instead.

Once the Second World War began, Rootes picked up more contracts to produce aircraft, including one to build the Handley Page Halifax. The Speke factory was not big enough to build Halifaxes and Blenheims side by side so production of the latter was planned for the new factory at Grindley Lane.

The main building was 400 ft by 660 ft and was known as No 10 Factory. Closer to Grindley Lane, three Bellman hangars were built, initially known as No 8 Factory, the entire site occupying 120 acres of land. A silk mill at Cheadle was also requisitioned for use by Rootes as a component store. Across the lane on the airfield side four more hangars (two pairs) were built; one pair was known as the Trials Installation Sheds and the other, the Flight Preparation Sheds.

The main factory was completed by April 1942 and it was built to a very high specification with every conceivable facility. This included canteens, offices, a surgery and full air conditioning specifically installed in the event of gas attack, which was still considered a possibility. Below the offices, a cellar was constructed for the use of the local Home Guard Unit and the Air Raid Precautions (ARP) headquarters. The building was also fitted with a highly efficient and powerful heating system to compensate for the fact that the factory was 630 ft above sea level and incredibly cold during the winter months.

While the Grindley Lane factory was being built, Rootes had already taken over a hangar at Shawbury, named No 9 Factory, for Blenheim production. Conditions were poor and as soon as the Grindley Lane site was ready, No 9 Factory was closed down. Production of the first Blenheim IVs began in No 8 Factory with the main component parts of the aircraft being supplied from Speke and Burtonwood in Lancashire. By the time No 10 Factory was ready, No 8 Factory was already completing five aircraft per week. Production of the Blenheim IV was carried out between May and October 1942, followed by a contract to build the Blenheim V.

The grass runways were sufficient for the operation of 5 EFTS's Magisters and just about coped during wintertime as well, but the continuous flying activities of the larger, heavier Blenheims were taking their toll on the airfield, especially with winter approaching. In

The first aircraft to be produced by Rootes at Grindley Lane was the Bristol Blenheim IV.

The Blenheim V was the next mark to be assembled at Meir, including AZ930 pictured in January 1942 at Boscombe Down, Wiltshire.

early 1942, a decision was made to construct a 3,000 ft by 150 ft concrete runway running in a north–south direction. The runway was completed by May and an additional ash perimeter track was laid from the flight sheds to the original EFTS hangars on the northern side of the airfield.

On 26th February 1943, a strange decision was made when 30 OTU at Hixon was given the responsibility of becoming the Parent Station to Meir. The RAF Care and Maintenance Party and a Flight of the RAF Regiment had been at Meir since 5 EFTS's disbandment in December 1941. The RAF Regiment had provided security for the airfield but in March 1943, the entire RAF contingent handed control of the airfield over to Rootes and 30 OTU's short parental duties were over.

By May 1943, the Grindley Lane factory was employing 3,799 staff. Production of the Blenheim V continued until 1st June 1943 when the last, EH517, was flown out of Meir. Alongside, the company carried out modification work on 362 Blenheim IVs for service in the Middle East. Blenheim production at its peak was reaching between 50 and 60 aircraft per week, but this did not stop MAP (Ministry of Aircraft Production) from landing Rootes with another aircraft contract. Rootes built Blenheims totalled 250 Mk Is, 2,230 Mk IVs and 940 Mk Vs, an incredible achievement in such a short space of time.

From January 1943, another Bristol aircraft, the Beaufighter VI, was built by Rootes at Grindley Lane. The Beaufighter was a complicated aircraft, which received over 60 modifications during its production

Two hundred and sixty Beaufighter VIs and torpedo-carrying TFXs were assembled at Grindley Lane by Rootes.

run. Despite this the workforce adapted quickly to building the new aircraft. Halfway through the run, production was changed to the torpedo-carrying Beaufighter TFX.

A 24-hour shift was in place by this time, which was only interrupted when the factory closed at 1200 hrs on a Saturday and re-opened again at 2200 hrs on the Sunday. Staff were trained in all aspects of the aircraft's production, giving every employee the necessary skills to work in every department of the factory.

Every single aircraft that left the factory up until 1943 was test-flown by production test pilot Mr E G Shulz. His responsibilities also included being the commander of the factory Home Guard unit. Eventually, Mr Shulz was joined by a RAF test pilot to cope with the amount of aircraft that were being produced.

The factory was visited by the Minister of Aircraft Production, Sir Stafford Cripps, with several MAP officials, on 3rd February 1944. Cripps chaired a meeting with management and addressed the staff about the importance of the Beaufighter production. He also stated that once this work was completed, the factory would be concentrating on supporting the large number of Canadian and American-built aircraft, which were being supplied to the RAF via the 'Lend-Lease' scheme. With the latter statement in mind, the factory came under the control of the Directorate of Repair and Maintenance, which among other things controlled the reassembly of 'Lend-Lease' aircraft.

Approximately one-third of the factory was reassigned for the

Under the 'Lend-Lease' scheme, North American Harvards flooded into Meir during the war years and remained a familiar sight for long after.

storage of engines, with another third for propellers. A large proportion of the workforce was released, the bulk to other shadow factories in order to exploit the skills already learnt. Rootes still kept control of the factory but the main task from now on would be the assembly and modification to RAF standard of the North American Harvard and North American Mustang. Every single new arrival was delivered, after a long sea voyage, in a large packing case. Discarded cases quickly filled all the free space around the factory and the roads leading to it.

Rootes handled the Mustang III and Mustang IV, the equivalent to the P-51C and P-51D. The earlier marks of the fighter had been restricted to low-level fighter reconnaissance because of their Allison engines. These later marks were fitted with a 1,680 hp Packard Merlin engine, resulting in greatly improved performance in all departments.

Rootes at Grindley Lane built 260 Beaufighters between the serials KV896 and KW416. Beaufighter X KW416 was the last, flown out on 30th April 1944, going on to serve with 27 Squadron at Agartala in India before being shot down by American P-38 Lightnings later in the year.

May 1944 at Meir saw 354 aircraft either in the factory or on the airfield, 94 of which were Mustangs flown in from Burtonwood and Speke awaiting modifications by Rootes to RAF standard. The Mustang had a high landing speed and, to deal with this, 600 ft of PSP (Pierced Steel Planking) was added to the southern end of the main

The Mustang IV, equivalent to the P-51D, was a superb all-round fighter. Conversion to RAF standard was one of the last wartime tasks carried out by Rootes at Grindley Lane.

runway. Some of the many empty packing cases which were littered all around the airfield were put to good use – the result was a new control tower constructed on the western side of the airfield. Completely unique to Meir, the new tower received a full-time air traffic controller by the name of Sqn Ldr Man, who was appointed to cope with the increase in flying traffic.

Rootes were also tasked with producing Lobelle jettisonable canopies for the Republic P–47 Thunderbolt. The initial order was for 500, but this was carried out with such efficiency that it was raised to 1,000, produced at an average of 35 per week. When the task was completed, a letter of thanks was received from the US Director of Maintenance, Brig Gen J T Morris.

The workload at the Rootes factory was never higher than during 1944. Throughout the year, 560 Harvard IIbs and IIIs were assembled; one of them, Harvard FX411, for the personal use of King Peter of Yugoslavia. Some 356 Mustangs were modified, painted and test-flown and, including the Beaufighters that were completed at the beginning of the year, Rootes built or assembled 1,025 aircraft during 1944. Other tasks included a large quantity of aircraft spares and modification sets for the Harvard, Liberator, Mustang, Thunderbolt and Beaufighter.

Considering the number of aircraft coming and going from Meir, the accident rate was incredibly low. A few Blenheims had been involved in minor accidents during the early part of the war but it was not until 9th September 1944 that a Mustang III crash-landed on the airfield.

KH449 was being delivered by an ATA pilot when, on approach, the undercarriage struck an unmarked steam road roller at the end of the runway. The roller was being used on the PSP extension in an effort to stop the planking from curling up, which was a permanent problem. The impact tore off one of the Mustang's main wheels but the pilot only suffered a bump on the head. The road roller driver was thrown fifteen feet across the grass.

Nine days later, another Mustang III, KH552, overshot in poor visibility and crashed into some obstructions beyond the end of the runway. A Hurricane 'nosed over' on 26th October, followed by Mustang IV KH687 which landed heavily on 29th November. The final incident at Meir took place on 7th December 1944 when Mustang IV KH722 landed heavily enough to collapse the tail-wheel, which caused the fighter to ground-loop.There is no record of KH722 having served with a squadron and, probably as a result of this accident, it was struck off charge on 16th December 1946.

With the end of the Second World War, the requirement for Harvards and Mustangs dwindled to a halt. The RAF needed transport aircraft to ferry troops and equipment from both Europe and the Far East. To fill the gap, the Air Ministry decided that 300 Liberator bombers, which were now redundant, should be converted to trans-porters. Rootes were commissioned to carry out some of these conversions and, in May 1945, Liberators carried out a series of touch and go tests, to see if the runway at Meir could take them. Not long after, the first American-built bomber arrived, with a crowd from the factory to watch the test pilot taxi the four-engined aircraft up to the flight sheds. The wingspan of the Liberator was 110 ft and the gap between the two sets of hangars was only 120 ft. The inevitable

Many Liberator bombers were given a second lease of life as transporters. Rootes converted several to CVI standard as shown here.

happened and a wing struck one of the hangar doors, resulting in a wingtip change for the first arrival. After VJ Day, work at the factory wound down rapidly. Liberator work was completed by the beginning of 1946 but the company remained at Grindley Lane until 1960.

The airfield was now completely at the disposal of 45 Gliding School (GS) under the command of Sqn Ldr W Nadin, RAFVR. He also owned and operated a BAC Drone from the airfield and later an Auster as well for Air Training Corps (ATC) duties.

A limited amount of civilian flying returned to Meir but only the occasional Auster. Staffordshire Potteries, who had taken over a pair of Bellman hangars, operated a Dragon Rapide for a short while and then a more modern de Havilland Dove up until 1960 when the aircraft was sold.

The Rootes factory was vacated by 1960 and not long after was taken over by Simplex–Creda for the production of household domestic appliances; they are still there today. Other parts of the factory and the flight sheds were used by various industrial companies.

Several attempts were made to introduce commercial aviation to Meir and for a time Dragon Airways operated a scheduled service on both its Jersey and Isle of Man routes, using the de Havilland Heron. The service was not destined to last for long, however, because the surface of the runway had deteriorated almost beyond use.

When the RAF gliding school left in 1963 their place was taken by the Staffordshire Gliding Club, who remained at Meir until the airfield's closure in 1973. Meir quickly succumbed to housing and today the most visible relic of the old airfield is the large factory built for Rootes in 1941. One connection with the past is to be found within the housing estate that occupies the main airfield site. While the aircraft named would not have flown from Meir, names such as Lysander Road, Siskin Place, Canberra Crescent and Hermes Close will always preserve a link with the past.

9
PENKRIDGE
(Pillaton)

This small Relief Landing Ground (RLG), once swarming with Tiger Moths, was one of the busiest of its kind within Staffordshire during the Second World War.

It is quite possible that the site for a new RLG for the ever-growing number of Elementary Flying Training Schools (EFTSs) was found by accident. On 15th January 1941, LAC J F Ford, in a 5 EFTS Magister I from Meir, became lost. Ford managed to make a good force-landing, causing very little damage to his aircraft, in a field east of Penkridge. Within weeks of this unscheduled visit, Air Ministry officials and personnel from 5 EFTS were looking at the potential for constructing a RLG on land one mile south-east of Penkridge, south of the B5012.

The landing ground was constructed west of a ruined fortified house known as Pillaton Old Hall and 'Pillaton' was the name that local people associated with the RLG. The small airfield had more facilities than most, with two hangars, temporary accommodation for up to 126 airmen, and several brick-built technical buildings. A single grass runway of 850 yards in length was marked out in an east–west direction.

The exact date for the opening of Penkridge is a little sketchy. It was first allocated to 29 EFTS, based at Clyffe Pypard in Wiltshire, in September 1941. This seems strange considering the two airfields were approximately 100 miles apart. There is little evidence of the unit's use of Penkridge but it is possible that they kept it for cross-country, navigation and diversion exercises.

The second and most prominent unit to use Penkridge was 28 EFTS, based at Wolverhampton. The school needed an additional RLG for

The ubiquitous de Havilland Tiger Moth was the most common aircraft to be found at Penkridge during the Second World War.

night-flying training and, from 19th May 1942, two Flights were installed with nine Tiger Moths each. Night flying did not officially begin until 17th June and in response to the new activity, more equipment was moved to Penkridge.

Probably the world's most famous training aircraft, the Tiger Moth served the RAF from 1932 to 1955. A development of the Gipsy Moth, the prototype first flew on 26th October 1931 and within twelve months was ordered for the Central Flying School (CFS). One thousand had been delivered before the Second World War began and British production alone totalled 4,668, all for the RAF. In 1939 Tiger Moths equipped 44 E&RFTSs and during the Second World War 28 EFTSs. Approximately 250 are still flying today, thanks to their appeal to the civilian market.

As flying increased, it was recognised that the RLG had virtually no medical facilities and on 20th June 1942 a new Emergency Station Sick Quarters (SSQ) was established. A wing of a wooden barrack block was converted into three rooms with two beds and medical equipment available. Running water and stoves were also provided. By the end of the year, the SSQ had been moved from the wooden hut to a more luxurious Nissen hut which had the addition of an electric light.

The first Tiger Moth was lost operating from Penkridge on 6th October 1942. Whilst practising aerobatics near the airfield, pupil pilot LAC Smith entered a spin and was unable to recover. Smith managed to abandon the aircraft but sadly he was too low for his parachute to open in time.

Night flying at Penkridge did not officially begin until 22nd January 1943. This continued without incident until Sgt Dennis and Cpl Cass crashed their Tiger Moth through a hedge on 5th April. Six other Tiger Moths were lost while operating from Penkridge before the war's end. Luckily none of them caused injury to the aircrew aboard.

Aircraft visiting the RLG included at least one Hawker Hurricane and an Anson I, DJ634, from 9 OAFU based at Penrhos, Caernarvonshire. The Anson made a forced landing after an engine failed during a cross-country flight.

No 28 EFTS stopped using the RLG at Penkridge from 9th July 1945 and it can only be presumed that the airfield was abandoned not long after. It was briefly back in the aviation limelight when, in 1950, the King's Cup Air Race came to Wolverhampton. No aircraft actually landed there but, like Wheaton Aston, Penkridge was used as a turning point during the race.

Today, a great deal of the airfield remains, including the landing ground, several wartime buildings and the entrance road. The local farmer has put all of them to good use. The three Robin hangars are not thought to be original, but arrived post war from the ex-SLG at Teddesley Park. On the very southern edge of the old RLG, aviation continues in the shape of Otherton airfield, the home of the Staffordshire Aero Club. This thriving club mainly operates microlights from an impressive well-equipped little airfield with three grass runways.

10
PERTON

Roads in the heart of a housing estate on the north-western edge of Wolverhampton have names such as Gaydon, Biggin, Scampton and Benson Close, as well as Shawbury Grove and Manston Drive. These references to the RAF airfields of the Second World War are the only indications today of the existence here of a wartime airfield, which has sadly disappeared under expanding suburbia.

Perton's association with aviation can be traced back to the First World War. In response to the increasing Zeppelin raids, several Home Defence squadrons were formed to shoot down the giant raiders. No 38 (HD) Squadron, with its headquarters at Melton Mowbray in Leicestershire, was tasked with the colossal responsibility of defending the Midlands. A landing ground was used at Fern Fields, next to the Perton to Pattingham road, by the squadron's FE.2b fighters from 1916 to early 1918.

The same Fern Fields briefly came into use again during the 1920s with the arrival of several joyride and barnstorming aircraft. Alan Cobham, in his de Havilland DH.61 Giant Moth G–AAEV, named *Youth of Britain*, visited the small airfield on 22nd June 1929. Cobham visited many local towns in a nationwide attempt to demonstrate the advantages of municipal airports and hopefully the benefits to the local economy. His visit on this occasion was aimed at the mayors and officials of Wolverhampton, Walsall, Wednesbury and Stourbridge. The following day, Cobham opened his aircraft up to the general public, who could pay ten shillings for a short flight. Cobham returned to Perton on 22nd September 1935 as part of his *Astra* flying tour.

Not long after Cobham's first visit to Perton, the small airfield received an unexpected military visitor. Hawker Hind (India) K2097 was on a delivery flight from a Packing Depot on 14th September 1931 when the engine began running roughly. The pilot made for Perton but

Hawker Hind K2097 at Perton in September 1931 after its undignified arrival. Local people helped to extricate the pilot while others looked on!

on landing, bounced and overturned. Dragged clear by onlookers, the pilot was uninjured and four days later the Hind was dismantled and left by the road for repair.

The site for a new airfield was surveyed not long after war broke out in late 1939. The requisitioned land was under the management of the Agricultural Land Commission and was occupied by farmers on tenancy agreements. Perton, like several others in the county, was intended for fighter operations and construction began in the spring of 1940. The location was further east than the First World War site – west of Tettenhall, sandwiched between the A41 to the north and the Pattingham road to the south. On the western border was another minor road giving access to the majority of the living accommodation in the general area of Cranmore Farm, which still exists today. Mr Alex Finlow remembers the airfield being constructed: 'Most of the ash came from Gibbons at Dibdale, Lower Gornal. It was loaded by an army digger. At the peak 73 vehicles were carrying loads; each load laid 8 square yards. The top layer of road stone came from Blue Rock Quarries, Oldbury. Mr Pugh was the manager at the time.'

Mr S J George was a transport driver for Pensnett Transport, High Oak, Pensnett in 1941 before his Army call up: 'We hauled a lot of runway material for the airfields at Perton and Cosford. The Lower Gornal ash certainly enabled the planes at Perton and Cosford to take off from some very fine runways.'

The design of the airfield itself was unremarkable with two runways of 1,100 yards and the main runway at 1,400 yards in traditional triangular formation. Only a few concrete hardstandings were built (some with earth-banked protection), a flying control and a single Type T2 hangar.

By July 1941, work at Perton was virtually completed, but no decision had been made by the higher echelons as to what the future held for the airfield. Its role as a potential fighter station had long passed and it quickly slipped into a state of limbo that would have been more appropriate in peacetime conditions.

On 2nd August 1941, instructions were issued by Headquarters Army Co-Operation Command that RAF Perton would officially open on 28th August. The airfield would come under 70 Group's control pending a decision on its future. Orders were also given that Perton was to organise a station headquarters and a defence force would be allocated.

An opening-up party, under the command of Plt Off H W Parsons, commenced formation at Castle Bromwich on 10th August. The party, which was made up of clerks, cooks and drivers, took up their duties at Perton on 18th August. A few days later, brick-built accommodation, located near Cranmore Lodge Farm, was taken over by a brigade of the Dutch Army. The soldiers, apart from their usual training duties, were employed for a variety of tasks on the airfield. They would go on to fight their way through France in 1944 and then onwards to liberate their home country.

Perton was now under the command of Flt Lt M Gordon, who also took charge of 764 (Defence) Squadron when they arrived from Firbeck in Yorkshire on 27th August. The squadron included an Anti-Aircraft Flight, which quickly took up positions around the perimeter of the airfield. The official opening day on 28th August came and went with the only highlight of the day being the opening of a NAAFI-run airmen's mess, which did not have enough food to operate properly!

A detachment of the 381st (Searchlight) Battery took up a position on the eastern side of the airfield on 2nd September. The next day, the defence force gained more equipment in the shape of an Armadillo armoured vehicle designed for mobile airfield defence. More weapons

Dutch soldiers at Perton in 1942 working amongst the huts near Cranmore Farm. (Via Ron Balding)

arrived including Vickers machine guns and Tommy guns. It was not long after this influx that one of the defence force, AC2 Pacitto, was shot and killed. A Court of Enquiry was arranged and as a result of its findings, the inquest found that tragically he had committed suicide.

It was not until 2nd November 1941 that the first aircraft arrived at Perton, although admittedly the pilot had not planned its arrival. Miles Magister I N7627 had to make a forced landing but, just before the aircraft touched down, the tail wheel struck a pile of rubble. The little trainer was later repaired and continued on to its parent unit of 8 FTS (Flying Training School) at Montrose in Angus.

Just to add to the increasingly confusing situation that Perton was finding itself in, more construction work began at the end of November. A bomb storage area, of the same proportions as that of an operational bomber station, was constructed on the north side of the airfield. The bomb dump straddled both sides of the minor road (today known as Wrottesley Park Road) and like most areas of this type it was carved out of natural woodland. Perton's future was now swinging towards being a bomber station, for either training or perhaps even operations? In the state that it was in at the time, the airfield's runways were far too short to operate such aircraft, though they could all be extended to cater for bomber types.

Wg Cdr D S Radford, the officer commanding 11 SFTS (Service

Flying Training School) at Shawbury in Shropshire, envisaged a more realistic use for Perton. An inspection in November, followed by a second on 8th December, concluded that the airfield was suitable for both day and night flying. Shawbury was having new runways laid and this had caused a lot of disruption to the training programme of 11 SFTS. The school needed as many airfields as possible to cope with the training backlog. It looked like Perton had found its future unit.

Two representatives, Sqn Ldr Romanoff and Flt Lt Ward, from the yet to be officially formed Parachute Training School, inspected the airfield on 27th December. Their home airfield at Ringway, on the southern edge of Manchester, was not an ideal location from a security point of view and suffered from industrial haze. The two officers concluded that Perton was in no better position than Ringway, a location that the school was destined to stay at for the entire war.

A letter of confirmation was received on 8th January 1942 which stated that Relief Landing Ground (RLG) facilities had been granted to 11 SFTS. A few days later, Wg Cdr Radford, Sqn Ldr Selby-Lowndes and Plt Off Jeremy visited to discuss moving the personnel from Shawbury. Plt Off Jeremy was to be in charge of the advance party, with 16 officers, 50 to 60 senior NCOs and pupil pilots, 120 airmen and 14 Airspeed Oxfords following close behind. Heavy snow disrupted the move, with the first of the 11 SFTS contingent arriving on 24th January under the command of Sqn Ldr Cor. The fourteen twin-engined Oxford trainers duly arrived on 26th January and two days later flying training began from Perton for the first time.

The Airspeed Oxfords of 11 SFTS from Shawbury, Perton's first flying unit.

156

A Miles Master II very similar to those operated by 5 (P)AFU at Perton in 1942.

The snow continued to fall heavily throughout the remainder of January and on into February. Perton's defence personnel, who were now in the renumbered 2764 Defence Squadron, were tasked with clearing snow from the perimeter track while two snow ploughs kept the runways open.

The 11 SFTS detachment came to a swift end when it returned to Shawbury on 28th March 1942. After a few more days of uncertainty, Sqn Ldr M C Adderley and Flt Lt J S Robinson arrived by air from 5 (P)AFU at Ternhill in Shropshire. Many visits like this continued through April and May with specific attention being paid by Flying Training Command.

Under the command of Flt Lt Hale, 2764 Defence Squadron moved to Snailwell in Suffolk on 7th May 1942. The defence of the airfield was now in the hands of the newly-formed 4035 Special Flight, RAF Regiment, under the command of Flt Lt Allden, MC. These new flights were the building bricks for the RAF Regiment, which still carry out airfield defence today.

By the end of May 1942, Perton was under the control of 21 (Training Group) within Flying Training Command, whose headquarters were at Cranwell in Lincolnshire. By 1st June, Ternhill had become the airfield's parent unit and 5 (P)AFU began flying instruction from 14th June. Only five Miles Master trainers operated from Perton, although a few Magisters joined them later in the month. Over the next fortnight various personnel from Ternhill were posted into Perton. Flt Lt Charles was the attachment's officer commanding and Chief Flying Instructor (CFI).

Whilst at Perton, 5 (P)AFU lost one aircraft in a flying accident. A Master II was one of three taking off together when, just after take-off, the engine failed. The trainer quickly lost height and crashed into a ploughed field not far from the Dutch Army camp. The pilot was unhurt and the Master was repaired to fly another day.

The placement of a Link trainer at Perton meant that a synthetic night-flying training programme could be put into action at the airfield. This started daily from 1st July although it was destined to be short-lived as 5 (P)AFU's association with the airfield came to an end on 22nd July 1942.

Perton remained under Ternhill's control until 4th August, despite no aircraft or personnel being resident. The same day, control was handed back to Shawbury in Shropshire and 11 (P)AFU (originally known as 11 SFTS), still operating the Airspeed Oxford. Perton now served as an RLG and the original aircraft, which arrived from Shawbury in January, took up permanent residence along with instructors, pupils and ground personnel. The single T2 hangar was used for servicing and Perton became a self-contained extension of the main unit at Shawbury.

With only a few 11 (P)AFU Oxfords operating from Perton, accidents were few and only minor. When accidents did occur they usually involved visiting aircraft that were unfamiliar with the airfield. Spitfire Va BL660, flown by 1st Lt Woodrow Hopkins of the 1st GTF (Gunnery Training Flight), 6th Fighter Wing, crash-landed on the airfield on 18th February 1943. The Spitfire was returning to Atcham in Shropshire but developed engine trouble over Perton. Luckily the pilot was uninjured and the fighter was eventually repaired.

The training activities of 11 (P)AFU came to an end on 1st August 1943 when the small detachment returned to Shawbury and then moved on to an alternative RLG. Their place was taken by another Oxford-equipped unit, 21 (P)AFU from Wheaton Aston. A flight of aircraft was located at Perton for the first stages of the course, including night flying and eventually blind approach training. The latter was catered for on the arrival of a few aircraft from 1511 BATF (Blind Approach Training Flight), which moved into Wheaton Aston on 28th September. Like 21 (P)AFU, the BATF was only a small detachment with both units' headquarters remaining firmly lodged at Wheaton Aston.

Now officially a satellite of Wheaton Aston, the unit at Perton was processing 30 pilots per course who arrived regularly every Tuesday. The majority of them came from Canada as part of the Empire Training

Scheme and the realities of flying in the more crowded and often weather-beaten skies of Great Britain came as a shock to many.

Perton was not equipped with any kind of illuminated flare path, until 1511 BATF's arrival. The unit was unique for the time because it actually travelled with its own mobile flare path! Fitted to converted bomb trolleys, the unit possessed several mercury–sodium 2kw flares which were used during pupil training. When in operation during the day, the pupil pilots wore goggles with adjustable lenses to simulate varying stages of darkness. At night the flares, which could be moved to the runway in use, would double as an emergency landing aid. In Perton's case, these flares came in very handy for several aircraft in trouble at night including at least one Wellington and several Hurricanes, Spitfires and C–47s.

Several B–17 Flying Fortresses were also involved in incidents at Perton during the Second World War. Certain areas of Perton, like most airfields, were prone to flooding. Aircraft as large as the B–17 would easily become stuck and on one occasion an aircraft was bogged down for two days. Only brute force and the combined power of a pair of tractors managed to moved the machine. The main runway at Perton had a notorious dip in the middle, significant enough for the pilot to lose the end of it from his line of sight. Another B–17, one of many which landed by mistake at Perton, fell foul of this dip when a civilian lorry crossed the end of the main runway unaware that the large bomber was hurtling towards them. When the B–17 appeared, the occupants of the lorry abandoned their vehicle and ran for their lives. The bomber struck the cab of the truck and now with a potentially fatally damaged aileron, the pilot just managed to stop before the end of the runway. The American four-engined bomber was filled with airmen going on leave via Prestwick who fixed the damaged aircraft themselves, being so desperate to leave the country!

In November 1944, the airfield gained a new station commander by the name of Sqn Ldr Harold (Mick) Stone. An experienced night intruder pilot, Stone recalls his first impressions of Perton:

> On arrival I was dismayed to find the airfield in such a neglected state. The flying was done from a flight office adjacent to the main gate and in a quite dilapidated condition. There was another office about 200 yards further round the perimeter which was in a much better situation, so I obtained paint, rollers and brushes etc, and had the pilots and ground staff get to work to completely redecorate the building inside and out. I had them

Trainee pilots walk out to their Oxford. A scene so typical of any training unit and one which would have been seen on an almost daily basis at Perton from 1942 to 1946.

make vegetable and flower beds and got the gang-mower to run over the area between the perimeter and runway in front of the office each morning so anyone so inclined could practise their golf or tennis. As the office was only separated from a lane by a barbed wire fence, I had the Salvation Army come twice a day to supply us with tea and buns on the house.

Although there was no requirement that I personally do any flying, I tried to make a point of test-flying with a pupil whenever I could spare the time. On these flights I would ask the pupil to carry out an emergency procedure such as precaution-ary or forced landings, overshoots, cross-wind landings, single-engined flying, precision landings etc. I did in excess of 30 of these tests, and I must record that there was not a single instance where the pilot carried out the test to my satisfaction, but their logbooks showed that they had been shown and practised these emergencies.

My own explanation for this was that for some years now, pupils had been taught by ex-pupils, who then taught pupils, who again taught pupils and so on. I see from my own logbook that the only times I carried out any emergency practice whilst at the Central Flying School was when I myself was showing the procedures to a fellow pupil. It may not have been possible to have a different system, but the fact remains that I was disturbed to see these young pilots going on to operations so ill-prepared for emergencies and not being able to do anything about it.

I would occasionally come across a pilot who would grip the control column as if his life depended on fighting the aircraft. It was known as 'white knuckle flying'. In these cases, after warning them not to attempt this themselves, I would take over and demonstrate how you could take off, complete the circuit and land with hands off the control column, using only the throttles, rudder and trim control.

Another regular sight at Perton were the Douglas Bostons and Havocs assembled at the Helliwells factory at Walsall. A permanent detachment of civilian personnel worked on the aircraft as they arrived for air-testing, Walsall being too small for such work. It was not uncommon for Boulton Paul-modified or built aircraft to use Perton as well. Like Walsall, its own airfield at Pendeford was very small and Perton offered a safer environment for flight-testing.

Mr P Bibb was stationed at Perton during the bulk of 1943 until spring 1944 and he remembers it well: 'Apart from the RAF, a civilian team worked at Perton doing final adjustments and flight-testing of American Boston and Havoc twin-engined fighter bombers which had been assembled at Helliwells at Walsall Airport. Perton was a very happy unit and a welcome change for many airmen from other airfields who had received some rough treatment from German bombers and fighters. I came from Sullom Voe (Shetland) so you can imagine the pleasure of a posting to civilization at Perton.'

The demand for pilots was obviously curtailed dramatically at the end of the Second World War. No 1511 BATF's small detachment of aircraft left the airfield not long after, leaving just a few Oxfords from 21 (P)AFU.

During this post war period, visitors were becoming few but Mr J A Douglass remembers one particular flight to Perton: 'On 2nd October 1945 I landed at Perton in Hurricane 'H' PZ802 which was a Mark IIC. My logbook says that the visibility at the time was 600 yards and I recall that no flying was taking place. Ostensibly my flight was a low flying exercise from Langham in Norfolk but in actual fact it was to enable me to visit my wife who was in hospital at West Bromwich. I stayed the night and left Perton next morning at 1030 hours. The squadron codename was "Panton" and the radio code for my destination was "Bushranger".'

Douglas Bostons and Havocs assembled by Helliwells at Walsall were air-tested from Perton.

The few remaining 21 (P)AFU Oxfords remained at Perton until 16th July 1946, bringing military flying to a conclusion at the airfield. On 1st August, the airfield was effectively cleared of equipment and personnel and placed under Care and Maintenance. On 10th July 1947, the Air Ministry abandoned the site and the airfield was taken over by the Agricultural Land Commission, the original owners of the land. It was passed to another Government organisation on 1st July 1949 and to the land's original owner, Sir Charles Mander-Bart. By this time several of the airfield buildings, mainly around Cranmoor Farm, were occupied by Latvians, Lithuanians and Poles. Many of the buildings

Dedicated on the 19th September 1982, this memorial to all members of the RAF is positioned on the airfield's main runway. (D Willis)

were converted into dwellings by Seisdon Rural District Council, and were occupied until at least 1962.

A single light aircraft operated from the airfield during the 1960s and McAlpine & Sons Ltd tried to reopen Perton after Wolverhampton Airport closed in 1970. The company operated a Beech King Air at the time but, unfortunately, Staffordshire County Council had other plans for Perton.

Planning permission for a residential development on the old airfield was initially applied for in 1964 and refused. This was appealed against and planning permission, on green belt land at the time, was granted and work began on a large housing estate. The 500-acre site became a new town with enough houses to accommodate 12,000 people. Today, with the exception of a few buildings around Cranmoor Farm and off Wrottesley Park Road, nothing remains; the entire airfield is now covered in houses. Thankfully, a memorial has been laid by the RAF Association Wolverhampton and District Branch on the site of Perton's main runway. Dedicated on 15th September 1982, the memorial is located close to the Sainsbury supermarket in Perton centre.

11
SEIGHFORD

It was obvious from the start that 30 OTU (Operational Training Unit) at Hixon, with its Vickers Wellington bombers on strength, would need an additional airfield to operate from. A site between the village of Ranton and Seighford had been surveyed in late 1941, the latter name being adopted for the new airfield.

Work began in early 1942, with hopes and pressure from senior staff that Seighford would be operational by the summer. The hastiness of the construction eventually reduced the airfield's effectiveness as many repairs and modifications would disrupt the future flying programme. However, as promised by the contractors, a three-runway 'A' class airfield, complete with a pair of T2 and single B1 hangars, technical site and accommodation for over 1,300 RAF and WAAF personnel had been constructed by July 1942.

This did not mean that the airfield was ready for aircraft. The main technical site and the three hangars were separated from the main airfield by a minor road (the B5405 today), which was often closed as aircraft were moved to and fro. Unlike Hixon, Seighford was not penned in by railway lines, allowing full-sized runways to be built. A pair of runways at 1,400 yards in length and the main runway at 1,800 yards were constructed (this was extended to 2,000 yards in the late 1950s). Runways of this generous length would attract several major aircraft diversions in the future.

The first RAF personnel arrived on 29th July 1942. Under the command of Plt Off Staniland, a group consisting of one corporal and 37 airmen from 30 OTU were tasked with cutting down trees, collecting and storing wood ready for the forthcoming winter. These airmen travelled daily from Hixon and it was not until late August that permanent staff began to arrive. Despite the fact that 30 OTU had been

The Wellingtons of 30 OTU were the main users of Seighford during the war years. The Wellington III, pictured here, and Wellington X were the most common marks.

providing the bulk of personnel for the new airfield, Seighford was not officially designated as a satellite for the unit until 16th September. It would still be several weeks before aircraft arrived. Defence personnel followed in November, consisting of 5 NCOs (Non-Commissioned Officers) and 31 gunners of the RAF Regiment.

The forthcoming disbandment of 25 OTU at Finningley in Yorkshire resulted in an influx of personnel into Seighford between 1st and 19th January 1943. All of these airmen, who were divided between 27 OTU at Lichfield and 30 OTU, were technical staff and were familiar with the Wellington. No 25 OTU was disbanded on 1st February and, like its airmen, the unit's 50-plus Wellingtons and 12 Avro Ansons were divided between Lichfield and Hixon. The latter airfield already had at least 54 Wellingtons crammed into it, hence the need for Seighford, which began to attract its own aircraft from 5th February 1943.

Only two days later, the first of many training accidents occurred when Wellington III X3332, a veteran of many operational sorties, crash-landed near the airfield. No injuries were caused and the Wellington was repaired and continued to serve with 17 OTU at Upwood, Huntingdonshire until it was scrapped in July 1945. Minor incidents occurred in both March and April, with two major crashes in May. Plt Off Birkbeck crashlanded Wellington III DF546 on 22nd May and Sgt Lydon made a similar arrival the following day in BK251. Both aircraft were extensively damaged but luckily, once again, no injuries were caused to either crew.

The final part of the bomber crew's operational training consisted of dropping propaganda leaflets over enemy territory, known in RAF circles as 'Nickels'. Whether the leaflets did anything to raise the morale of civilians in occupied Europe or indeed to lower the morale of the enemy is open to debate. However, these raids, usually flown over France, gave fledgling crews a taste of what the enemy would throw at them.

The first of many Nickel raids from Seighford involved eight aircraft on the night of 1st/2nd July 1943. While over France, 'C' BK255 flown by Sgt L W Fisher was hit by flak, causing the starboard engine to catch fire and then stop. Fisher diverted to Exeter in Devon where the airfield's personnel were well-used to aircraft in trouble descending upon them. A searchlight was used to indicate the position of the airfield to the crippled bomber. Unfortunately though, the port engine failed on approach and the Wellington crashed into Deep Meadow, Spain Farm, south of the airfield. All the crew were killed except the rear gunner, Sgt B S Sheldon, who was seriously injured. The same searchlight, which was intended for BK255, helped the pilot of Wellington X HE413, on the same Nickel from Seighford, to land safely at Exeter. One aircraft landed at Hixon, with five others returning safely to Seighford. There was no denying that experience was gained quickly on these raids.

Another part of OTU training was the 'Bullseye' exercise. This involved bombers from several other OTUs forming up into a 'bomber stream' at the same time as an operational raid by front-line squadrons of Bomber Command. The training aircraft would fly towards the enemy coast, close enough to be detected by the enemy, who would put up their night-fighters thinking it was a large raid. The theory was that, while the enemy night-fighters returned to their home bases to refuel and possibly re-arm, the main raid would take place. As the war progressed Bullseyes gave aircrew experience of flying for a long period of time in formation, following navigation points all around the country. The first of several Bullseyes from Seighford began on the night of 28/29th July, when seven aircraft took part. One of them, DF460, flown by Sgt Aspin, had to land early at Harwell in Berkshire with an overheated engine. The others returned safely to Seighford.

Despite there being dedicated Air-Sea Rescue (ASR) squadrons scattered around the country, OTUs provided aircraft in this role on a regular basis. Six of Seighford's Wellingtons took part in an ASR operation in the early hours of 30th July. The operation was in support of a big raid on Hamburg involving 777 aircraft. If a bomber or its crew came down in the North Sea, it was hoped that their chances of survival would be increased by the presence of ASR aircraft.

The skies over England were filled with hundreds of aircraft almost every day during the Second World War, but despite this aerial collisions were not as common as you may think. Those that did happen would often occur within the airfield's circuit, where the aircraft were in close proximity to each other. It was near the airfield that an air-to-air collision did occur on the morning of 11th August 1943. The weather was not particularly good that day, with the cloud base down to approximately 800 ft, allowing only a few 30 OTU Wellingtons to carry out circuit training. Unit instructor Flt Lt L W Metcalfe, DFC, was flying Wellington X HE390 when suddenly, out of the clouds, appeared Miles Master II W9073 from 5 (P)AFU at Ternhill in Shropshire. Neither aircraft had time to avoid the other and the resulting collision caused the Wellington to crash in flames on land belonging to Derrington Farm. The Master crashed near Vicarage Farm, both on the edge of the airfield. The two men in the Master, Flt Sgt C A Simmons and Sgt J W Mudie, RAAF, and the Wellington's crew of five were all killed. HE390 could have been described as an unlucky machine, as it had already been involved in a ground collision with a unit Lysander a few months earlier.

Nickels, Bullseyes, ASRs and the training of the new bomber crews quickly became daily routine at Seighford, although inevitably accidents occurred on a regular basis. As mentioned earlier, the airfield was built in great haste and, by the summer of 1943, the wear and tear on the runway and perimeter track began to show. Contractors returned to the airfield from early August, making the operations from Seighford more hazardous with building equipment and workmen all around. On 11th August, Flt Sgt Mace was taxiing Wellington 'Z' around the perimeter track when it collided with a contractor's tractor. No one was injured, but the disruption caused would have been better avoided.

A more dramatic incident, which also involved the contractors, occurred on 26th August 1943. Plt Off H A Vernon, RCAF, was tasked with ferrying Wellington III BK359 'F' on a short flight to Hixon. Vernon lined up on runway No 1, and opened the throttles. All seemed well until he was approximately 300 to 400 yards down the runway, but then the bomber began to swing. The Wellington ran onto the grass, but Vernon continued to attempt the take-off, clipping the front of a contractor's lorry. The bomber carried on, heading straight for a gang of civilian workers with Vernon still trying to get it into the air to avoid any casualties. It was to no avail, Vernon lost control and BK359 crashed onto another runway, miraculously avoiding the workmen.

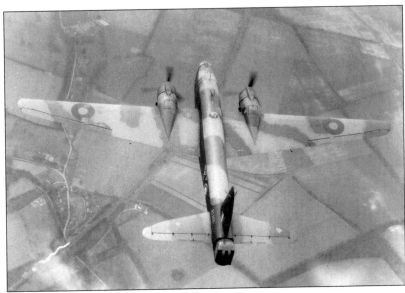

An excellent air-to-air view of a Wellington III. Several were lost in flying accidents from Seighford during the war years.

The only injury was to the driver of the lorry that had been struck by the bomber but he got away with a badly lacerated leg and Vernon was uninjured despite BK359 being a total write-off.

The unit flew 17 Nickels and 25 Bullseye exercises during September 1943. One aircraft, flown by Sgt Kipson, had to jettison its bombs onto the Cannock range in the early hours of 1st September. The same day Wellington X HE222, piloted by Flg Off F A Whitehead from Hixon, crashed four miles north-west of the airfield between Bishop's Offley and Eccleshall. Single-handedly, his crew having already baled out, Whitehead was attempting to reach Seighford after both engines lost power. Wellington III BK366 had to crash-land at West Freugh in Wigtownshire after the port engine failed on a navigational exercise on 20th September, with several other aircraft returning to various airfields with technical faults.

All of the Wellingtons on the OTU had seen at least one or more tours of duty with front-line squadrons. By the end of 1943, 30 OTU's Wellington IIIs were very tired and, by the beginning of 1944, the last bomber variant of the Wellington, the Mk X, was arriving at Seighford. Basically an improved version of the Wellington III, over 3,000 were delivered to the RAF. Many were converted into the T10 trainer by Boulton Paul at Wolverhampton and several remained in RAF service until 1953.

Seven aircraft from Seighford took part in a Nickel raid over France on 2nd January 1944. Three aircraft in all had to return early, with Wellington III BJ761 and BJ988 experiencing the same engine overheating problem. Both aircraft had seen their engines appear to glow as if on fire but the bomber's instrumentation gave no indication of a problem. It turned out that general wear and tear had caused the anti-glare paint to flake off the exhaust pipes, giving the impression in the dark that the engines were on fire!

A Command Bullseye, which would have involved aircraft from other OTUs within Bomber Command, was one of the most regular exercises that Seighford took part in during 1944. Seighford contributed nine aircraft to one such exercise on 21st January. By the end, only five aircraft returned to the airfield. Two had to land at West Malling in Kent; one with engine trouble and the second with instrument failure. One aircraft had to belly-land at Warmwell in Dorset with five of the crew baling out safely, and finally another Wellington had to land at Bruntingthorpe in Leicestershire, low on fuel.

The aircraft loss rate at Seighford was fairly typical of a bomber OTU flying the Wellington. Up until early 1944, the fatality rate was below average but sadly this was to change from 24th February. Flg Off E Ryan and his crew in Wellington X HE903 had just taken off from Seighford as part of a Special Command Bullseye. At 2222 hrs, the bomber dived vertically out of cloud and plunged into the ground not far from the airfield perimeter fence; all six on board were killed instantly.

Another five crew were killed when Wellington III BK437, piloted by Flg Off Barrett, crashed into a hill at Whernside in North Yorkshire on 21st April. Miraculously, the rear gunner, Sgt Marks, survived with only minor injuries.

A freak accident claimed four more lives over Staffordshire on 16th July 1944. Wellington X NC678, with Sgt Phillips at the controls, was flying in formation over Cannock when a flash bomb from an aircraft flying above struck it. The Wellington quickly caught fire and Phillips ordered his crew to bale out. Only two managed to get out, including the pilot, before the bomber plunged into the ground at Cannock Chase.

Seighford's potential role as a diversion airfield began to be fulfilled from mid-1944 onwards. Two Armstrong Whitworth Whitleys from

The Wellington X was the most produced variant of this successful bomber. Later versions operated by bomber OTUs had the nose turret removed and faired over.

Ashbourne in Derbyshire arrived on 20th July and five Halifaxes from 1662 HCU (Heavy Conversion Unit) at Blyton in Lincolnshire, landed on 6th August; more would follow.

The last Nickel operation, and the last loss of a 30 OTU aircraft as a result of enemy action, took place on 9/10th August 1944. Four aircraft set out for a target in Northern France and at approximately 0230 hrs Wellington X HE828 with Flt Sgt Jolly at the controls was hit by enemy flak. Jolly managed to maintain control of the aircraft and set course for home. On crossing the south coast, a decision was made to abandon

The Airspeed Horsa was the RAF's main assault glider and the main equipment for 23 HGCU at Seighford.

the aircraft and all six crew escaped the damaged bomber. HE828 plunged into the ground at Burl Farm, south-west of Holywell, near Dorchester in Dorset.

Every OTU had support aircraft which were used for a variety of tasks, including fighter affiliation. Seighford had a single Hawker Hurricane IIC LF170 for this task. On 24th October 1944 it was LF170, flown by Flg Off Brown, that became 30 OTU's last loss from Seighford. The fighter, which was making a low pass over the airfield, struck a tree, lost part of its wing and crashed near the officers' mess at Seighford. Brown was killed instantly. Four days later, Seighford ceased to be a satellite for Hixon and the airfield was transferred to Flying Training Command.

Some fifteen miles to the west of Seighford at Peplow in Shropshire, 23 HGCU (Heavy Glider Conversion Unit) was formed on 28th October and it was in need of a satellite airfield of its own. The unit was formed as a direct result of the heavy losses incurred during the Arnhem operation which, as with all glider operations, was a one-way trip for the crews and aircraft. As the name implies, the unit trained glider pilots and instructors on the Airspeed Horsa and the American-built Waco Hadrian (known as the CG–4A 'Haig' in USAAF service). To tow the gliders aloft, the unpopular Armstrong Whitworth Albemarle was employed, one of the main roles the type had been relegated to.

On 1st November 1944, the first of two flights of Albemarles arrived and glider training commenced two days later with a single tug aircraft and glider. The unit trained new tug pilots as well, so usually both

Not one of the most popular types in the RAF's inventory. The majority of Albemarles spent their last flying days towing gliders from units like 23 HGCU.

crews were under flying instruction. Seighford's unintentional role as a diversion airfield disrupted 23 HGCU's operations on 4th November. A pair of Boeing B–17 Flying Fortresses returned from a daylight raid and found sanctuary on Seighford's main runway. One of the American bombers became bogged down at the end of the runway in use. It remained there for another two days, further complicated by an Albemarle which blocked another runway when it landed with a flat tyre.

A semblance of order was reached by 8th November with sixteen tows being completed by day and twelve by night. These first tows at Seighford were for the benefit of new instructors, who would go on to train new glider pilots themselves. Only one glider, Horsa RX647, got into difficulty during this period of instructor training when staff instructors Flg Off Cave and Flt Lt Moorhouse had to make a forced landing at Ellenhall Park on 13th November. Both the crew and their aircraft were unharmed.

Course No 7, the first to be allocated to Seighford, arrived on 14th November. The course was made up of 23 First Pilots from 1 GTS (Glider Training School) at Croughton in Northamptonshire and 22 Second Pilots from 21 EFTS at Booker in Berkshire. This course was meant to begin the next day but, once again, airfield disruptions made it difficult. Despite being warned by Flying Control, a group of civilian workmen blocked the runway in use and another day's flying training for the HGCU was lost. The following day, 16th November, was even worse when 30 B–17s, once again returning from a daylight raid, descended upon the airfield. The American crews stayed the night at Seighford, the majority being accommodated five miles north, at Stone. The next day 25 of the four-engined bombers departed but 23 HGCU's training was still disorganized, with only two tows being achieved during the whole day.

The first of several Hadrian Is were ferried from Peplow to Seighford on 20th November, with training tows beginning the next day. Over 700 Hadrians were supplied to the RAF, with over 14,000 being produced in total. The RAF preferred the Horsa for front-line operations and the Hadrian was only used in action once, during the invasion of Sicily by British forces in July 1943. However, many were used for training purposes and 500 were shipped to India in late 1944 for potential airborne operations against Japan.

The first of many 'massed landings' took place at Seighford on 22nd November. The airfield was effectively turned into a landing zone as Albemarles from Peplow unhitched their gliders over Seighford. The landings took place during the day and night to give glider pilots a realistic idea of what it would be like to come down in a tight area in enemy territory. On the afternoon of 24th November, Flg Off Marsh in Albemarle VI V1847 was towing Horsa I RX614 with Flt Sgt Garner at the controls. At only 500 ft, the port engine of the Albemarle failed, giving Marsh no choice but to release the glider to give any hope of both aircrews surviving. Garner made a successful forced landing in a field while Marsh, struggling to maintain control, spun into the ground near Standon, eight miles north-west of the airfield.

With regard to flying the Horsa, the training programme was broken down into eight parts. This usually totalled approximately eight hours of instruction. The course was as follows:

Part 1. Familiarisation; Take-off; Low Tow; Stalling; Use of Flaps; 3,000 ft release and landing.

Part 2. Circuit and Landing with a release at 1,000 ft on the downwind leg (45 minutes of IF (Instrument Flying)).

Part 3. Circuits and Landings, with a release at 1,000 ft on the downwind leg (15 minutes of IF Dual).

Part 4. Solo, Circuits and Landings (Second Pilot to receive at least fifteen minutes of flying).

Part 5. Local Flying, Instrument Practice and 500 ft low release across wind.

Part 6. 500 ft low release across wind and solo IF 15 mins.

Part 7. Mass Landing Dual.

Part 8. Mass Landing Solo.

As you can see from this very compressed syllabus, it was not long before an inexperienced pilot was let loose at the controls of a Horsa.

Routine maintenance of all gliders, which were usually stored outside and at the mercy of the elements, was essential. An example of the simplest of checks being missed occurred on 3rd December 1944, when Flg Off Johns was being given instruction on Hadrian 319829. Whilst under tow by Albemarle VI V1875 at 1,000 ft, Sgt Glaghorn, a passenger in the Hadrian, noticed a small tear developing in the bottom of the glider's fuselage. The instructor on board the Hadrian, Flt Sgt Garner, tried to contact the Albemarle by R/T (Radio Transmitter) without success. An attempt to attract the tug's attention by flying further out to the left also failed. During this period of time, the tear turned into a large hole and the increased airflow into the fuselage caused the tail to balloon in size. With the Hadrian rapidly destroying itself, the crew released from the Albemarle and made a swift forced landing in a field at Hyde Lea near Stafford, luckily without serious injury or further damage to the glider, but it had been a close-run thing.

The hazards of massed landings were highlighted during one particular exercise on 4th December. Two large landings had already been carried out when a third took place in the late afternoon. Three Horsas had successfully landed when the last of the group, RX678 piloted by Sgt Wells, touched down. Approaching without his flaps down, Wells landed a mere 150 yards from three other gliders. With brakes applied, the large glider skidded along and with no attempt to turn, Wells crashed into RX625 and RX608. The wooden aircraft clattered together, causing damage to all three machines but fortunately with no injuries to aircrew or the personnel scurrying for safety on the ground. All three gliders were repaired, RX608 eventually taking part in Operation *Varsity*, the crossing of the Rhine, on 24th March 1945.

Various forced landings occurred around the airfield involving both Horsas and Hadrians but none caused serious injury or damage to the gliders. By the end of 1944, with a rapidly achieved but sufficient number of trained glider pilots now available, 23 HGCU operations began to wind down at Seighford. The last massed landing took place

Albemarle VI, V1875, served with 23 HGCU. Note the glider towing equipment fitted within the rear fuselage.

on 30th December 1944 and it is a shame that a fatal accident marred it. At 1125 hrs, Albemarle VI V1934, piloted by Flg Off Johnson, was preparing to tow Horsa RX629 on the second exercise of the day. Five minutes after take-off, and at only 250 ft, the port engine failed. The Albemarle crew had no chance to recover the situation and the aircraft made a rapid force-landing but tragically hit a wall near Wincote Farm and burst into flames. Johnson, Flg Off Flack and Sgt Terssa were killed instantly. Plt Off Scrase and Sgt Oultram in the Horsa reacted quickly to the situation and managed to force-land not far from the burning wreckage of the Albemarle. This was the last major incident and the last operation involving 23 HGCU at Seighford and on 17th January 1945 the unit's short, but important, contribution to the Second World War was over.

With both Peplow and Seighford now empty of all aerial activity, 21 (P)AFU, which still had nearly 150 Airspeed Oxfords on strength, was looking for additional Relief Landing Grounds (RLGs). Peplow was first choice, but the Admiralty had other plans for the Shropshire airfield and Seighford became the unit's new RLG on 28th February 1945.

English Electric Canberra B6, WH967, is towed across the B5405 towards the Boulton Paul Type B1 hangar. (Via D Willis)

For the next fifteen months, the sound of Armstrong Siddeley Cheetah engines reverberated around the airfield. The Oxfords of 21 (P)AFU would fill the circuit and the inevitable spate of accidents continued despite peacetime rapidly approaching.

With the end of the war in Europe still two weeks away, Bomber Command began a repatriation exercise known as Operation *Exodus*. The object of the exercise was for Avro Lancasters, mainly operating from Brussels, to collect British and Commonwealth prisoners of war who had already been liberated – 469 flights carried over 75,000 men back to airfields in England. Seighford was one of the many airfields chosen and a special processing reception centre and additional medical centre were constructed to receive the POWs. The first flights arrived on 18th April 1945 and steadily increased in number, especially when VE Day finally arrived. One of the biggest flights came into Seighford on 10th May when 41 Lancasters delivered 917 soldiers, sailors and airmen.

With hostilities now at an end in Europe, 21 (P)AFU appeared to be unaffected by world events and training continued as normal. However, 21 (P)AFU steadily reduced in size during 1945, partly because of the number of aircraft being written off and, more significantly, the lessening demand for trained RAF aircrew. During the remainder of the unit's stay at Seighford, a further ten Oxfords were lost in accidents, with one airman killed and many more injured.

No 21 (P)AFU's tenure of Seighford officially came to an end on 16th July 1946. However, Oxfords would still use the airfield for circuits until early December when the main unit moved to Moreton-in-Marsh in Gloucestershire.

Now clear of aircraft, a unique event took place on the airfield's deserted runways on 23rd August 1946. The RAC (Royal Automobile Club) organised a practice to see if the airfield was fit for future racing events. Gp Capt LeMay and several senior Air Ministry personnel attended the meeting which, although a success on the day, did not come to fruition as the RAC did not find Seighford suitable for conversion to a racetrack.

Seighford fell silent for a few years although it was still retained by the Air Ministry, then the airfield attracted the attention of the Boulton Paul Aircraft Company (BAC). The company's grass airfield at Pendeford was becoming unsuitable for their latest jet-powered projects. They extended the runway in the late 1940s and built additional hangars. The bulk of flight testing carried out by Boulton Paul took place at Boscombe Down in Wiltshire, but aircraft such as the

A deserted Seighford in 1991 prior to the arrival of the Staffordshire Gliding Club. The bulk of the runways have been lifted but a large section to the right of the picture still remains in situ. A few 'frying-pan' dispersals and large sections of the perimeter track can also be seen. The technical site, complete with surviving hangars, is top left with the B5405 splitting the two areas.

BP.111, more affectionately known as the 'Yellow Peril', visited Seighford on several occasions. The airfield's main role was to carry out a variety of sub-contract work that Boulton Paul gained. Work included modifications on Canberras and Lightnings but sadly came to an abrupt end in 1964 when the BAC TSR.2 was cancelled. As a direct result of this cancellation, BAC now struggled to find work for its own employees and sub-contracting work was moved to its own 'in-house' divisions. The last aircraft to be overhauled by Boulton Paul, a

Canberra T4, left the airfield in December 1965 and Seighford closed the following year.

In 1969 an attempt was made to bring aviation back to Seighford but Stoke-on-Trent City Council unfortunately refused planning permission. The airfield languished for many years, the only changes taking place on the western side as several businesses began to make use of the vacant T2 and B1 hangars.

Aircraft returned to Seighford in 1992 when the Staffordshire Gliding Club made the airfield their home. Originally formed at Meir, the club moved to a moorland site near Leek before arriving at Seighford. The club has several gliders of its own plus several private aircraft, which are stored on the airfield.

Only small sections of the runways and perimeter track remain, but many wartime buildings still do. The most interesting is the increasingly rare Type 13079 control tower, with emergency and operations buildings alongside. Many technical buildings still stand with only livestock for company alongside the B5405. On the western side of this road hangars remain, all being put to good use. One of the Type B1s was actually built by Boulton Paul during their time at Seighford because the wartime hangar of the same type was in such poor condition. Several wartime Nissen and Maycrete huts still stand behind these hangars and many provide a use for local businesses.

12
TATENHILL

While hundreds of other, possibly more important, Second World War airfields have disappeared, Tatenhill lives on. Used as a convenient Relief Landing Ground (RLG) during the war for several different local units, the airfield now supports the East Staffordshire Flying Club, Heli Air Limited and Tatenhill Aviation, with high hopes for the future.

Work began on the new airfield in 1940 on land known as Needwood Forest, south of a minor road (B5234) between the small villages of Newchurch and Needwood. Its namesake, Tatenhill village, was two-and-a-half miles south-east. The initial role of the airfield was not clear, although it is logical to assume that it was planned as an additional fighter station to protect the industrial Midlands.

Any possibility of the airfield becoming a fighter station was removed when 27 OTU (Operational Training Unit) was formed with Vickers Wellingtons at Lichfield in April 1941. Tatenhill had been earmarked for 27 OTU's use and this was reflected in the design of the airfield. A traditional three-runway layout was built with a main runway at 1,600 yards in length and two subsidiaries of 1,100 and 1,000 yards. Nineteen 'frying-pan' dispersals (this was later increased to nearly thirty), all approximately 125 ft in diameter, were attached to an all-encompassing perimeter track. Several dispersals were built on the north side of the B5234, which called for the road to be temporarily closed while aircraft were taxied or towed across it. A single T2 Type hangar was built in late 1942 and a pair of Blisters provided the only cover for aircraft needing maintenance. A permanent control tower was built along with temporary accommodation for over 1,100 personnel, although this would never be fully used. A bomb dump was provided on the south-eastern side in the grounds of Byrkley Park.

The first unit credited with using Tatenhill was 16 EFTS (Elementary Flying Training School) based at Burnaston in Derbyshire and

Two of the three runways are in regular use today, with the third serving as a parking area. The airfield is virtually complete in all respects as the early 1990s' view shows. The 'frying-pan' dispersals on the north-western side of the airfield, north of the B5234, are now the home of the Lancaster Business Park.

operating the Miles Magister. At the time, the airfield would have still been under construction, but a Magister did not need much room to manoeuvre. A single aircraft is recorded as having been lost while 16 EFTS were using Tatenhill, when Magister I T9707 stalled on approach, hit wires and crashed. By April, the unit was using Meir as a RLG and later Abbots Bromley and Battlestead Hill as well.

The airfield was then silent while 27 OTU at Lichfield built up its strength and organized a training programme and it was not until August 1941 that the airfield became a satellite under its control. A further three months passed before an aircraft descended onto the unused runways. In November 1941, a single flight of Wellingtons was detached from Lichfield with the intention of training the crews for night operations. Immediately, despite Lichfield being no bigger, the airfield was found inadequate for the safe operation of Wellingtons. With no alternative on the horizon, the OTU had to make do, but did not move any more personnel to Tatenhill until 5th February 1942 with the arrival of 'D' Flight.

The subsequent arrival of 'A' Flight of 27 OTU on 27th April increased the flying activity at Tatenhill and the airfield began to gain a more purposeful appearance. More than twenty Wellingtons and a few Avro Ansons could be seen sitting on the frying-pan dispersal during the early hours of the day, many still ticking as they cooled down from their night-training sorties. Despite the Wellingtons being the busiest aircraft at Tatenhill, the first significant accident involved an Anson. Pupil pilot Sgt Steer was taking off in Anson I N5026 on 6th April 1942. The twin-engined aircraft developed a swing and, before the pilot had a chance to recover, the Anson careered off the runway. Luckily, no one on board was hurt but the aircraft suffered bent propellers, port engine damage and severe damage to the port wing. Despite this, the veteran Anson, which had already seen service with three operational squadrons, was repaired and eventually served with two further training units before crashing on the Isle of Man in December 1943.

It was not uncommon for Wellingtons on 'Nickel' operations to arrive at a different airfield on their return, including Tatenhill. A pair of 30 OTU Wellington ICs arrived in the early hours of 14th September from a raid on Bremen. T2475 with Plt Off Edwards had to return early with an unserviceable compass and X9801 diverted to Tatenhill after successfully attacking the target from 14,000 ft. Both aircraft returned later in the day to their home airfield at Hixon. One of Tatenhill's own aircraft, Wellington IC Z8949, became the last from 27 OTU to be involved in an accident at the airfield on 6th October. The bomber hit the runway hard causing the port tyre to burst, quickly followed by the collapse of the undercarriage. Loaded only with half-pound practice bombs, the Wellington was repaired and remained in service until July 1944.

No 27 OTU were never entirely happy with the facilities during their stay at Tatenhill. From the outset, an alternative had been sought and the newly constructed Church Broughton, over the border in Derbyshire, was deemed as being far more suitable for the operation of

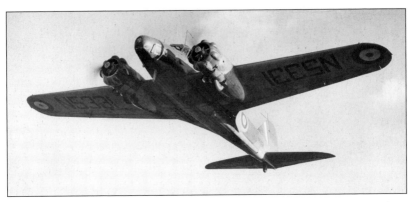

Used as a satellite airfield by the Wellingtons of 27 OTU, the most common sight at Tatenhill during early 1942 would have been the unit's Avro Ansons.

Wellingtons. The first signs of the unit's departure came on 12th October 1942 when the Maintenance Wing left for Church Broughton. The same day 'B' Flight flew out with the majority of the resident Wellingtons and Tatenhill was placed under Care and Maintenance for the first of many occasions. Despite this, the airfield was maintained with full flying facilities available. The last personnel and remaining aircraft of 27 OTU left on 14th October for Church Broughton, where they would remain until virtually the end of hostilities in Europe.

The limited emergency services retained at Tatenhill were made use of when Blenheim IV V5920 got into difficulties on 21st October. The Blenheim, which originally belonged to 6 OTU at Andover in Hampshire, was on its way to 42 OTU at Ashbourne in Derbyshire when the port engine failed. The pilot attempted a single-engine approach, but then the starboard engine partially failed. The bomber struck a tree before crashing on the end of one of the airfield's short runways, blocking it completely. The Blenheim's back was broken, and with damage to the propellers and the port engine smashed, it would never fly again.

Resigned to the fact that the airfield would only be used from now on by a training unit, it was simply a case of which one and when. This was confirmed on 7th November when Tatenhill was transferred on loan to Flying Training Command specifically for the use of 15 (P)AFU. This was a large unit that operated the Airspeed Oxford as its main equipment. Originally formed at Leconfield in Yorkshire, 15 (P)AFU was forced to find a new home when Bomber Command took over.

No stranger to many of the county's airfields, the Airspeed Oxford was the main user of Tatenhill until January 1945.

Since April 1942, the unit had been moved from RLG to RLG and Tatenhill became the latest when the first of many Oxfords arrived on 13th November. The unit's headquarters remained at Leconfield until 15th December when it moved to Andover and this in turn, opened up more local possibilities for RLGs.

The Oxfords of 15 (P)AFU operated out of Tatenhill without any serious incident until their departure on 1st May 1943. A reshuffle of units resulted in 15 (P)AFU moving to Grove in Berkshire and Tatenhill being handed over to 5 (P)AFU at Ternhill in Shropshire, which needed RLGs for its Miles Master operations. 'E' Flight were resident at Tatenhill from 4th May and the unit's main task was to teach navigation night-flying techniques.

Over 3,200 Miles Masters were built, making it the most prolifically produced aircraft from the Shoreham-based company. This single-engine, low-wing monoplane was an excellent stepping-stone between the primary trainer and the single-seat fighter. No 5 (P)AFU operated all three marks of the Master, the main difference being that each variant was fitted with a different engine. The Mk I was powered by a Rolls-Royce Merlin, the Mk II by a Bristol Mercury and the Mk III by a Pratt and Whitney Twin Wasp. The Mks II and III had a similar

185

Prevalent at Tatenhill between mid-1943 and early 1944, the Miles Master trainer was used by 5 (P)AFU.

appearance as both their engines were radials, but the Mk I had completely different lines. Production of the Masters ended in 1942 to make way for the Martinet target tug.

No 5 (P)AFU was a large unit which, by mid-1943, had nearly 200 Masters spread across three different airfields. Many of these aircraft operated over Staffordshire and inevitably many came to grief within the county border. Not all of these came from Tatenhill, but at least three did crash on the airfield for a variety of different reasons. The first incident occurred on 1st June 1943 when Master I T8756 landed heavily, causing the undercarriage to collapse. On 18th August, Master II AZ694 landed in a similar way but on this occasion was carrying far too much speed, bounced back into the air, stalled and overturned. Master II DL120 also came to grief at Tatenhill on 18th October when the engine cut immediately after take-off.

Considering the amount of flying that 5 (P)AFU achieved from Tatenhill, the accident rate was very low, especially compared to the parent unit at Ternhill. No further accidents occurred involved the unit's Masters, although Wellington III BK546 from 27 OTU at Lichfield kept the emergency services on their toes on 4th December 1943. The starboard engine caught fire and the pilot, Sqn Ldr M Powell, made a forced landing near the airfield. The bomber could not have been seriously damaged because it went on to serve with the Royal Aircraft Establishment (RAE) until February 1947.

The Masters of 5 (P)AFU left in late January 1944 and control of Tatenhill was passed on to 21 (P)AFU at Wheaton Aston. It was the return of the twin-engined Oxford and the unit's advance party, consisting of a single officer, 10 NCOs and 25 airmen, arrived on 10th February. This first batch of personnel actually arrived from Dalcross (now Inverness Airport) where 19 (P)AFU had just been disbanded.

The first 21 (P)AFU pupils arrived at Tatenhill on 22nd February. Like their instructors and aircraft, they were originally from 19 (P)AFU, their course still only partly completed. The weather was poor that day and this was highlighted by the unexpected arrival of de Havilland DH.60G Gipsy Moth BK827. The visibility was particularly bad and the pilot, Flt Sgt L A Burn, overshot his landing without causing too much damage to his ex-civilian hack aircraft.

The weather continued to play havoc with the flying programme throughout March 1944. On 2nd March, Plt Off Rouse in Oxford I L9703, ended up in the snow with the aircraft on its nose, but a more serious accident occurred the following evening. Instructor Flg Sgt Maybee was conducting an air test at night in Oxford II V3723 when the ex-19 (P)AFU machine inexplicably dived into the ground near Wood House Farm, Yoxall, three miles south of the airfield, killing him instantly.

A further thirteen Oxfords were lost in a variety of accidents between March and August 1943. Many involved collisions either on or near the ground; with so many Oxfords operating within close proximity of each other, this was inevitable. One particular incident on 17th August was a typical example, but on this occasion the pilot was lucky enough to survive. Sgt Bond in Oxford I EB731 was on approach to land, completely unaware that another Oxford was only feet below him and slightly in front. The runway controller ran out of his caravan and fired a red Very light to warn Bond to abort his approach. Bond responded immediately by banking steeply to starboard, but lost control in the slipstream of the other aircraft. The starboard wing of the Oxford struck the ground and the twin-engined trainer cartwheeled across the airfield. EB731 never flew again, but thankfully Sgt Bond lived to tell the tale. Flt Sgt Wigley in Oxford I LX513 was not so lucky on 28th August. Having returned successfully from a night-navigation exercise, inexplicably Wigley decided to go around again. It was to be a fatal decision; as he climbed away, the Oxford stalled at only 200 ft and crashed one mile west of the airfield.

187

Before 21 (P)AFU's departure, a further five Oxfords were lost in accidents, with the loss also of two flying instructors and one student pilot. The unit was steadily reducing in size and the last Oxford left the airfield a week later for Seighford.

Back in November 1944, the local countryside had been shaken to its core when the underground bomb store at 21 MU (Maintenance Unit) at Fauld exploded. Ever since this tragic accident, the unit had been looking for an alternative location. Tatenhill was chosen and the MU officially made the airfield a sub-site from 23rd December 1944. When 21 (P)AFU moved out on 26th January 1945, the MU began to move ordnance onto the airfield from Fauld and to receive it from other units for open storage.

The RAF School of Explosives moved into Tatenhill from Llanberis in Gwynedd on 1st October 1945. Tatenhill would have seemed an appropriate move considering the amount of explosives available from 21 MU's stockpile. The school was disbanded on 20th January 1947 and absorbed into 6 School of Technical Training (SoTT) at Hednesford.

The bombs that now covered the runways, perimeter track and dispersals were steadily disposed of during the post war years. The

One of many original wartime buildings, located on the northern edge of the airfield at Tatenhill. (Author)

The Second World War control tower was demolished many years ago. This modern equivalent is attached to the side of the original Type T2 hangar on the northern side of the airfield. (Author)

189

airfield was clear of wartime bombs by mid-1954 and 21 MU's sub-site was officially closed down on 27th November 1954. This marked the end of the RAF's presence at Tatenhill and after a few years of being placed under Care and Maintenance, the airfield was sold off in the late 1950s.

Approaching Tatenhill today, from either east or west on the B5234, you will see an abundance of aircraft long before you have arrived at the airfield. Light aircraft, twin-engined and warbirds make an interesting mix of flying machines. The single T2 hangar still survives and remains in use for maintenance work. The wartime control tower has been demolished and a relatively modern replacement has been attached to the T2. A large variety of wartime buildings still survive along the roadside; quite a few are in use by a local farmer but as many more are in a state of dereliction. On the north side of the B5234 many more buildings survive as far as the eye can see, as well as dispersal areas. A new industrial park has been built alongside the B5234 and has been named Lancaster Park. The purist may have preferred Wellington or Oxford Park, but at least an aviation name will live on, just in case the airfield itself does not.

13
TEDDESLEY PARK

Over 50 Satellite Landing Grounds (SLGs) were surreptitiously built throughout the country during the Second World War. Many were only known to the Air Ministry, the landowners and a few locals; their locations and very existence were always top secret.

No 48 SLG Teddesley Park was a classic example of a well-camouflaged 'off the beaten track' airfield. It was located two miles north-east of Penkridge, with Cannock Chase on its eastern side. Requisitioned by the Air Ministry in late 1940, Teddesley Hall, built by Sir Edward Littleton c.1750, stood semi-derelict within beautiful parkland. The last owner and occupant of the hall, the third Lord Hatherton, had died in 1930, so removing a large portion of any opposition to the military takeover. The current owner of the land tried to object but was forced to yield, with arguments for the war effort winning the day.

Several trees had to be felled to make room for a pair of 850-yard runways and thousands of sections of Square Mesh Tracking were laid. Great care was taken to blend the small landing ground into the resident, natural camouflage.

The SLG was officially opened on 14th July 1941 for the use of 27 Maintenance Unit (MU) at Shawbury, Salop. The unit had no use for Teddesley Park, however, and it was immediately handed over to 29 MU at High Ercall, also in Shropshire. No 29 MU, like its sister unit at Shawbury, was a civilian-manned aircraft storage unit handling a variety of military aircraft during the Second World War and for many years beyond. SLGs were essential to these kinds of unit, which quickly filled with aircraft, all of which needed to be dispersed to protect them from potential air attack.

The Curtiss Seamew was one of the Second World War's more unusual aircraft. Only 13 reached this country and the majority, if not all, were stored at Teddesley Park.

Teddesley Park was the second of three SLGs used by 29 MU. The first Hinstock (Ollerton), Salop, opened as 21 SLG in May and the third at 46 SLG, Brinklow in Warwickshire in September 1941.

Some of the first arrivals were twin-engined Lockheed Hudsons, all of which had been in service with front-line squadrons. More American types followed, including examples of the Grumman Avenger, Lockheed Ventura and rarer types like a Brewster Bermuda and Curtiss Seamew reconnaissance aircraft. The latter was known as the 'Seagull' in the USA and, under the Lend-Lease scheme, 250 were destined for delivery to the Royal Navy. Only thirteen ever reached this country as the vast bulk of the original order was sent to Canada instead.

British-built aircraft dispersed at Teddesley included a batch of Hawker Typhoons, a few Percival Proctors and a large amount of General Aircraft Hotspur gliders. Many of the latter remained at the SLG until 1945, when it is presumed that they were broken up and burnt.

The land surrounding the SLG was also used for other military purposes. The 446th Quartermaster Troop Transport Company, which was attached to the US 7th Armored Division, made Teddesley their home from 6th April 1944 to 18th May 1944. Also, land was used for Prisoner of War Camp No 194, which would have continued to operate until at least 1946, possibly later.

With the end of the war, 29 MU reduced in size and the need to disperse aircraft was removed. Hundreds could now be crammed close together at High Ercall and 48 SLG Teddesley Park was officially closed on 6th February 1946.

Today only a single military-built road gives any clue that the site had a purpose during the Second World War. Quickly returned to farmland during the post war years, no trace can be found of the old SLG and the important role it played.

14
WALSALL
(Aldridge)

Sprawling suburbs and the demands for industrial land have obliterated many of our wartime airfields. In contrast, not only does the site of Walsall Airport still exist, it still looks like an airfield and would easily accommodate modern light aircraft today. Thankfully, a sympathetic local council protects the site as a park open to the general public.

Riding on the back of huge public interest and support for aviation in the 1920s, Walsall Council suggested that the town needed an airfield of its own. A visit by Alan Cobham to Walsall in 1929 sowed the seed and he recommended a site at Aldridge Lodge Estate. Some 230 acres of land were purchased on the north-eastern side of Walsall, south of Aldridge. The exact location was east of where Walsall Road meets Longwood Lane, with Bosty Lane running along the northern edge. Work began on levelling a runway in late June 1933, which was a difficult task considering the western end of the runway was 485 ft above sea level and the eastern end rose to 530 ft! The main advantage to this was a short landing run when approaching from a westerly direction. Civilian aviation rules at the time stated that a 1:25 incline was the very maximum tolerated. The end of the runway was 1:25.5 with the rest being an acceptable 1:46, comparatively speaking.

The main runway was initially 830 yards long and a generous 150 yards wide with scope for extension at the eastern end. A hangar and clubhouse were constructed at a cost of £1,460 and £1,250 respectively. They were located on the northern side of the airfield, set well back from the flying field on high ground and accessed from Bosty Lane. An alternative location was suggested for a control tower and clubhouse nearer to the runway and Walsall Road, even before construction was completed.

The first occupants of the airfield were the Walsall Aero Club, who acquired their first aircraft, Miles M.2 Hawk G–ACRB, for the princely sum of £425. A flying instructor was hired by the name of Bill Holmes. He was paid £250 per year and 5 shillings an hour 'flying pay'. Initially the club struggled and a take-over did little to improve the situation. The Hawk was sold for a plane that was cheaper to buy and operate – the Avro Avian G–ABMW – and a Desoutter I G–ABMW was also introduced. By October 1934, the club was facing closure and members held an emergency meeting. The following June, it was reformed and the South Staffordshire Flying Club was created to run the airfield. Under new management, the club began to thrive and on 4th July 1935 an air show was organised to open Walsall Airport officially.

Not long after, a Dudley-based engineering company by the name of Helliwells Ltd looked at a site on the western edge of the airfield for possible construction of an additional factory. Established in 1889 in Fountain Street, Dudley, Helliwells originally produced fire irons, fireguards and various pieces of ironmongery. Construction of a new factory began in late 1935, accessed from Walsall Road on the western boundary of the airfield.

Designed by Henri Mignet, the Flying Flea was presented as a light aircraft which could be built and flown by virtually anyone. Several were constructed throughout the county, and the first was registered by Wolverhampton men, R and D Weaver on 26th August 1936 with G–AEME. Three more Flying Fleas, G–AEBT, G–AEFI and G–AEOH, were built in Birmingham but test-flown at Walsall Airport. Two members of the flying club, Harry Griffiths and Jock Ogilvie, began construction of a Flying Flea at Walsall. Unfortunately though, the Flying Flea was a particularly dangerous aircraft to fly and several had been involved in fatal accidents. Before Griffiths and Ogilvie finished their project the Flying Flea had been banned.

An additional hangar was built for the flying club near to the Walsall Road factory in September 1937 and an extension of 200 yards to the existing east–west runway was discussed. A large amount of tree cutting was also implemented in an attempt to make the airfield safer during take-off and landing.

One of the highlights of Walsall's pre-war history occurred on 2nd July 1938, when an airshow was organised in conjunction with the resident Staffordshire Flying Club and the Midland Gliding Club based at Handsworth, near West Bromwich. The highlight of the day

195

The Mignet Pou du Ciel or 'Flying Flea' was an early attempt to introduce home-built aircraft to the masses. Unfortunately, after several fatal accidents, aviation legislation grounded all UK-registered machines.

was a display by Amy Johnson, the celebrated solo flier, in a Kirby Kite glider. Over 6,000 people watched her perform three displays during the day. Unfortunately, on her third landing, the Kite was caught in a down draught, clipped a hedge and overturned. Miss Johnson was not seriously injured but was still taken to hospital as a precautionary measure.

An unexpected military visitor made an undignified arrival on 14th July 1938 – Handley Page Harrow II K6982 of 215 Squadron from Driffield in Yorkshire. The twin-engined transport plane was probably the biggest aircraft to attempt a landing since the airport opened. With only 950 yards of runway available, on a downhill slope and with wet grass, the Harrow could not stop in time. The transport ended up straddling Longwood Lane with only minor damage but a very embarrassed pilot. K6982 was later repaired and remained in RAF service until December 1943.

In July 1938, the Air Ministry established a new organisation called the Civil Air Guard. Flying clubs and schools throughout the country were subsidised to train civilian pilots who would be employed by the Air Ministry in the event of a national emergency. The creation of the new guard was obviously influenced by events on the Continent. Within weeks of the new scheme being launched, 35,000 applied, of

A 215 Squadron Harrow from Driffield in Yorkshire became the biggest aircraft to arrive at Walsall on 14th July 1938. Unfortunately for the pilot, who had underestimated the slope and length of the runway, the transport ended up straddling Longwood Lane.

whom 4,000 already held a pilot's licence. Walsall played its part in training many new pilots and the aero club benefited from the increased throughput of flying training.

Another flying display was held on 24th September 1938. In conjunction with a garden party, the display included a demonstration of instructor–pupil flying, an air race, crazy flying, and a height and speed judging competition, as well as balloon bursting, picking up a handkerchief with a hook on the wing tip, aerobatics and bombing with bags of flour. The day was marred when de Havilland DH.83 Fox Moth G–ACEY, which was carrying out passenger flights throughout the day, crashed into trees on the edge of the airfield. The aircraft was being operated by Utility Airways Ltd and flown by Flt Lt William Hill. One of the four passengers aboard, a Miss Margaret Part, was slightly injured.

Another accident, which was recorded in the *Daily Sketch* as 'Pilot's Escape', occurred at Walsall on 14th March 1939. The type of aircraft was not mentioned but it belonged to a London publicity firm. Capt V N Dickenson, with Flt Lt Grey as passenger, piloted the aircraft; both men escaped without serious injury.

A final club air show and garden party was held on 1st July 1939 but within a few weeks the country was at war and Walsall Airport was closed to flying. Only three days after the Second World War began, a frantic letter was written to the Under-Secretary of State from the directors of South Staffordshire Aero Company Ltd. The main complaint was the fact that a considerable number of Civil Air Guard trainees had had their training cut short. The directors had to confess that the trainees had effectively kept the company going and the 'no civilian flying' ruling removed all income going into the airfield. Pleas like this were sent to the Air Ministry from all of the country's now defunct flying clubs and schools and Walsall's plight was a familiar story, which fell on deaf ears in London. The Civil Air Guard was disbanded and the South Staffordshire Aero Company was out of business.

Now well-established in their new factory, the work of Helliwells Ltd was the only significant activity at Walsall Airport in late 1939. Already employed by the Air Ministry to produce a variety of small aircraft components, since the factory's opening the company had been producing component parts for the Anson, Blenheim, Gladiator, Hart, Hurricane, Wellesley and Whitley. From 28th July 1940, the company became one of the many cogs within the complex machine known as the Civilian Repair Organisation (CRO). The CRO was set up specifically to relieve the pressure on RAF units responsible for aircraft repair work and the manufacturers themselves. Helliwells was just one of 43 different companies employed throughout the United Kingdom for this purpose.

At the outbreak of war, the Air Ministry requisitioned the airfield and all resident civilian aircraft. All flying during the war years was the responsibility of Helliwells and much of it from July 1940 was carried out by Peter Clifford, the company's resident chief test pilot. Helliwells' first major and longest running task was the uncrating and assembling of hundreds of North American Harvards. This contract was originally carried out by North American Aviation using a pair of hangars at Shawbury. The Harvard was easy to build, durable and a reliable tandem trainer which was the perfect stepping stone for many pilots from elementary types like the Tiger Moth to fighter types like the Hurricane or Spitfire. Over 17,000 Harvards were built and, by the end of the Second World War, more than 5,000 had been supplied to the RAF and Commonwealth air forces. One of the first American-built aircraft to serve with the RAF when first ordered in June 1938, the Harvard, with a characteristic rasping sound caused by its direct-drive propeller, was a familiar sight throughout the country until the mid-1950s.

The largest wartime contract won by Helliwells at Walsall was the uncrating and assembly of hundreds of North American Harvards. Post war the company was called upon again for refurbishment work with the American-built trainer.

Repair contracts for Hawker Hurricanes ran side by side with the Harvard work and more American-built types followed later in the year. Known in the USA as the Douglas DB–7, these twin-engine bombers were supplied to the RAF as the Boston and Havoc. Like the Harvards, Helliwells uncrated and assembled the aircraft which were all skilfully flown out of Walsall's very tight runway. The aircraft were then flown direct to Perton, where a full air test would be performed. This contract was shared with Boulton Paul whose grass-covered Pendeford airfield was unsuitable for such work; they also used Perton for full air tests.

The Havoc served the RAF as a night fighter or night intruder. The Boston performed the role of a light day bomber, carrying out many attacks at very low levels and suffering high losses as a result. Unlike the Havoc, which had left RAF service by late 1942, the Boston served throughout the Second World War.

The airfield's limited size called for an inspection on 18th and 19th June 1941 by Lt F C H Kirby of the Ministry of Aircraft Production (MAP). Kirby submitted several recommendations to the Air Ministry for extensions of the landing area and improvements of the flying approaches. As the airfield stood, despite innumerable flights being made by Bostons and Havocs, Walsall did not reach the limitations set for such an aircraft. It seems remarkable that the airfield's runway seems to have come secondary to the actual work carried out by Helliwells.

During his inspection, Lt Kirby was accompanied on several occasions by Peter Clifford who was quite candid about flying from

Alongside the Douglas Havoc, the Boston was assembled by Helliwells and flown out to Perton for air test.

Walsall. Clifford stated 'that he had been flying at Walsall for over a year and was quite prepared to continue, he had been fortunate in that he had never had an engine cut or brake failure which would almost inevitably cause damage to the aircraft by running into the hedge. He had raised the question because of the ease with which the length of run could be extended in various directions with very little cost or inconvenience.' Seeing the proposals, the local council was in agreement with all proposed extensions and in the spirit of the war effort declared 'the aerodrome was already a heavy loss and burden to the rate'!

In early 1942, the Air Ministry issued plans and materials to all Air Training Corps (ATC) squadrons for the construction of a glider. Flt Lt Woodhead, the Commanding Officer of the Walsall Wing, approached Helliwells for permission to fly the glider from Walsall. The company was enthusiastic, Peter Clifford offered his services as a tutor and two other ATC officers from the Wing went on glider courses. Gliding by the ATC took place from the airfield for the first time on 5th March 1942. The airfield's licence was re-issued a few weeks later and, to cater for the ATC operations, an additional entry of 'including instruction to pupils in flying' was added.

By September 1943, all of Lt Kirby's recommendations had finally been implemented. The new runway ran in a north-east/south-west direction, the northern end towards Bosty Lane and the southern end to Hayhead Wood. A third runway was also laid from the Walsall road to the eastern edge of Hayhead Wood. This triangular pattern now gave pilots considerably more options for landing and taking off. Overhead telephone wires were removed along Walsall Road and Bosty Lane and placed underground, a task that had first been recommended in 1938. A tarmac apron was built in front of the Helliwells hangars and, unbelievably, the word 'Walsall' in large white letters across the middle of the airfield was finally removed. MAP also built additional buildings near to the Helliwells factory comprising a new hangar, a works canteen and a kitchen. It was about this time that a large concrete circle was laid on the southern side of the airfield, probably for aircraft compass calibration.

The Air Ministry did not overlook the importance of gliding as a good general introduction to flying. With the ATC already operating their own glider, Walsall was selected as one of eleven units within the Midland Area to form No 43 Gliding School in October 1943. The school flew a variety of gliders including the Kirby Kite and Cadet, remaining at Walsall until the unit was disbanded in December 1946.

By late 1943, more inspection reports criticised the gradients of the

Refurbishment of the Supermarine Seafire was another post war contract won by Helliwells.

201

Aerial view of the airfield at Walsall in May 1948. Helliwells' factory is on the western edge with Hayhead Wood on the southern side. Note the compass circle shining white at the bottom of the photograph.

runway but nothing could be done. These reports continued until the war's end, with the Air Ministry continually quoting regulations about runways and gradients. A compromise was reached with an additional crash tender and more medical equipment being installed at the airfield, so at least Walsall was ready if an accident did occur. Luckily, no aircraft produced by Helliwells was involved in an accident at Walsall during the Second World War. However, a visiting Blenheim overshot on landing, crashed through a hedge onto a road and struck a passing lorry. Sadly, the lorry driver was killed.

Post war, Helliwells won another contract, this time for the refurbishment of the Supermarine Seafire, and the Harvards which it

Sadly plans fell through to produce the American-designed Globe Swift. Helliwells operated a single example, G–AHUV, until they left Walsall in the late 1950s. (Via author)

was already very familiar with. The Seafires were delivered by road from storage and returned to flying condition by Helliwells. The naval fighters, refurbished at Walsall, all took off from the grass airfield but landed at Castle Bromwich where air tests would take place. Havoc work continued as well, but this time rather than constructing them, they were dismantled and scrapped.

Ambitious plans were revealed in 1947 for Helliwells to set up a production line for the Globe Swift. This American aircraft was designed and already being built by the Globe Aircraft Corporation at Fort Worth in Texas. The Swift was the world's first low-wing, two-seat aircraft with retractable undercarriage built specifically for the civilian market place. The aircraft built at Walsall would be known as the Helliwell Globe but sadly despite such high hopes the project did not materialize. The company actually operated a Swift of its own, G–AHUV. Helliwells also operated a pair of Tiger Moths and a Percival Proctor, G–AHGT.

In 1948 the Council renewed Helliwells' lease for a further ten years, probably in response to the workload generated by the Harvard alone. Other component contracts included work for the Avro Ashton, of which only six were ever built. In 1956, the last Harvard to be

Walsall Aero Club and later the South Staffordshire Flying Club hangar still in situ and now in use by Walsall County Council. It is still referred to as the 'Top Hangar'. (Author)

refurbished at Walsall, KF448, left the airfield and within a few months Helliwells moved to Elmdon (Birmingham Airport) and the airfield closed to flying.

The airfield, which is still known as 'The Airport', is a remarkable sight, having been preserved as a sports field and local park. Helliwells' factory is long gone, now replaced by modern buildings but the road leading to them has been sympathetically named 'Airfield Drive'. A walk from the car park at Hayhead Wood towards Aldridge Lodge Farm really gives you an idea of the gradients that the Air Ministry was unhappy about. Standing at the top of the hill near the farm, it is easy to work out the positions of the three runways and Helliwells' factory near the Walsall Road. Also near the farm, two hangars still survive and within the coppice several remnants of wartime buildings remain derelict in the woods. Remains of possible military buildings can be found on the south side of the airfield within Hayhead Wood and the compass circle described earlier is also still in place.

15
WHEATON ASTON
(Little Onn)

A typical training airfield in all respects, Wheaton Aston remained active throughout the war years and was second only to Lichfield with regard to aircraft movements. Its remote location attracted several units who enjoyed relatively uncluttered skies to train thousands of aircrew for a variety of tasks.

Construction began in early 1941 on the new airfield, which was located between the tiny villages of Marston and Little Onn. It was locally known by the latter name but the village of Wheaton Aston, positioned one-and-a-half miles south-east, became its official namesake. On the eastern border flows the Shropshire Union Canal, with the Church Eaton to Wheaton Aston road bordering the western side. The airfield was built in a typical triangular pattern with a main runway of 1,310 yards in length and two shorter runways at 1,100 yards; all three were the standard 50 yards wide. The runway lengths indicate that the airfield was planned potentially as a fighter station; however, by the time construction was under way, Wheaton Aston's future was already destined for training.

Three Type T1 hangars were constructed and eight 'Extra-Over' Blisters were spread around the airfield's perimeter. Another indication that the airfield's requirements had changed was the fact that only four round concrete aprons and a single fighter pen were built. The control tower, which still stands today, was the standard design for an OTU or training airfield for the period.

The airfield's first intended role was to be a satellite airfield for 30 OTU at Hixon. It was ready by late November 1941, six months before Hixon and seven months before 30 OTU was even formed! A swift opportunity presented itself to 11 Service Flying Training School

The Airspeed Oxford, which was to become a common sight at Wheaton Aston, was a development of the Envoy, depicted here

(SFTS) at Shawbury in Shropshire, where new runways were being laid, causing great disruption. They took over Wheaton Aston as a Relief Landing Ground (RLG) on 15th December 1941, mainly operating the Avro Anson and Airspeed AS.10 Oxford under the command of Gp Capt Divers.

The Oxford was the RAF's original twin-engined monoplane advanced trainer, first entering service in late 1937. A development of the Airspeed Envoy, 8,586 had been built by July 1945, all seeing service with Britain, Canada, Rhodesia, Australia, New Zealand and the Middle East. The most common versions that would have been seen at Wheaton Aston were the Oxford I and II. The Oxford I was designed to cater for every aspect of aircrew training including gunnery. An Armstrong Whitworth dorsal turret was fitted to the Oxford I while the Oxford II was devoid of the turret and was mainly used for pilot training. This long-serving and generally overlooked aircraft served the RAF until 1954 when 10 Advanced Flying Training School (AFTS) at Pershore in Worcestershire was disbanded.

Despite being nineteen miles (as the crow flies) from Shawbury, Wheaton Aston was by far the closest RLG that 11 SFTS had in use. With this in mind, the airfield was taken over permanently by the SFTS on 14th March 1942 when it was redesignated 11 (Pilots) Advanced Flying Unit ((P)AFU).

At least two 11 (P)AFU Oxfords came to grief at Wheaton Aston, the first on 11th November 1942. Oxford I N4596 was carrying out night circuit training when it flew into the ground approximately one-and-a-half miles east of the airfield. A slightly less serious incident followed on 15th January 1943 when Oxford II N4832 retracted its flaps prematurely after take-off and crashed.

By early 1943, 11 (P)AFU was a massive unit with at least 150 aircraft spread over three flights at Shawbury and three more at Condover in Shropshire, Perton and Wheaton Aston. The flight at Wheaton Aston was rapidly approaching a state of self containment by the summer of 1943, with only major aircraft servicing being carried out at Shawbury. The airfield now provided accommodation for all instructors, ground personnel and course pupils. In all, accommodation was available for over 1,400 RAF and 440 WAAF officers, senior NCOs and other ranks. Wheaton Aston was now ready to support its own unit and had established the need for RLGs of its own. With Perton in a similar position, it was time for a new Advanced Flying Unit to be formed.

No 21 (P)AFU was formed on 1st August 1943 from a nucleus of aircraft and personnel provided by 11 (P)AFU. The new (P)AFU would grow to over 200 Oxfords, with a pair of Ansons and a single Miles Magister also on strength, all under the command of Wg Cdr J H Brown. The unit's headquarters were at Wheaton Aston and Perton was the main satellite airfield affiliated to it along with Bratton in Shropshire. On formation of the new unit, only 35 Oxfords and a single Magister could be seen on the airfield, but this would increase rapidly during the remainder of the year. The general plan for the training programme was that all pilots under training would continue as they had under the 11 (P)AFU regime. All junior flying would be carried out at Perton, followed by one week's training with 1511 BATF (Beam Approach Training Flight) at Greenham Common, Berkshire, and then senior flying at Wheaton Aston. This equated to two flights at Perton and two more located at Wheaton Aston. Only weeks later, this plan was contradicted by Flying Training Command who also increased the training course from six to eight weeks. The command also ordered 21 (P)AFU to carry out complete training at Perton and Wheaton Aston, removing the need to move pupils around. On 15th August 1943, all 141 pilots under training at Wheaton Aston and Perton were officially posted (on paper) from 11 (P)AFU to 21 (P)AFU.

The need for a resident BATF was clearly apparent with a unit the size of 21 (P)AFU. It was logical that 1511 BATF, based at Greenham Common and already affiliated to the unit, should be the choice. On 6th September, Wg Cdr Coleman from Flying Training Command and the officer commanding 1511 BATF, Sqn Ldr King visited the airfield to arrange for the transfer of the unit from its Berkshire home. No 1511

All five flying units which regularly operated from Wheaton Aston used the Airspeed Oxford.

BATF arrived on 28th and 29th September 1943, made up of three officers, fifty-nine airmen and seven Oxfords. The unit's move was completed on 1st October when a final batch of stores and equipment was delivered by rail and road to the airfield.

It was not long before 21 (P)AFU suffered its first flying-related loss. On 29th September, whilst flying under dual instruction at low level and in poor weather, Oxford I LW959 crashed near Henbury in Cheshire. The instructor, Sgt Munro, was killed instantly while his pupil, Sgt Donnelly, RCAF, died of his injuries not long after the crash.

Another string was added to Wheaton Aston's bow on 4th October when Meteorological officers arrived from Ramsbury in Wiltshire. The group established a Meteorological Office at the airfield, a useful facility that remained in use until beyond the war's end. By this time, 69 Oxfords, 2 Ansons and a Magister were on strength and up-to-date weather information was invaluable to all who wanted to fly from the airfield.

A larger than usual visitor made a precautionary landing on 7th October. Wellington III from 30 OTU at Hixon was low on fuel when, in poor visibility, the bomber landed on a taxiway rather than the runway. The pilot got away with it and although the bomber ended up straddling a public road, little damage was caused. Minor repairs were carried out and the Wellington returned to Hixon a few days later.

An example of how easy it was to get lost at night occurred on 18th October 1943. Plt Off D P Kyne was detailed to fly a short cross-country exercise to the airfield at Condover in Shropshire (twenty miles due west of Wheaton Aston) and back. The final contact with Kyne was a radio message at 2100 hrs stating that he was setting course for Condover; this was the last 21 (P)AFU ever heard. Incredibly, his aircraft was found five days later, wrecked, on Howden Moor, overlooking Derwent Reservoir in South Yorkshire. Sadly, Kyne's lifeless body was found in the wreckage, which was 60 miles north-east of Condover and approximately 50 miles north of his home airfield.

A loss of a different kind, but not involving a unit aircraft, took place over Germany on the night of 20th/21st October. It was common practice to attach Staff Instructors to front-line squadrons to gain operational experience, which could, in turn, be passed on to the trainee pilots. Flt Sgt E H Willcocks of 21 (P)AFU had only been attached to 103 Squadron at Elsham Wolds in Lincolnshire for a few days when the unit took part in a large raid on Leipzig. Willcocks was on board Lancaster III ED881 when the aircraft was lost without trace, complete with seven other crew members.

Wheaton Aston was becoming no stranger to unexpected visits by aircraft in trouble. One unusual visitor made an emergency landing on 4th November. Fairey Swordfish NE862 being flown by Miss Fergusan of the Air Transport Auxiliary (ATA) suffered an engine failure whilst over Kiddemore Green, only four miles south of the airfield. Wheaton Aston must have been a welcome sight for Miss Fergusan, who was ferrying the biplane torpedo bomber from Sherburn-in-Elmet, Yorkshire to 29 MU at High Ercall in Shropshire.

By the end of 1943, 21 (P)AFU officially claimed to have 64 Oxfords, 2 Ansons and 2 Magisters. The total number of Oxfords obviously fluctuated as aircraft were lost in accidents or received back on strength after being repaired.

Wg Cdr Brown was succeeded as Wheaton Aston's station commander and officer commanding the 21 (P)AFU detachment on 10th January 1944. His replacement was Gp Capt J J Williamson, AFC, who originally joined the service back in 1917 as a pilot with the Royal Flying Corps. One of Williamson's first tasks was to host a visit by three officers from the Brazilian mission. No pilots from that nation have been recorded as flying from Wheaton Aston.

No 1511 BATF achieved a milestone on 15th February when the unit

No 21 (P)AFU's main equipment was the Oxford but while stationed at Wheaton Aston the unit operated several Avro Ansons as well.

instructed its 100th course since its formation at Upwood in Huntingdonshire in September 1941. No 21 (P)AFU, which had only recently reorganised several of its flights between the home airfield and its RLGs, underwent a bigger change at the end of February 1944. The RLG at Bratton was relinquished to another unit and, on 15th February, Tatenhill was allocated as its replacement. To add to the confusion, 19 (P)AFU at Dalcross in Invernesshire was disbanded on 25th February with all trainees, instructors, ground personnel and aircraft being placed under the control of 21 (P)AFU. Within days, the unit almost doubled in size and the establishment was raised to 148

Oxfords, of which the unit actually had 101 on strength by the end of February.

This increase in size also justified the need for a second BATF affiliated to 21 (P)AFU. No 1545 BATF was formed at Wheaton Aston on 6th March 1944 under the command of Sqn Ldr L F D King who was posted from 1511 BATF two days later. Like its sister unit, the BATF only had eight Oxfords on strength and occasionally they were also used for communication and liaison flights. One such flight took place on 17th March 1944 when Sqn Ldr King and Flt Lt Marshall flew Gp Capt Williamson, AFC, to Reading to take up a new appointment as Air Officer Commanding 50 Group. Gp Capt Oliver, AFC, took over as station commander at Wheaton Aston a few weeks later.

The services of 1545 BATF were deemed to be more useful at Halfpenny Green from 21st March 1944. The small unit was now affiliated to 3 (O)AFU and, on 25th April, the ground personnel, closely followed by their aircraft, left Wheaton Aston.

A potentially serious accident occurred at Wheaton Aston on the night of 5th April. Sgt Beckett, a pilot under training, landed his Oxford I LW964 successfully, but before he could taxi off the runway both engines inexplicably cut out. Plt Off Myers, in Oxford I LX484, had landed close behind and was completely unaware that Beckett's aircraft sat powerless on the runway. Myers, now down to taxiing speed, crashed into the stationary LW964, ripping the starboard wing off his own aircraft. Luckily, there were no injuries to either pilot but both Oxfords were seriously damaged. Despite this, both were repaired and each continued to serve until long after the war's end.

No 21 (P)AFU was at such a size by May 1944 that it had three BATFs affiliated to it simultaneously. Nos 1511, 1515 and 1534 BATF were now performing duties for 21 (P)AFU, all with an average of eight Oxfords each.

A pilot under training, Flt Sgt Jarvis, became very unpopular on 19th May when landing in Oxford I LW736. The aircraft developed a swing and too slow a response from the pilot resulted in the Oxford leaving the runway and colliding with two other Oxfords, NM273 and LX476. These were parked over 100 yards from the runway and Flt Sgt Jarvis was suspended from flying pending a test on single-engine aircraft. LW736 could not have been seriously damaged as it was repaired and remained in RAF service until 23rd August 1954!

To give an idea of how busy Wheaton Aston had become, the total flying hours during May 1944 had reached an impressive 8,773 by day and a further 2,605 by night. The following month achieved a similarly large total and aircraft on 21 (P)AFU strength were recorded at 130 Oxfords, 4 Ansons and 1 Magister with a further 15 Oxfords serving with 2 BATFs.

American Independence Day, 4th July, was not worth celebrating for the pilot of Republic P–47C Thunderbolt 41–6538 when the engine failed whilst 3,000 ft over the airfield. Richard M Dunlop was flying the big fighter from the 552nd Fighter Squadron of the 495th Fighter Group based at Atcham in Shropshire. On approach into Wheaton Aston, Dunlop undershot his landing and crashed into the Shropshire Union Canal. The pilot escaped with only a shaking but the P–47 was condemned on 7th July due to 'non-battle damage'.

Wheaton Aston had its fair share of sporting stars who, like tens of thousands of others, had to serve their military time. In 1944, Eric Boon, the 1937 British Lightweight Boxing Champion, ran the gymnasium at the airfield. The Cambridgeshire-born fighter was joined by another great name of the time. Freddie Mills, who won the British Light-Heavyweight title in 1942, served at Wheaton Aston at the same time. Anyone who wished to improve their boxing skills would obviously have benefited from being at Wheaton Aston!

The attrition rate continued throughout the summer of 1944 with a serious accident occurring on average once a week. The dreaded high tension cables claimed another victim on 28th September when Oxford I HN592 crashed on Dunstan Heath, south of Stafford. Flt Sgt Smit, the instructor, Sgt Wright, the pilot under training, and Flt Sgt Beasty, the bombardier, were all killed instantly.

Facilities continued to improve at Wheaton Aston, which was no less busy and looked as if it would stay so for the foreseeable future. A new Corporals' Club was opened by the Station Commander, Gp Capt Oliver, AFC, on 16th October 1944. Gp Capt B Caswell, who was just about to take over the station from Gp Capt Oliver, pending the latter's promotion to Air Commodore and posting overseas, accompanied him.

No 21 (P)AFU's Chief Flying Instructor, Sqn Ldr L E Speer, AFC, was a popular character who was affectionately known as 'Dagger Speer'. He worked as ground staff before the war broke out, converted to a pilot and steadily rose through the ranks. All who flew or worked with Speer liked him and all who served at Wheaton Aston received the news of his death on 29th November 1944 with shock and sadness. 'Dagger Speer' was tasked on the fateful day to fly the Station Commander to an undisclosed destination but, on getting into his aircraft, he realised he had forgotten his map so returned to the flight office to retrieve it. On his return to the aircraft he had to walk along the perimeter track past several Oxfords with engines running. Still wearing his helmet, Sqn Ldr Speer failed to notice a visiting Spitfire taxiing too fast behind him in a straight line rather than zigzagging from side to side as he should have been doing. The propeller of the fighter caught Sqn Ldr Speer on the nape of his neck, sending him flying across the ground. Sadly, he had died before anyone had a chance to help.

The following year, 1945, began with no decline in the amount of pilots passing through their advanced flying training ready for posting to a front-line squadron. Even with the war approaching its finale the average monthly flying hours remained above 10,000.

A reshuffle of the unit's RLGs took place on 19th January when Peplow in Shropshire replaced Tatenhill. Peplow was only used until 28th February and was replaced by Seighford, which was used as an RLG with Perton until 16th July 1946.

VE Day on 8th May 1945 brought a well-earned rest day for Wheaton Aston, as for so many other airfields. Gp Capt Caswell addressed all station personnel in No 1 hangar, thanking them for all their efforts over the previous three years.

On 14th May, all Canadian instructors left the unit for repatriation to their home country, followed by the first RAF and WAAF personnel to be released from service on 18th June.

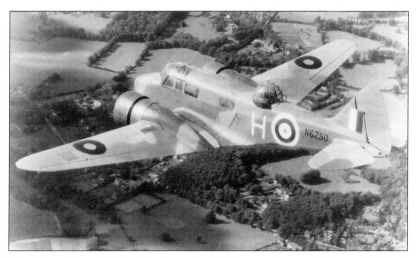

The sight and sound of the Oxford remained at Wheaton Aston until August 1946 and not long after the airfield was abandoned.

From the air, the old airfield looks complete but all three runways are in an advanced state of deterioration. The Shropshire Union Canal can be seen following the eastern border and the surviving control tower and several wartime buildings are extant on the western side.

While other units disbanded or were reorganized, 21 (P)AFU continued and actually grew, reaching a peak strength in June 1945 of 148 Oxfords plus the 4 Ansons and sole Magister which had served the unit since its formation. Two BATFs still remained – 1511 BATF and newly arrived 1517 BATF from Chipping Norton in Oxfordshire, each with a further nine and ten Oxfords respectively. This was the most aircraft ever allocated to 21 (P)AFU and with a further 9,600 flying hours achieved during the month it appeared that peacetime would have very little effect on the unit.

Yet another BATF was affiliated to the unit on 4th December 1945. No 1547 BATF from Watchfield in Berkshire operated with 21 (P)AFU until the unit's departure from Wheaton Aston. The same day, both 1517 and 1545 BATF were disbanded at their home airfields, reducing only slightly the number of Oxfords operating from the airfield.

In January 1946, the establishment of 21 (P)AFU actually rose to 164 Oxfords but, despite this, only 128 were on strength with the unit; still a very high figure for a peacetime training unit.

On 1st July 1946, 1511 BATF was disbanded and Course No 193 became the last to pass through the unit since 21 (P)AFU's arrival at the airfield. The unit was rapidly shrinking in size by August 1946 with a mere 71 Oxfords, a single Anson and one Magister on strength.

No 21 (P)AFU experienced its last fatal accident from Wheaton Aston on 1st August when W/O Orr crashed in Oxford I LW788 near Lichfield. The aircraft lost a propeller and became uncontrollable before hitting the ground with fatal consequences.

Only a fraction of its former self, a signal was received for 21 (P)AFU to move out of Wheaton Aston in late November 1946. On 5th December, the main party departed for Moreton-in-Marsh in

The airfield's Type 12779 control tower, once the heart of this very busy airfield, still stands in 2007, 60 years after the airfield closed. (Author)

Gloucestershire and Wheaton Aston fell silent for the first time in five years.

By July 1947, this once very busy airfield had been abandoned but it was quickly occupied by a collection of Polish families who were housed in the old WAAF accommodation. In 1954, the Ministry of Agriculture and Fisheries installed a poultry progeny testing centre on the old airfield. A few years later, the centre and a large portion of the airfield was sold to the current resident pig farmers, Midland Pig Producers, with the motto 'More Perfect Pigs'.

Today, the airfield's Type 12779 control tower still stands with several technical buildings also extant and in use around it. From the air, all three runways and perimeter track appear intact but on a closer ground inspection, they show an advanced state of deterioration.

16
WOLVERHAMPTON
(Pendeford)

Opened in the 1930s, riding the wave of the public enthusiasm for municipal airports, it seems ironic that Wolverhampton was closed over 30 years later by a wave of equally forceful public pressure. Now, like so many airfield sites located on the fringes of towns and cities, Wolverhampton has succumbed to the ever increasing demand for new housing.

From the start, the local Town Council, seeing Stoke-on-Trent and Walsall gaining their own airports, obviously felt that Wolverhampton also warranted such a facility. The council, like so many others, called upon the knowledge and experience of Sir Alan Cobham who had visited Wolverhampton on several different occasions. Cobham surveyed 25 sites around the town, eventually stating that an area of land at Barnhurst Farm was the most suitable.

The proposed site was located on the northern side of Wolverhampton, between the Shropshire Union and Staffordshire and Worcestershire Canals north of Pendeford. In June 1933, the town mayor, Sir Charles Mander, proposed that 178 acres of land at Barnhurst be considered for the construction of a Municipal Airport. Despite some opposition from the council, the land, which was actually owned by the Sewerage Committee, was released, as well as funds to begin construction of the new airport.

After a more thorough survey, it was discovered that the land would need extensive drainage. It would take up to two years to make it suitable for aviation, but in the meantime work could begin on all the ancillary buildings that were needed. A single hangar, small terminal and integrated clubhouse, concrete hardstandings and refuelling

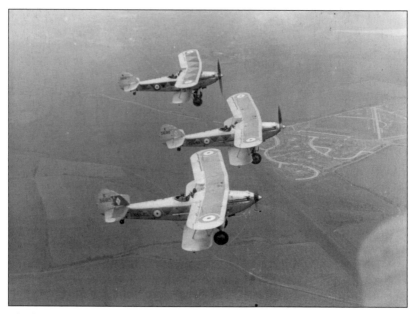

The first aircraft to be built by Boulton Paul at their new factory at Pendeford was the Hawker Demon.

pumps were built over the next eighteen months. The flying ground itself at the time had no defined runways, with aircraft taking off into the prevailing wind.

With over £80,000 having been spent, the airfield was ready for operations by the Midland Flying Club in early 1936. However, the first aircraft that made use of the new airfield was a product of the Boulton Paul Aircraft Ltd factory, which was being built simultaneously. The vast factory complex was on the western edge of the airfield on the very edge of the Shropshire Union Canal. Initially, the factory and airfield were connected by a grass taxiway, which would eventually be replaced by a more substantial perimeter track.

Boulton Paul Aircraft Ltd, who had relocated from their original home in Norfolk, were subcontracted to build the Hawker Demon light bomber at the time. The first of these flew from Wolverhampton on 21st August 1936. The Demon was developed from the Hart bomber, the main differences being that the rear cockpit provided a better field of fire, and there were twin front guns and a super-charged engine. The clouds of a potential war in Europe were already gathering at this

The prototype Boulton Paul Defiant K8310, at Pendeford in 1937 without the four-gun turret fitted.

stage. The original woodworking and steelwork firm of Boulton Paul remained in Norwich while the aircraft wing of the company, which had been sold off, looked further west because of the increasing possibility of it being targeted by German forces.

The company's most famous product was already designed and being built by the time Boulton Paul had arrived in Staffordshire. The Air Ministry issued specification F.9/35 for a two-seat fighter with its main armament contained in a power-operated turret. In 1935, three contenders were put forward: the Hawker Hotspur, the Bristol 147 and the Boulton Paul P.82 Defiant. The Defiant easily won the contract and the half-built prototype was transported by road to Wolverhampton along with the rest of the company. The first Defiant, K8310, was flown from Wolverhampton on 11th August 1937 in the capable hands of the company's Chief Test Pilot, Flt Lt Cecil Feather. The Air Ministry's keenness for this type for aircraft was emphasised by the fact that an order for 87 aircraft had been placed in March 1937, five months before the prototype flew.

The Defiant, which was of similar proportions to the Hawker Hurricane, was a pleasant aircraft to fly. Powered by a 1,030 hp Rolls-Royce Merlin I engine, the Defiant continued flight trials from the airfield throughout 1938. By this time, a second prototype had been

Defiant K8620 with the four-gun turret fitted. The factory and a Blackburn Roc are in the background.

produced with a more powerful engine and a slightly larger tail. The final production variant, which had even more power with a Merlin III engine fitted, first flew on 30th July 1939. Capable of over 300 mph, the Defiant I had arrived just in time for squadron service as war broke out in Europe.

Wolverhampton, locally known as Pendeford, was officially opened on 25th June 1938 by Flg Off A E Clouston. The New Zealander, along with Mrs B Kirby-Green, was famous at the time for achieving a record-beating return flight to South Africa in a de Havilland DH.88 Comet. A well organised and well attended air show was arranged by the Midland Aero Club. There were displays by Amy Johnson in a Kirby Kite glider as well as by the RAF's Gloster Gauntlets of 46 Squadron and Hawker Hinds from 605 Squadron. The latter took part in a mock attack with the airfield defended by enthusiastic personnel from 209 Anti-Aircraft Battery, a Territorial Army Unit based in Wolverhampton.

The airfield then settled into a routine with a steady increase in privately owned aircraft at Wolverhampton as well as the aero club's three de Havilland Tiger Moths, which were a regular sight. Private aircraft included a Taylorcraft C2, British Aircraft Swallow, de Havilland Leopard Moth, General Aircraft Monospar and many more.

When the Demon contract was completed, Boulton Paul began production of the Blackburn Roc. L3057 was the first of 136 produced by the company.

Virtually all were destined to enter military service in the rapidly coming Second World War.

With the Demon contract finished, Boulton Paul's next task was to produce 136 Blackburn Roc naval fighters. Of a similar design to the Defiant, the first of many rolled off the production line at Pendeford on 23rd December 1938. All were test-flown and delivered from the airfield between February 1939 and August 1940.

When Britain entered the Second World War on 3rd September 1939, all civilian flying throughout the country was stopped. The only aviation activity which occurred from the airfield was the flying of Rocs and Defiants fresh off the production lines. The latter had achieved a total production order of 363 aircraft when war broke out. Some 150 more Defiants were ordered in December 1939, followed by another 50 in February 1940.

King George VI and Queen Elizab ᵻ ʾisited the Boulton Paul factory in April 1940. They visited of offices, viewed the production lines and were entertain ˡ ᵼnt aerobatic display.

Luckily for Boulton Paul and it˪ rₛ force, only one raid on the factory occurred. A large dun ᵼad been constructed at Brewood, five miles west of the P ginal in order to distract would-be raiders. At around 190ᶜ ˥eptember 1940, a single

The factory, now camouflaged, once again provides a backdrop for a line of brand new Defiants. (Boulton Paul Heritage Project)

Junkers Ju 88 did not take the bait and attempted to bomb the real factory. Up to five bombs were dropped, but all missed the Boulton Paul works and exploded in the Barnhurst sewage plant. The factory's own anti-aircraft defences did not respond until the bombs started falling, by which time the Ju 88 was hastily departing towards the south-east. Apparently, the Ju 88 was hit and could have been the same aircraft which came down near Nuneaton in Warwickshire the same evening.

A host of modifications, many in response to RAF requests, resulted in the Defiant II being introduced in early 1941. Now fitted with a 1,260 hp Merlin XX engine, the Defiant could reach a speed of 313 mph at 19,000 ft. This was to be the final armed version of this much-maligned fighter, which served with distinction on thirteen front-line squadrons in both day and night-fighter roles.

Since late 1939, the hangar which belonged to the Midland Aero Club had found a temporary role as a packing depot. Tiger Moths, many belonging to the local club, were dismantled and packed for shipment to the Far East and South Africa. At the same time, Wolverhampton's role as a military airfield was being decided. It

222

Operated by 28 EFTS at Wolverhampton, the Tiger Moth was a common sight throughout the Second World War.

would become home to a new Elementary Flying Training School (EFTS) and the sound of Tiger Moths was to return.

Work began on expanding the area north-west of the flying ground, which was already the location of the old clubhouse and aero club hangar. Four Bellman hangars were built next to the original club hangar and seven different types of Blister hangar were constructed around the airfield. The main technical area was constructed behind the Bellman hangars. This consisted of administration, sick quarters, a Motor Transport (MT) section plus the usual host of class and lecture rooms, which go hand in hand with a training airfield. Accommodation was provided for 800 RAF personnel.

Wolverhampton's first training unit was 28 EFTS, whose main equipment was the ubiquitous Tiger Moth and a few Hawker Hinds. Air Schools Ltd, who were already operating 16 EFTS at Derby airport, ran the school at Wolverhampton. The first personnel arrived on 1st September 1941 and its new officer commanding, Wg Cdr West, took charge a few days later. Flt Lt R Hanson was posted in as Chief Flying Instructor and on 12th September, Flg Off Cock arrived for duty as the Chief Ground Instructor.

While Boulton Paul continued to produce Defiants and the last few Rocs left the production line, a more secret project was proceeding in the background. As far back as 1936, the Air Ministry issued specification F.9/35 calling for a twin-engined, three-seat fighter fitted

Boulton Paul P.92 V3142 on approach into Wolverhampton in 1941. The P.92 was built to an Air Ministry specification calling for a heavily armed three-seat fighter. The aircraft was fitted with a large dorsal/barbet type turret equipped with high calibre guns.

with a four-cannon turret. The heavy armament was being called for because it was suspected already that lower calibre weapons were insufficient to bring down a modern bomber. Boulton Paul responded to the specification immediately because this new aircraft was effectively in direct competition with the Defiant.

It was simply designated the P.92 and construction began on the first of two prototypes in mid-1939; however, the first flying version was half the size of the proposed original. The P.92 prototype was to be made of wood and Boulton Paul's lines were set up for the all-metal Defiant production, so Heston Aircraft built the first P.92 instead. Designated P.92/2 by Boulton Paul and J.A.8 by Heston Aircraft and given the military serial of V3142, the aircraft flew for the first time at Heston in Middlesex, during the spring of 1941.

Unfortunately, the Air Ministry had already cancelled the specification, but the aircraft was still flown to Wolverhampton for further trials. Here it remained, becoming a regular and unusual sight for those lucky enough to see it. The A&AEE (Armament & Aircraft Experimental Establishment) at Boscombe Down in Wiltshire, received the P.92/2 for trials on 3rd July 1943. Returned to the company, V3142 was stored but broken up by the war's end. If the P.92/2 had not been cancelled so early it probably would have been developed into an aircraft of similar performance to the Northrop P–61 Black Widow, which was a formidable machine in its own right.

The first intake of pupils for 28 EFTS arrived on 13th September and two days later flying training began. Despite a spell of poor weather, the new EFTS found its feet very quickly and the sight of camouflaged Tiger Moths in the circuit quickly became commonplace. On 1st October, the airfield saw the unexpected arrival of Hurricane IIA Z2962 of 316 (Polish) Squadron based at Churchstanton in Somerset. It is not known whether the pilot, Sgt R Gadus, had a problem but, sadly, after take-off, the fighter's engine failed and the aircraft stalled and spun into the ground just outside the perimeter fence. Gadus had no chance of escape and was killed instantly.

To cater for pupil pilots who were ready to be posted to their next stage of training but had not yet received their posting notices, a new unit was attached to 28 EFTS. No 3 Pupil Pilots Pool (PPP) was formed on 3rd November 1941 and, to keep the pupils current, the new pool used the EFTS Tiger Moths. The unit was eventually renamed the Pupil Pilots School but its role never changed until it was disbanded in April 1947.

The school suffered its first fatality on 8th December when two Tiger Moth IIs, T7918 and T7455, collided north of Coven, three miles north of the airfield. LAC Howard and Cpl Sexton, both student pilots flying solo, were killed instantly. An equally serious accident followed on 4th January 1942 when Tiger Moth II T7179 crashed near Featherstone. The trainer, with Flt Lt A B Mobley and Plt Off W J S Wright, hit a tree and burst into flames. Luckily for the crew, an army unit was practising Co-Operation manouvres nearby and dragged the two officers clear of the wreckage. Both were injured but survived to fly another day.

The fighter variant of the Defiant was reaching the end of the line by the middle of 1941. A new role came its way when a production order for 140 target tugs was placed in July 1941. Based on the Defiant II, the new version was designated the TT Mk 1, and first flew from Wolverhampton on 31st January 1942. A second order for 150 aircraft began the same month. This batch was based on the Defiant I, receiving the designation TT Mk III. The last of 1,062 Defiants left Wolverhampton in February 1943, but Boulton Paul's most successful product remained in RAF service until July 1945.

There was no shortage of other work for the Boulton Paul employees throughout the Second World War. However, an order for 200

The Defiant TTIII was the last version to be produced at Pendeford. The last of 1,062 Defiants rolled off the production line in February 1943.

Beaufighters fell through in early 1940 and a contract to build 100 Halifaxes with Fairey was also cancelled in early 1941 in favour of the Defiant, while a separate order was received from Fairey's to produce 300 Barracuda IIs at the Wolverhampton factory. The first aircraft, DP855, flew from the airfield in early 1943 and before the first contract was completed, a second was received for 600 Barracuda IIIs. The company managed to produce 392 before the order was cancelled at the end of the war.

A harsh winter took hold in January 1942, causing massive disruption to 28 EFTS's flying programme. Heavy snow had virtually closed the airfield and the resulting quick thaw and subsequent deep freeze made the situation even worse. Despite this, the school, which was now simply grading pilots for further training overseas, managed to despatch nearly 60 pupils and received a further 90 at the beginning of February. The objective of a grading school was to establish whether a pupil could fly solo within twelve hours. Those who made it were sent overseas to complete their pilot training, while those who did not were remustered to other flying trades, including Navigator and Air Gunner.

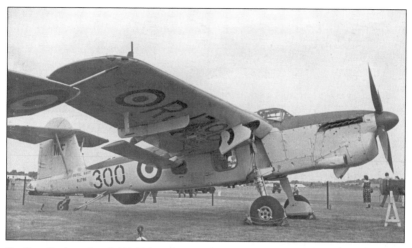

Boulton Paul produced 692 Fairey Barracudas at Pendeford during the Second World War. Barracuda III RJ796, seen here after the war, was one of them.

With the worst of the weather behind them, 28 EFTS knuckled down in an attempt to increase the unit's flying hours. On 10th February alone, the unit managed to achieve a record figure of over 187 flying hours. Training was also given a lift earlier in the month with the arrival of a Link trainer (a primitive but highly effective synthetic trainer) from St Athan in Glamorganshire.

On 19th May 1942, an already busy Wolverhampton became busier with the arrival of 36 Tiger Moths from 17 EFTS at Peterborough (Westwood), Northamptonshire. No 17 EFTS was being closed down and, as well as the influx of aircraft, 28 EFTS gained eleven officers and nine senior NCO flying instructors. It now had over 100 Tiger Moths on the strength and it was obvious Wolverhampton could not cope with so many aircraft. The unit had had time to prepare for this expansion, as a new Relief Landing Ground (RLG) at Penkridge was ready for two new flights of eighteen aircraft each. Night-flying training was the most common exercise flown from Penkridge; the first reference to this taking place was on the night of 17th June 1942. No 28 EFTS aircraft also briefly used Battlestead Hill for night-flying training; this was an RLG for 16 EFTS based at Burnaston in Derbyshire. In response to the increase in aircraft and throughput of pupils, 3 PPP naturally grew in size as more future pilots awaited their next posting.

Even with two RLGs at the school's disposal, other sites were looked at for flying training. A site near Codsall was inspected on 1st July 1942 and another at 'Walley's Field' north of Wolverhampton was also considered. Neither was ever developed although the Air Ministry retained the latter until 1956.

October 1942 was not a good month for 28 EFTS. One pupil was killed at Penkridge and Plt Off Hill and his pupil pilot LAC Franks lost their lives on 8th October. Their Tiger Moth II, N6878, struck a chimney while flying at night. On 17th October, LAC Shinn was making a powered approach when suddenly his Tiger Moth dived into a wooden pavilion on the edge of the airfield. Shinn survived but his aircraft did not, and the pavilion probably did not fare too well either! LAC Watson did nothing to further his career on 21st October when carrying out circuits at Wolverhampton. On landing, he crashed into another stationary Tiger Moth, with Plt Off Spiers and Sqn Ldr Hazell, the unit's Chief Flying Instructor (CFI) on board. Watson's aircraft caught fire but, luckily, all three managed to scramble clear of the wreckage unhurt.

An increase in the demand for night-flying training resulted in the practice being performed at Wolverhampton in addition to the RLGs. Weather permitting, flying was carried out from the airfield every weekday night.

Up to 1942, Turkey, an ally of Germany during the First World War, still remained neutral. Political pressure was being applied from both sides but a Churchill-supported offer by the RAF to train 80 pilots of the Turkish Air Force swung the balance. The first batch of 40 Turkish officers arrived at Wolverhampton on 4th November 1942 for their basic flying training. By the end of their first week at the airfield, almost all had visited the Station Medical Officer (SMO) who immediately dismissed them as having not one serious medical complaint between them! The very same SMO inspected some civilian-manned huts in mid-December describing them as follows: 'I have not seen such filthy conditions before except in slums.' The culprits were evicted from the camp and told to find accommodation elsewhere!

Only 60 Turkish officers in total actually made it to 28 EFTS for the flying training. Sadly, 20 were killed when their ship was sunk by a torpedo in the Mediterranean. Several were also killed or injured before they completed their training course. The first was Lt A Aksu in Tiger Moth II BB816 on 21st January 1943. Aksu collided with LAC De'ath in Tiger Moth II R5101, both aircraft falling on Watling Street near Lapley village, not far from the airfield at Wheaton Aston.

Plt Off (later Wg Cdr) Charles W Cornish was posted to 28 EFTS in 1943 as a flying instructor with only 250 hours of flying experience. He recalls a few of his experiences:

I was posted to an EFTS in the Midlands, where I discovered to my great surprise that my contribution to Britain's war effort was to be teaching not young RAF aircrew cadets, but officers from the Turkish, Iraqi and Iranian Air Forces!

I had just sent a Turkish student on a one-hour detail to carry out spinning and aerobatics in aircraft number 98. I observed him land safely halfway across the airfield, but was astonished to hear a tremendous roar from the engine as the propeller came flying off. I ran 200 yards across the airfield to the now stationary aircraft. My student was still in the cockpit, with helmet removed and a puzzled look on his face. The engine was still revving like mad. My shout of 'Switch off!' went unheeded, so I clambered up onto the wing and did so, the student still having a look of total surprise on his face. After interrogation it would appear that he had carried out the detail in accordance with the briefing. He had carried out three spin recoveries before starting aerobatics and had attempted several loops and rolls. No, he had had no trouble, although he did not think his rolls were very good. He had no idea why after landing, 'The prop, she come off and lie sleeping on the ground!' The engineers were adamant that the propeller bolts could only have sheared as a result of the engine being over-revved, but we could get no indication from the student that he might inadvertently done this. The mystery was solved about three weeks later.

An occasional visitor to our Mess was the Boulton Paul Aircraft Company's test pilot who flew Fairey Barracuda aircraft from the factory at the far side of the airfield. One evening in the bar, he let slip the remark, 'I didn't really believe it at the time and I meant to ring up your Chief Flying Instructor to register my disbelief, but I became involved with more important matters over the following couple of days and it slipped my memory. I was cruising at 3,000 ft with 200 mph on the clock when I was *overtaken* on my left side by a Tiger Moth, which then peeled off to the left. I mentally recorded the number on the cowling – it was 98'! There was a great chortle from the three of us present who knew the sequel to that brief encounter!

I now have to explain that the entry speed for a loop is

120 mph and maximum permissible diving speed of the Tiger Moth was 170 mph and the engine revs at 2500 rpm, so one can only guess what speed the engine revolutions of aircraft number 98 were doing on that occasion. The young Turkish officer was lucky that only the propeller fell off on the ground rather than the wings falling off in flight. Speaking to him the next day he admitted with no sign of remorse or guilt that on completing his aerobatics at 5,000 ft, he had seen a 'fighter airplane' way below and had carried out a dummy attack on it. Nothing wrong with that was there? I suppose it was a substitute for a cavalry dash for him.

An international flavour continued when several officers from the Soviet military inspected the operations of the EFTS on 28th January. A Chinese military party followed on 9th March, a visit that was well publicised and documented by six representatives from the *Birmingham Gazette* and *Dispatch*, *Birmingham Post* and *Mail* and the *Wolverhampton Express* and *Star*. On 10th November, a Brazilian mission carried out a similar visit. In all cases, no pupil pilots from those nations were training at Wolverhampton at the time.

Another collision between a pair of 28 EFTS machines took place on 5th February 1943. The pupil pilot of Tiger Moth T7971 made a hash of his take-off and crashed on top of stationary Tiger Moth N6875 with instructor W/O J D Loach and his pupil on board. Loach sustained serious burns in the ensuing fire while his student suffered from minor injuries; all were lucky to have survived the accident.

Considering the large number of pilots who were passing through 28 EFTS, the accident rate was probably below average. While the odd minor accident continued to occur, there was only one more fatal incident in 1943. Whilst attempting a practice forced landing on 23rd December, Tiger Moth T7739 crashed at Lapley, not far from Wheaton Aston. The instructor, Flt Sgt Higgs, was killed and his pupil AC Rix was seriously injured.

It was quite common for training school instructors to be attached to front-line squadrons to gain valuable experience to pass on to their students. Instructor Flg Off A D Critchlow, for instance, was attached to 53 Squadron at St Eval in Cornwall flying the Consolidated Liberator V. No 28 EFTS received the news on 16th April 1944 that Flg Off Critchlow had been posted missing.

A BBC recording unit and British Movietone News descended on Wolverhampton on 29th June 1944. The team was at the airfield to produce a film about the Iranian officers passing through 28 EFTS at the time.

The only fatal accident during 1944 took place on 26th August. Tiger Moth T6039, with Sgt A Wilkinson and Sgt W Woodward, crashed at Llwynamapsis Field, Morda near Oswestry. Sgt Wilkinson was killed and Sgt Woodward seriously injured.

More missions arrived at Wolverhampton in early 1945. The first was French on 9th March, followed by the Yugoslavs under the command of Col Savitch on 31st March. This was the final such visit of its kind before the end of the Second World War.

No 28 EFTS's long-serving commanding officer, Wg Cdr West, was posted to Kenley in Surrey on 14th March 1945. Wg Cdr H A Roxburgh, who was destined to remain working at Wolverhampton as a civilian, replaced him.

The war ended with little fuss at Wolverhampton – 28 EFTS continued as usual but on 9th July a sign that the unit was reducing in size took place. The long-serving RLG at Penkridge was closed down followed by a change of controlling group on 19th July to 50 Group. Nationalities passing through the unit during the month included Dutch, Czechoslovakian, Belgian and still a few Turkish.

On 15th August 1945, the unit reduced in size again when the aircraft establishment was adjusted to 45 Tiger Moths. By the summer of 1946, the unit was only carrying out daytime flying and the average monthly total was down to just over 1,000 hours per month. Post war training courses still retained an international flavour with Dutch, Greek, Iranian and Iraqi pupils. No 28 EFTS's days were nearly over but when disbandment came on 26th June 1947, the unit was immediately reincarnated as 25 RFS (Reserve Flying School).

Post war, Boulton Paul continued a variety of subcontract work including conversion of many Wellingtons into the T10 navigation trainer. One of these aircraft survives today at the RAF Museum at Hendon. The company achieved a first on 26th May 1947 when the world's first single-engine turboprop was flown from the airfield. The Balliol was accepted by the RAF as an advanced trainer and the company built three T1s, 166 T2s and 30 Sea Balliol T21s. A further 30 Balliol T2s were built by Blackburn. The Balliol bridged the transition from piston power to jet power and its career was cut short when the air training policy favoured advanced instruction on jets. This was to be the last significant mass-produced aircraft that Boulton Paul would build. The company also built several jet aircraft including the BP.111, BP.120 and BP.124, the latter in competition with the Hunting Jet

The most successful post war aircraft produced by Boulton Paul was the Balliol. This is the prototype Sea Balliol T21 VR599.

Provost which went on to serve the RAF as a primary jet trainer for decades.

Jet flying was carried out at Seighford, which had concrete runways and was also where the company had taken over several hangars for more sub contract work. The company merged into the Dowty Group in 1961 and still exists today in the same building as Smith's Aerospace.

No 25 RFS was still operating the Tiger Moth and run by Air Schools Ltd. The unit also used examples of the Percival Prentice, Avro Anson and de Havilland Canada Chipmunk. No 1954 Reserve AOP (Air Observation Post) Flight, flying various marks of the Auster AOP, was to be the last military unit formed at Wolverhampton on 31st March 1954. No 25 RFS was disbanded on 31st March 1953 followed by 1954 Flight on 10th March 1957, bringing an end to military flying at Wolverhampton.

Civilian flying during the post war period was prolific and permission was given for its revival at the airfield from 1st January 1946. Several air races were held there, including the Goodyear Trophy from 1948 to 1953. The King's Cup was held at Wolverhampton in 1950

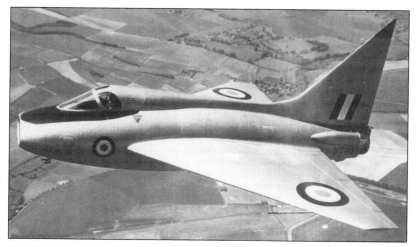

One of many post war jets was the Boulton Paul BP.111, nicknamed the 'Yellow Peril'.

with 36 entrants taking part – the race was won by Edward Day in Miles Magister G–AKRV, beating Gp Capt Peter Townsend in his Hawker Hurricane G–AMAU by a whisker.

Commercial aviation was evident in the late 1950s and early 1960s with aircraft such as the de Havilland Dragon Rapide and Douglas Dakota being operated. Wolverhampton's post war history is far too extensive for this publication and possibly represents the busiest period of the airfield's existence; even taking into account the combined wartime operations of 28 EFTS and Boulton Paul. Sadly though, by 1970 the airfield was closed, like so many others earmarked for urban development.

Today, a walk through Pendeford Wood on the south side of the old airfield is the best way to view what remains. Walking towards the Smith's Aerospace factory, remnants of a few wartime buildings can be seen and looking east up the hill, the keen eyed will spot a Battle Headquarters building just visible above the ground. Sadly, it is inaccessible, but this is probably the best-preserved wartime building. Its very existence is unusual for an airfield with only training in mind, as these buildings were usually found on operational airfields. Houses have covered the main airfield and flying ground and the northern edge hosts a collection of modern offices. Within the estate, a brick relief representing a Boulton Paul Defiant serves as a memorial to a brief but important period of the airfield's history.

Hawker Hurricane G-AMAU, which took part in the 1950 King's Cup Air Race at Wolverhampton.

The Smith's Aerospace factory has changed externally very little over the years and is also the home of the Boulton Paul Heritage Project. This small but very active museum will hopefully keep alive the spirit of Boulton Paul and aviation at Wolverhampton for many years to come.

17
MINOR
AIRFIELDS

Marchington Hall

Marchington, located in sight of the River Dove and the Derbyshire border, became the home of one of the largest USAAF Supply Depots within Staffordshire. Known as Marchington Hall, the depot was located to the east of the town, north and south of a minor road near the hamlet of Moreton. Officially designated Station No 193 by the Americans, the depot stored equipment for both the 8th and 9th Air Forces from 1943 to late 1945.

On the northern side of the depot, a grass landing strip of approximately 1,300 yards in length was constructed. It is quite possible that the vast array of USAAF liaison and communication aircraft available at the time were visitors and it has been suggested that gliders, probably Waco CG–4As were towed and unhitched over the airstrip. On landing, the gliders were dismantled and stored for future use.

During the post war years, the site remained in the hands of the Ministry of Defence and was eventually passed on to the Home Office for miscellaneous storage. The land was still in Home Office hands when the Burton and Derby Gliding Club, who had been operating from Church Broughton in Derbyshire, were looking for a new site. A piece of land, almost in the same position as the wartime strip, was purchased and the club changed its name to the Marchington Gliding Club. The strip hit the headlines on 19th August 1984 when Varsity T1 G–BDFT belonging to the Leicester Aviation Preservation group crashed after an engine failed. Sadly, eleven of the fourteen on board were killed when the aircraft tried to force-land on the glider strip.

In the early 1990s, the gliding club had to find another home because the Home Office needed the land for a new prison. HMP Dovegate now dominates the site. While remnants of the USAAF depot still exist, the small airstrip has disappeared.

Stafford

Stafford was famous as the home of 16 Maintenance Unit (MU) from its formation on 1st December 1939. Before the arrival of the vast equipment depot, an area near Beacon Hill was used as a landing ground by Home Defence squadrons between 1916 and 1918, during the First World War. It is unlikely that it was used between the wars.

Almost on the same site, a short grass strip was used during the Second World War purely for the use of neighbouring 16 MU at Stafford. The exact location of the small airstrip was from Beacon Hill in the west to the Staffordshire County Showground in the east. Light military aircraft such as the Magister, Tiger Moth and Auster types would have had little difficulty in landing here.

Today, the site of the small airfield has been virtually removed by the A518.

Stone

Forced landings by small trainers such as Magisters and Tiger Moths were not uncommon during the Second World War. Such events were usually safely performed and an instructor generally flew the aircraft out again. Some more organised training schools would have officially designated Forced Landing Grounds (FLGs) where pupil pilots could practise landing in a small area. One such landing ground was located on school playing fields at Stone, possibly belonging to Alleynes High School, although this has not been confirmed.

The first reference to a landing ground at Stone was made in June 1940 when 5 EFTS (Elementary Flying Training School) was formed at Meir. Not only was the playing field used for forced landing training but it was also used as an emergency diversion airfield. Magister I L8224 made a precautionary landing at the FLG on 15th October 1940. Whatever problem caused the trainer to land in the first place occurred again when the Magister tried to take off. The pupil pilot abandoned his take-off but not quickly enough to stop L8224 crashing into trees on the edge of the landing ground. Another example where Stone FLG proved useful was on 15th November 1940 when thick fog rapidly formed over Meir, leaving several aircraft unable to land. Three

Magisters made precautionary landings at Stone, only returning once conditions at Meir had improved.

On 11th January 1941, LAC R H Imeson from 'B' Flight, 5 EFTS, force-landed at Stone. This was followed by the last incident involving a 5 EFTS Magister on 27th May 1941, when LAC Horsham from 'C' Flight suffered an engine failure near to the playing fields and, on landing, damaged the undercarriage of the small trainer.

By December 1941, 5 EFTS had been disbanded and no further reference to the forced landing ground at Stone has been recorded. It is logical that it could have been used at a later date by USAAF liaison aircraft visiting one of the large American depots located on the edge of the town.

18
CIVILIANS
AT WAR

3rd September 1939 was a dark day for the nation, when Prime Minister Neville Chamberlain's announcement that Great Britain was once again at war with Germany was in stark contrast to his 'Peace in our time' statement on his return from Munich in 1938. But it came as no surprise to the many who had been watching and listening to the political and military developments on the Continent. Two days earlier, Air Raid Precautions (ARP) personnel had been mobilized and blackout regulations and strict rationing came into force overnight after an initial state of panic took over and many people bought extra supplies from their local shops.

It was the blackout that caused the most disruption to people's daily lives. All motor vehicles had their headlights covered with just a narrow slit for the beam to pass through. Streetlights were also extinguished, causing a rapid increase in motoring and pedestrian accidents.

Many senior politicians had vivid memories of the use of gas during the First World War. The government was convinced that the Germans would use gas against the population and in 1938 over 38 million gas masks, kept in brown cardboard boxes tied with string, were issued to the general public. Thankfully, the threat never materialised and, by late 1940, rather than being carried everywhere the boxes had disappeared.

Rationing was not officially introduced until January 1940 but then remained in force until 4th July 1954. Various commodities were rationed progressively. For example, the first foods to be rationed were bacon, butter and sugar. Jam followed in March 1941, eggs in June 1941, soap in February 1942 and sweets and chocolate in March 1942, just to name a few. It was reversed during the post war years when, as productivity and availability increased, flour came off ration in July 1948, tea in October 1952 and the sweets and sugar by 1953.

Government campaigns, including the very successful 'Dig for Victory', were designed to encourage people to turn their gardens into vegetable patches. Fresh vegetables on the table made life considerably more bearable and the population healthier. The Armed Forces also took part in the 'Dig for Victory' campaign, even though they were not under orders to do so. Often making use of good agricultural land, airfields lent themselves to the production of large areas of vegetables. The airmen stationed at Lichfield, along with several others in the county, were very successful amateur gardeners.

For the majority of civilians living in Great Britain during the Second World War, their only contact with the enemy was by an air raid. Staffordshire was no exception but compared to many other counties it was let off fairly lightly. Many people still had memories of the Zeppelin raids during the First World War but, while these attacks were terrifying, they did not compare to the efficiency of the Luftwaffe.

Photographic reconnaissance of the area by high-flying German aircraft soon revealed that, along with Coventry and Birmingham, Wolverhampton, Stoke-on-Trent and Newcastle-under-Lyme held significant industrial and military targets.

To navigate to a specific target, the Germans set up several Beam Stations across Northern France and the coastal regions of Belgium and Holland. The system was known as *Knickebein* and worked on the simple principle of projecting three beams – two were in parallel, for the bombers to fly between, while the third beam crossed the other two and marked the position of the target. Codebreakers at Bletchley Park in Buckinghamshire had already identified the German target numbers for the country's cities: No 51 was Wolverhampton, No 52 Birmingham and No 53 Coventry.

On 10th November 1940 a message was decoded that revealed beam settings had been placed on the three Midland targets – Wolverhampton, it was thought, would be the first. On 14/15th November, a large attacking force headed for the Midlands, but rather than Wolverhampton it was Coventry that was hit hard. Within hours, 554 civilians were dead and a further 865 were seriously injured. Birmingham was bombed a few nights later with similar results, leaving Wolverhampton to await its fate.

Professor R V Jones at Bletchley Park, who was responsible for investigating the German beam system, contacted Anti-Aircraft Command. Every available anti-aircraft gun was placed in a giant circle around the city in anticipation of a large raid. After a second raid on Birmingham it is presumed that the Luftwaffe flew further photographic reconnaissance over the area to view bomb damage and other potential targets and, whilst over Wolverhampton, the photographs would have revealed a massive increase in the city's defences. This resulted in there being no raid on Wolverhampton, purely because the Luftwaffe could not afford to lose great numbers of aircrew and their aircraft. Professor Jones was later criticised for 'upsetting' the defences of the country purely on a false deduction. Not long after, he was vindicated when he received a call from an RAF officer who said that a conversation between two German aircrew POWs had been overheard. They had been discussing the success of the Coventry and Birmingham raids and one stated that a similar attack was meant to have been carried out on Wolverhampton. The pair even gave the codename for the Wolverhampton raid, *Einheitspreis*, meaning 'unit price'. A Luftwaffe target map of Wolverhampton at the time revealed that priority targets within the city were Guy Motors Ltd, Ever Ready Ltd, the Gas Works, the Railway Workshops and Electric Construction Company. It was certainly a good example of a deterrent actually working.

Attacks were made on Staffordshire targets but not on the scale of those against the Midlands or the North West, such as the Liverpool Docks. Stoke-on-Trent was also a strategic target for the Luftwaffe with many important industrial targets within it. They included the Michelin factory, the large railway goods yard, the British Aluminium Works and the Radway Green munitions factory. Bombs aimed at Stoke fell on Chesterton on 14th December 1940 causing extensive damage. Bombs also fell onto the High Street at Pittshill on the northern fringes of Stoke on 14th March 1941. A single bomb destroyed several houses in Taylor Avenue, May Bank on 2nd June, one of only a few bombs to drop in the Newcastle-under-Lyme area. Several minor bombing raids, mainly by single aircraft, were inflicted upon Stoke during 1941; while casualties did result, they did not compare to other heavily populated areas in the country.

Bombs fell on Lichfield in 1940 and 1941, killing three people and destroying two houses; a further 390 homes were damaged, some beyond repair. Seventeen houses were destroyed in St Giles Crescent, off Willenhall Road, Wolverhampton when several HE (High Explosive) bombs were dropped on 31st July 1942. Many of the houses were repairable but it is recorded on the bomb damage register that five of them had to be demolished and rebuilt.

To protect the civilian population, personal Anderson air raid shelters were provided for back gardens. For families earning less than £5 per week, the shelter was provided free of charge. For the slightly better off, an Anderson could be purchased for £7. When war broke out, over two million families had a shelter and by the end of 1941 this had risen to two-and-a-quarter million. For those without a garden, the Morrison shelter was developed for protection inside the house. Named after the Home Secretary, Herbert Morrison, the shelters were made of very heavy steel and could be put in the living room and used as a table. One side lifted up for people to crawl underneath and get inside. Morrison shelters were fairly large and provided sleeping space for two or three people.

Large public shelters were built in town centres and almost every road, street and major bus stop had a shelter built on or near it as well. Public buildings often had a shelter underneath while all the major factories had shelters for their staff. The factories had their own ARP personnel, firewatchers, Royal Observer Corps (ROC), and the larger facilities had their own Home Guard detachment as well.

The mass evacuation from cities and big towns of schoolchildren, their teachers, mothers with children under five, pregnant women and some disabled people began soon after war was declared. Staffordshire was ready to receive evacuees but the planned influx did not materialise. Wolverhampton alone was prepared for over 6,000 evacuees. Only Lichfield received more than expected, with 2,000 having arrived by the end of 1940, causing overcrowding within the town. A number of Jewish tailors from London who could not find work were also evacuated to Lichfield, causing more housing problems. When the worst of the bombing came to an end, many evacuees who were unhappy living in the country returned to their homes.

War work was plentiful in Staffordshire with Wolverhampton alone housing four major companies who were producing for the war effort. H M Hobson Ltd had been in the Accuracy Works, Cousin Street in Wolverhampton since 1911 and had been involved in war work during the First World War. In 1939, the company bought land at north of Fordhouses for a new factory. Here, they produced thousands of carburettors for many aircraft types including the Lancaster, Spitfire and Sunderland.

Guy's Motors Ltd employed 200 full-time and 300 part-time women in the production of armour plate for tanks and military cars. The company also produced their own armoured cars which were of such high quality that they were used for the protection of Winston Churchill and the Royal family. Throughout the war, the company continued to develop armour-plate welding specifically for tanks. The old plate was riveted and Guy's was credited with saving the country over £100 million in production costs by welding the plates.

Just a few of the female civilian staff from 82 MU at Lichfield. Front row (left to right): Miss Hancox, Bird, Ramsell, Mrs Atack, Webb, Jones and Harvey. Middle row, Miss Shone, Mrs Johnson, Miss Shepherd, Mrs Parker, Rogers, Miss Page and Mrs Guest. Rear row, Miss Chinnock, Holloway, Mrs Putt, Miss Hodkinson, Harvey, Mullaley, Mrs Bailey and Heathcote.

The Goodyear Tyre and Rubber Company first arrived in Wolverhampton in 1927. The company seamlessly switched its efforts to war work when hostilities broke out in September 1939. Employees who had been used to a normal working week were now working twenty days on and one day off. Within twelve months, the company was Britain's second largest producer of aircraft tyres. All aircraft were catered for, from the Tiger Moth to the Short Stirling; the latter's tyres were nearly six feet high. Synthetic tyres were produced when there was a shortage of natural rubber. A 'run-flat' tyre was also developed and Goodyear produced hoses for all uses, including self-buoyant armoured ones for refuelling ships. An extra facility was built for the USAAF to repair self-sealing aircraft fuel tanks, wheels and brakes.

Another Wolverhampton-based company was Industrial Designs Ltd. The company specialised in planning the conversion of a company from peacetime to wartime work, such as when they converted a Scottish company more familiar with carpet production into a producer of torpedoes. By the war's end, the company had handled over 35,000 war production designs.

The aircraft factories in the region also provided work for many local people. Boulton Paul at Pendeford had recruited and trained workers since their arrival in the county in 1936. Helliwells at Walsall also employed civilian staff and many workers who were trained in the Potteries retrained in aircraft assembly for Rootes at Meir. No 82 MU at Lichfield was civilian-run with over 300 local people on its books by the war's end.

Throughout the country, committees and groups were formed with the aim of raising funds to help buy equipment for soldiers, sailors and airmen. The government met part of the enormous expense of the war by borrowing from the people through savings campaigns. They combined the appeal to save with patriotism and community spirit. 'Salute the Soldier' was one of the largest and most successful campaigns with towns encouraged to compete against one another to raise the most funds. Kidsgrove, north of Stoke, had one of many committees formed specifically to raise funds to buy equipment. Between July 1940 and March 1944, the Kidsgrove Local Savings Committee raised an astonishing £433,182. This equated to one RAF bomber, 28 Supermarine Spitfires, two heavy tanks and a motor torpedo boat – the latter was HMMBT (His Majesty's Motor Torpedo Boat) No 76, which, along with all the other equipment, was recorded as seeing active service.

A new threat from the air indirectly affected the county from mid

1944 onwards. The V1 'Doodlebugs' and V2s, rocket-propelled unmanned bombs, were falling on to south-east England with alarming regularity, causing a second wave of evacuees to pour out of London. Most of them had returned to their homes by September 1944 as the Allied forces advanced steadily east towards their goal of Berlin.

The blackout restrictions were partially lifted by October 1944 and another sign of an impending victory came when the Home Guard was disbanded on 1st November. VE (Victory in Europe) Day was declared on 8th May 1945 with Winston Churchill aiming his comment, 'This is *your* victory', at the country's civilian population.

Over 65,000 British civilians lost their lives in the conflict and another 86,000 were wounded on the home front. Civilian casualties tend not to be remembered on war memorials, but one dedicated memorial was unveiled in the corner of Brampton Park in Newcastle-under-Lyme in 2006. The small black monument commemorates the 78 people who were killed as a direct result of enemy bombing in Newcastle-under-Lyme and Stoke-on-Trent during the Second World War. Like the thousands of servicemen who lost their lives during the conflict, there were many in the civilian population who also made the ultimate sacrifice.

APPENDIX

Units and their aircraft located at airfields in Staffordshire
during the Second World War

Abbots Bromley
5 EFTS. RLG with main unit at Meir from 17th June 1940. Aircraft –
Magister.
16 EFTS. RLG for main unit at Burnaston. June 1941 to 9th July 1945.
Aircraft – Magister and Tiger Moth.
21 MU. Sub-site 14th May 1945 to 31st March 1949.

Battlestead Hill
16 EFTS. RLG for main unit at Burnaston. May 1941 to 9th July 1945.
Aircraft – Magister and Tiger Moth.

Halfpenny Green
3 AONS. Reformed 17th February 1941 at Bobbington in 51 Gp with
35 Bothas; July 1941 re-equipped with Anson; 7th July 1941 to 25 Gp;
redesignated No 3 AOS 18th October 1941. Aircraft – Botha and Anson.
3 AOS. Reformed 18th October 1941 ex-No 3 AONS at Bobbington with
an establishment of 66 Ansons and 12 Target Tugs; 31st January 1942
divided into 'A' Flt, armament, 'B' and 'D' Flts, day navigation, 'C' Flt,
night navigation; became No 3 (O)AFU 11th April 1942. Aircraft –
Anson, Lysander and Defiant.
3 (O)AFU. Formed 11th April 1942 ex-No 3 AOS in 25 Group at
Bobbington with 66 Ansons. Martinets introduced Spring 1943, but
withdrawn November 1943: training ceased 13th November 1945.
Disbanded 1st December 1945. Aircraft – Anson, Martinet and Defiant.
School of Flying Control. Unit moved to Bridgnorth on 15th November
1942, the aircraft with the school to Bobbington. Aircraft – Anson,
Dominie and Oxford.
1545 (BATF). Affiliated to 3 (O)AFU. From Wheaton Aston to Halfpenny
Green 25th April 1944. Re-affiliated to 21 (P)AFU 16th January 1944.
Disbanded 17th December 1945. Aircraft – Oxford.
Pilot-Navigation Instructors Course. Formed by 1945 at Halfpenny
Green. To Cark 29th October 1945.

Hixon
30 OTU. Formed 28th June 1942 in 93 Group at Hixon to train night
bomber crews (proposed satellite at Wheaton Aston; satellite at
Seighford 16th September 1942 to 28th October 1944); July 1942 unit

establishment 27 Wellingtons, 2 Target Tugs; 23rd July 1942 received first Wellington, these being flown on Bomber Command raids in 1942; December 1942 establishment 54 Wellingtons, 2 Target Tugs, 1 Defiant; February 1944 had 35 Wellington IIIs and 15 Mk Xs; October 1944 reduced to three-quarters status, establishment 40 Wellingtons, 5 Hurricanes; 2nd February 1945 to Gamston. Aircraft – Wellington, Defiant and Hurricane.

1686 B(D)TF. Formed 1st July 1943 in 93 Group at Hixon with 6 Tomahawks; disbanded 21st August 1944. Aircraft – Tomahawk.

12 (P)AFU. From Spittlegate 8th February 1945 (detachment at Cranage February 1945); disbanded 21st June 1945. Aircraft – Blenheim, Oxford and Beaufort.

16 MU. Main unit at Stafford (Equipment Supply Depot). 31st July 1945 to 5th November 1957.

Hoar Cross

32 SLG. Opened 1st August 1941 at Hoar Cross for 51 MU; closed June 1945. Dispersal for Beaufighter, Boston, Havoc, Hellcat, Hurricane, Wellington and Whirlwind.

Lichfield

42 MU. Commenced to form December 1939 as Aircraft Storage Unit in 41 Group at Lichfield but redesignated 51 MU 6th March 1940 to avoid confusion with 42 Maintenance Group.

51 MU. Formed 6th March 1940 ex-42 MU in 41 Group at Lichfield; opened 1st August 1940 as Aircraft Storage and Packing Unit; 21st April 1941 to 51 Wing (which disbanded 31st October 1942); 6th May 1941 storage section became 82 MU; (SLGs: No 32 1st August 1941 to October 1942, No 35 1st August 1941 to July 1942, No 29 April 1942 to 19th August 1942, No 38 August 1942 to 1943, also Nos 13 and 37 no dates); sub-sites at Church Broughton from August 1945, Stoke Heath from 15th November 1948. Disbanded 1st July 1954.
Aircraft handled included Hurricane, Spitfire, Magister, Tiger Moth, Wellington, Beaufighter, Defiant, Mosquito, Hellcat, Liberator, Flying Fortress, Oxford and many more.

82 MU. Formed 4th April 1941 as Aircraft Packing Depot in 53 Wing at Lichfield; disbanded 15th November 1945. Aircraft handled included Hurricane, Spitfire, Albacore, Airacobra, Wellington and Oxford.

27 OTU. Formed 23rd April 1941 in 6 Group to train night-bomber crews with Wellington ICs (satellites at Tatenhill from August 1941 to October 1942, Church Broughton from August 1942 to 8th May 1945); 2nd July 1941 began leaflet raids; August 1941 establishment 54 Wellingtons, 18 Ansons, 2 Lysanders; 11th May 1942 6 Group became 91 Group, trained many RAAF crews; in 1942, 117 aircraft took part in

Bomber Command raids; October 1942 Wellington Mk IIIs received, also one Albemarle (P1409) for trials; February 1943 establishment 54 Wellingtons, 5 Lysanders, 1 Defiant; August 1943 Wellington Mk Xs began to arrive; 1st September 1943 to 93 Group; 14th February 1945 returned to 91 Group; disbanded 22nd June 1945. Aircraft – Wellington, Anson, Lysander and Defiant.

93 Group. Formed 15th June 1942 as 93 (Operational Training, later Bomber Command OTU) Group in Bomber Command at Lichfield to control a number of bomber OTUs; to Egginton Hall 7th July 1942.

93 Group Communication Flight. Formed 17th July 1942 at Lichfield with 2 Moth Minors; disbanded 14th February 1945. Aircraft – Warferry, Proctor I and III, Dominie and Moth Minor.

93 Group Screened Wireless Operators' School. Formed 17th June 1943; fate unknown.

Meir

Rootes Securities. Established at Grindley Lane, Blyth Bridge as Nos 8 and 10 Shadow Factory; later merged into 10 Factory by early 1942. Produced Blenheim I, IV and V, Beaufighter VI and TFX. Assembled Harvard and carried out modification work on Mustang and later Liberator 1945/46. Postwar, Harvard work continued until closure. Factory vacated circa 1960.

28 E&RFTS. Formed 1st August 1938 at Meir in 26 Group; 1st February 1939 to 50 Group. Disbanded 3rd September 1939. [Operated by Reid & Sigrist Ltd.] Aircraft – Hart, Hind, Magister and Anson.

No.1 Practice Flying Unit. Formed 4th March 1940 after two postponements at Meir in 23 Group to provide flying practice for pilots trained at flying training schools but awaiting posting to Group Pools, initially with six Hectors, later supplemented by Hinds, the intended establishment being 27 Dominies and 27 Hectors or similar; disbanded into 51 Group 16th June 1940 with the establishment of OTUs, the need for a PFU having lapsed, its aircraft being taken over by 5 EFTS. [The unit was numbered because it was intended to form other PFUs but this did not happen.] Aircraft – Hector, Hind I, Gladiator II and Dominie.

5 EFTS. From Hanworth to Meir 17th June 1940 in 51 Group (RLG Abbots Bromley); October 1941 reverted to Class B due to airfield congestion; disbanded 23rd December 1941. Aircraft – Magister.

16 EFTS. RLG from April to June 1941. Aircraft – Magister.

45 GS. Formed August 1942 at Meir (detachment at Long Mynd); 20th May 1946 to 63 Group; redesignated 632 GS 1st September 1955; to Ternhill in 1963. Aircraft – Cadet I, II, TX3, Prefect TX1, Falcon III and Sedbergh TX1.

Penkridge

28 EFTS. RLG from 19th May 1942 to 9th July 1945. Aircraft – Tiger Moth.

29 EFTS. RLG from September 1941 to 9th July 1945. Aircraft – Magister and Tiger Moth.

Perton

11 SFTS. RLG January 1942 to 14th March 1942. Aircraft – Oxford.

5 (P)AFU. RLG from 1st June 1942 to 4th August 1942. Aircraft – Master and Hurricane.

11 (P)AFU. RLG from 4th August 1942 to 1st August 1943. Detachment at Perton from March 1942 to June 1942; airfield on loan. Aircraft – Oxford.

21 (P)AFU. RLG from 1st August 1943 to 16th July 1946. Aircraft – Oxford.

Seighford

30 OTU. Satellite from 16th September 1942 to 28th October 1944. Aircraft – Wellington, Ic, III and X.

23 HGCU. Satellite from October 1944 to January 1945. Main unit at Peplow. Aircraft – Albemarle II, VI, Horsa I and II, Hadrian I and Proctor III.

21 (P)AFU. RLG 28th February 1945 to 16th July 1946. Aircraft – Oxford.

Tatenhill

16 EFTS. RLG 1940 to April 1941.

27 OTU. Satellite August 1941 to October 1942. Aircraft – Wellington.

15 (P)AFU. RLG from 13th November 1942 to 1st May 1943. Aircraft – Oxford.

5 (P)AFU. RLG from 1st May 1943 to 1st February 1944. Aircraft – Master.

21 (P)AFU. RLG from 15th February 1944 to 19th January 1945. Aircraft – Oxford.

21 MU. Ammunition Storage Depot. Sub-site 23rd December 1944 to 27th November 1954.

Teddesley Park

48 SLG. Opened 14th July 1941 at Teddesley Park for 27 MU; closed 6th February 1946. Dispersal for Typhoon, Avenger, Hotspur, Proctor and Seamew.

Walsall (Aldridge) Airport

Helliwells Ltd. Factory established by 1936. Assembly of Harvard,

Boston and Havoc as part of the Civilian Repair Organisation (CRO). Post war Seafire and Harvard refurbishment. Company moved to Elmdon in 1956.

43 GS. Formed October 1943. Closed by December 1946. Aircraft – Cadet.

Wheaton Aston

11 SFTS. RLG 15th December 1941 to 1st April 1942. Aircraft – Anson, Oxford.

11 (P)AFU. RLG 14th March 1942 to 1st August 1943. Aircraft – Oxford.

30 OTU. Proposed satellite for this unit. Seighford used instead.

21 (P)AFU. Formed 1st August 1943 from a nucleus provided by 11 (P)AFU at Wheaton Aston (21 Group) with establishment 71 Oxfords, 2 Ansons (RLGs – Bratton 1st August 1943 to February 1944; Peplow 19th January 1945 to 28th February 1945; Perton 1st August 1943 to 16th July 1946; Seighford 28th February 1945 to 16th July 1946; Tatenhill 15th February 1944 to 19th January 1945); 25th February 1944 absorbed into 19 (P)AFU, establishment now 148 Oxfords, 4 Ansons; to Moreton-in-Marsh 5th December 1946. Aircraft – Oxford, Anson and Magister.

1511 BATF. From Greenham Common 29th September 1943; disbanded 31st July 1946. Aircraft – Oxford.

1545 BATF. Formed 6th March 1944 with 8 Oxfords at Wheaton Aston in 25 Group, affiliated to 21 (P)AFU; 21st March 1944 affiliated to 3 (P)AFU; 25th April 1944 to Halfpenny Green. Aircraft – Oxford.

Wolverhampton

Boulton Paul Aircraft Ltd. Established at Pendeford in 1936. Produced Demon, Roc, Defiant I, II, TTI & TTIII, Barracuda, Wellington conversion to T10 standard and Balliol. Innumerable test aircraft. Company merged into Dowty Group, 1961. Current as Smith's Aerospace on same site.

28 EFTS. Formed 15th September 1941 at Wolverhampton (Pendeford) in 51 Group as Class B (soon to Class A) and operated by Air Schools Ltd (RLG at Penkridge 19th May 1942 to 9th July 1945); 1st June 1942 to Class A+2 by the addition of 2 flights from the disbanded 17 EFTS; 14th July 1945 to 50 Group; 15th August 1945 reduced to 45 a/c; 21st April 1947 to 23 Group; redesignated 25 RFS 26th June 1947. Aircraft – Tiger Moth II and Hind.

3 Pupil Pilots Pool. Formed 3rd November 1941; redesignated Pupil Pilots School 8th March 1943. [Used aircraft of 28 EFTS Wolverhampton.] Aircraft – Tiger Moth.

BIBLIOGRAPHY

Action Stations 2, Smith, PSL
Aircraft of the RAF since 1918, Thetford, Putnam
Bomber Command Losses Vol.7, Chorley, Midland
Bomber Command Losses Vol.8, Chorley, Midland
Britain's Military Airfields 1939–45, Smith, PSL
British-Built Aircraft Volume 4, Smith, Tempus
Military Airfields in the British Isles 1939–45, Willis & Holliss

Public Records Office Documents:

Air 29/877	1545 BATF Wheaton Aston & Halfpenny Green
Air 29/2487	2 Air Signallers School Halfpenny Green
HLG 144/158	Proposed airport at HG Airfield
Air 29/672	30 OTU Hixon
Air 29/670	27 Lichfield
Air 29/671	27 Lichfield
Air 29/1009	51 Lichfield
Air 29/1025	82 Lichfield
Avia 5/26	Tempest 2
Air 28/529	Meir
Air 29/617	5 Meir
Air 29/631	1 FPU
Avia 2/779	Aerodromes
Avia 2/1197	Licences
Air 28/625	Perton
Air 29/549	21 (P)AFU, Wheaton & Perton
Air 29/1143	School of Explosives
Air 29/873	1511 BATF Wheaton Aston
Air 29/622	28 EFTS Wolverhampton
Air 29/1701	45 Wolverhampton
Avia 2/1155	Licence for Wolverhampton
Air 29/2098, 2783, 3268, 4029, 4030 for 27 MU Teddesley Park	
Air 29/619	16 EFTS

Air 29/1701   Wolverhampton
Air 29/526   23 HGCU
Air 29/544   Halfpenny Green 3 AOS
Avia 2/694   Walsall   1934–37
Avia 2/1199   Walsall   1937–44

RAF Bomber Command Losses OTUs 1940–1947, Chorley, Midland
RAF Flying Training & Support Units, Sturtivant, Hamlin, Halley, Air
  Britain
The Bomber Command War Diaries, Middlebrook & Everitt, Midland
The History of Burton-upon-Trent, Part I, The Edwardians
The K File, The RAF of the 1930s, Air Britain
West Midlands Airfields, Dunphy & Ellows Hall School, Dudley
Wolverhampton No.67 Airfield Focus, Welch

INDEX

Units connected with Staffordshire Airfields